DATE DUE

DATE DUE

WITHDRAWN

Paradigm Shift in the Church

How Natural Church Development Can Transform Theological Thinking

Christian A. Schwarz

Published by ChurchSmart Resources
Carol Stream, IL 60188

For a free catalog of our resources call 1-800-253-4276

Original title: Paradigmenwechsel in der Kirche
Published 1993 by C & P Verlag, Emmelsbüll, Germany

Manuscript edited by Ed Rowell

Cover design by Julie Becker

Printed in U.S.A.

ISBN 1-889638-05-6

Contents

Introduction:
What This Book Is About

E very reformation movement is confronted with an opposing force known as "orthodoxy." This was true in the days of the 16th century Reformation (when the opponent was Roman Catholic orthodoxy); it was true in the days of Pietistic revival in Europe (which was opposed by orthodox Protestants); and the same seems to apply to the different movements that fight for a reformation of their churches today. The stiffest opposition comes often from those who stand up for "doctrinal purity."

Why is this so? Are the renewal movements on the wrong theological track? Or is there something wrong with what we know as orthodoxy?

In conversations with many Christian leaders, I have come to the conclusion that the greatest obstacle to strategic church development is not a lack of methodological know-how, but deep-rooted theological blockages. By this, I am not referring to "God-is-dead theology," nor to groups that contest the absolute claims of Jesus or advocate a syncretistic theology. I am talking about theological blockages in Christian groups whose doctrinal "correctness" is beyond question. The fact that some of the greatest obstacles to church development are to be found in these circles is, in my estimation, the real dilemma.

Why People Talk at Cross Purposes

Over the last few years, in many countries a lot of theological battles have been fought on topics related to church growth. However, the *progress* made in these discussions has so far been surprisingly small. In many cases, people are talking at cross purposes.

The reason seems to me to be that some advocates of church growth—whether consciously or unconsciously—think in a different theological paradigm than their critics. They have another perspective from which they view their own experience and interpret the church (and the world). Different paradigms cannot be related to each other. Christians who think and act in different paradigms are, in effect, talking different languages. Even where they use the same words, they may mean something completely different. Thus it is easy to explain why the very same phrase that makes one person's heart beat faster can give another one a sinking feeling in the stomach. On both sides of the debate people make the same mistake of criticizing theological statements that originated in another paradigm from the point of view of their own paradigm—without realizing how hopeless a task it is. Different paradigms are mutually incompatible.

Perhaps a simple illustration may clarify this. Let us suppose that the only eating utensils we have are knives and forks. The foods (topics) to be "dealt with" are steaks on the one hand, and soup on the other. Research in this area would probably come up with the result that steaks are a highly suitable type of food, whereas soup is rather dubious and completely unfit for human consumption.

This illustration shows us the dilemma we are facing. To understand what church growth is about, we need the appropriate theological utensils. If we do not have them, the subject *must* seem, at best, irrelevant, and at worst, a real threat. There is a limit to the applicability of those illustrations, but even this caricature—and it *is* a caricature—highlights a real aspect of the issue involved. In this case, it is the fact that the theological paradigm that stands in the background of what we call *Natural Church Development* is incompatible with conventional theological thought patterns.

A lot of contributions to the debate have, in the last analysis, been expressions of a different (and, for some, completely new) paradigm. But those of us who presented their theses were insufficiently aware of that reality. Some may have wondered: *What in the world makes these people reject this tasty, wholesome soup (and be so aggressive about it)?* As long as we remain within the illustration, the answer is simple. People who only have knives and forks *cannot* appreciate the value of soup. It seems to me that this is the reason why discussions about isolated theological topics are often so fruitless. We spend our time wondering whether the soup might be better accepted if we were to spice it a little more, but we overlook the fact that the real problem is on a completely different level.

Is Numerical Growth the Key?

In the last few years, there have been a large number of publications on the theology behind church growth.[1] However, most of these publications were surprisingly one-sided in their focus on the aspect of the "numerical growth"—as if this were the theological key to understanding the essence

---

1   A lot of these discussions, however, have taken place outside the English-speaking world. In this book I want to reflect those parts of the debate which I believe are most relevant for everybody who is interested in evaluating the theological presuppositions behind supposedly "value-neutral" methodologies.

of the subject.[2] The scant attention paid to this issue on the following pages is due, first of all, to the fact that so much has been written and said about it that I probably couldn't add anything new. But second, and more important, the question of numerical growth seems to me to be just a side issue—albeit an important one—of church development. It is not the strategic goal, but one of many natural consequences of a church's health to experience growth. The concentration on numerical growth goals overshadows the fact that, at the heart of the debate there are far more fundamental issues concerning our basic theological understanding, and in the last analysis, even our picture of God. Decisions in this area—they may be reflected or not—shape our approach to church growth, and not the methodological question of whether or not we have numerical growth goals.

In this book, I try to link church development with some of the *loci classici* of the systematic theological discussion.[3] What is its relevance in relation to doctrine, ethics, the understanding of Scripture? What is the effect of the underlying paradigm on the discussion about baptism and communion, on church traditions, on the question of church planting and ecumenism? What concept of spiritual gifts is the consequence of this approach, on what understanding of conversion is it based, and what is the outcome of this paradigm when related to social and political questions? Finally, are the movements that put "church growth" or "church development" on their agenda restricted to a particular school of theological thinking, or do they present a method which is theologically neutral? Is this "school of theology" (or "method") orthodox?

All of these questions are fundamentally theological ones which require a theological answer. This is a challenge which the church growth movement—in the estimation of its critics and some of its leading proponents—has not faced up to sufficiently.[4]

---

2   The most thorough discussion of this subject I know of is still the dissertation by the Reformed theologian Charles van Engen, "The Growth of the True Church. An Analysis of the Ecclesiology of Church Growth Theory" *(Engen: 1981)*. Here, the concept of growth is related to the classical *notae* of the true church. This book, however, is a typical example of the way the numerical approach is seen as the essence of the church growth movement.

3   This approach means that I deliberately use the technical terminology that has become customary in the theological debate. However, as I hope that this book will not only be read by theologians, I have endeavored to use the technical terms in such a way that their meaning becomes largely clear from the context.

4   For example, C. Peter Wagner: "It should be admitted that it (i.e., church growth theory) has not yet been wrapped in a recognizable theological package ... The theory itself must be translated into 'theologese.' No one has yet done this because few missionaries are made in the image of the stereotyped theologian" *(Wagner: 1971, p. 37)*. Compare also Michael Herbst: "The church growth movement hopes to enable as many denominational positions as possible to identify themselves with its basic ideas, so it does without precise dogmatic definitions. That the dogmatic question cannot be left out permanently is bound to be clear to everyone involved in church growth ... The church growth movement cannot permanently be spared a controlled doctrinal reflection on these questions" *(Herbst: 1987, p. 265)*.

The Need for Boundaries

In the past, the church growth movement has been relatively strong in the area of building bridges, in its famed "both-and" approach—and I see this as its divine purpose. When there have been struggles between "evangelicals" and "charismatics" or between proponents of "church renewal" and advocates of "church planting," it has refused to take sides. It has tried to expose the theological and strategical futility of an "either-or" approach. It would have nothing to do with the divisions, segregations, and accusations of heresy that are common in so many Christian circles—and I thank God for that!

But at the same time, this strength is related to a major weakness. Where is the boundary for the "both-and" approach? I believe that advocates of church growth have not spoken out clearly enough at this point. It would be easy to (mis)understand them as proposing the unspoken maxim, "As long as a church is growing, we won't ask too many questions about its theology." In other words, the church growth movement may be a world champion in bridge building, but when it comes to setting out the standards for necessary, theologically justified boundaries, there is a lot of work still to do.

I am convinced that we do not so much need to tackle the assertive and often superficial anti-church-growth slogans of our time; the real task is to identify the far more subtle presuppositions. These are particularly devastating in their effect because they are accepted without question by the majority of Christians. The problem is that these presuppositions—in contrast to the slogans themselves—can be recognized only after considerable analytical effort.

The Theological Background of Natural Church Development

This book does not focus on practical issues, yet it has a practical intent. It aims to present the theological background of what we have chosen to call *Natural Church Development.*[5] The practical books based on this approach are consciously kept free from theological arguments (in the narrow sense of the word). I considered it to be more appropriate to present the paradigm at the root of natural church development *in context*, rather than working with isolated theological statements whose motives may be difficult to comprehend, or trying to give an impression of "biblical correctness" by quoting a number of fairly random Bible verses.

---

5   Explained in more detail in "Natural Church Development" *(Schwarz: 1996)* and "Implementation Guide to Natural Church Development" *(Schwarz/Schalk: 1998).*

The work presented here follows on from the book "Theologie des Gemeindeaufbaus" (*Theology of Church Development*), first published in 1984, which was my initial attempt at a theological discussion of the church growth approach.[6] After publication, this book acquired a number of friends and a host of critics. The most important critical comments were collected in the book, "Diskussion zur Theologie des Gemeindeaufbaus" (*Discussion of the Theology of Church Development*).[7]

I have learned a lot from the criticism voiced over the last few years. I hope this new general survey of the subject will overcome some of the misunderstandings that have accumulated, and even in those areas where the reader remains somewhat skeptical towards natural church development, at least he or she will understand better the background of what we present in our practical tools.

On the following pages, the "I" form is used fairly liberally. This is not usual in theological books, but I feel it appropriate because of the nature of the subject. When I speak about natural church development, I do not wish to pretend that I am able to present a sort of "objective" theology—with gloves, so to speak, so that no fingerprints can be seen. On the contrary! I wish the reader to sense that I am deliberately and consciously presenting theology as it inevitably must be: However impersonal and abstract the language it is clothed in, however consistently the authors take refuge in the passive verb form and use pronouns like "one" and "we," theology always remains the attempt of one finite individual human being to communicate with the reader.

A New Reformation?

This book speaks about nothing less than a reformation. Some critics suggested that this term sounds rather lofty. That may be true. But I am convinced—as I hope the following pages will make plain—that we will make no significant progress in our churches without changes as radical as those of the Reformation.

When I use the term "reformation principle" on the following pages, I want to express my conviction that our task today is not to delete 2,000 years of church history and create something completely new. We would do well to identify ourselves with the great reformation movements that have had a lasting effect on the history of Christianity. Anyone who longs for a reformation of the church today—and any fundamental change of church structures or theology is, after all, a form of reformation—has every reason to be humble and learn from their "fathers in the faith." What

---

6   *Schwarz/Schwarz: 1987.*
7   *Weth: 1986.* The book includes critical contributions by Falk Becker, Ako Haarbeck, Michael Herbst, Eberhard Kochs, Christian Möller, Manfred Seitz, Reiner Strunk, Rudolf Weth, and others.

we need today—and what I understand by natural church development—is nothing less than the *application* of the principles of the Reformation to the present situation.

If we refuse to tackle this task, we spurn one of the central principles
of the Reformation, that the church must constantly go on in reforming
itself *(ecclesia semper reformanda)*. Cultivating a "Reformation heritage" is
definitely not the same as applying the reformation principle in practice!

I believe, however, that the ideas involved in the phrase "reformation principle" will remain nothing more than a nice theory unless there
is a radical paradigm shift in church and theology. The practical tools of
natural church development will not help us until our thought patterns
are in line with the theological paradigm which is in the background of
any reformation movement.

Will we really experience something like a new reformation in our
days? Yes, in many churches around the globe there are signs that this is
far more than a vague hope.

Christian A. Schwarz
Institute for Natural Church Development

Part 1

Church Growth Between Spiritualism and Institutionalism

One of the most characteristic marks of any reformation movement is that it subjects all institutional forms to the question: How useful are they for developing the church as an organism? This approach is in competition with two other thought patterns which are far more widespread within Christianity: First, a "spiritualistic" paradigm ("Institutions aren't important"), and second, an "institutionalistic" paradigm ("You must use these forms, methods, programs"). In part 1, I will describe the thought pattern which forms the paradigm of natural church development, and I will contrast it with these two competing systems. This book argues that if we understand the presuppositions behind the different paradigms, which are often not explicitly stated but nevertheless present, many (if not most) of the modern theological controversies can be explained in a way that may be surprisingly simple.

1

The Starting Point of Natural Church Development: Bipolar Ecclesiology

Working out the theological consequences of a bipolar ecclesiology—i.e., the distinction and interrelationship between the church as "organization" and the church as "organism"—is, as simple as it may sound, the most important contribution made by our book *Theology of Church Development*. This distinction, which draws primarily on the systematic theological work of Emil Brunner,[1] Hans-Joachim Kraus[2] and Helmut Gollwitzer,[3] is in my opinion an important foundation for a theological reflection on church development.

Unfortunately, the implications of this bipolar approach were usually not really understood in the discussion that followed publication. This was partly due to our lack of terminological clarity at that stage. Thus, this distinction was variously understood as a "strict division,"[4] a "dualistic theory of the church,"[5] an "angry attack on the state church,"[6] a "theological neutralization of the church,"[7] a "mystification of shared

---

1   *Brunner*: 1951. However, in our book we did not take over the one-sidedness of Brunner's concept of the church. Following the church law specialist Rudolph Sohm, Brunner regards the institutional element of the church—at least in one strand of his argument—as basically negative, and incompatible with the nature of *ekklesia* (cf. *Brunner*: 1960 c, p. 46). It then really is a feat of intellectual acrobatics to assign to this same institution the task of "serving the becoming of *ekklesia*" (*Brunner*: 1951, p. 106f). In a second strand of the argument, Brunner develops a relaxed and constructive approach to the institutional side of the church, which is nearer to our position, but he does not manage to bring the two aspects into harmony with each other.
2   *Kraus: 1975; Kraus: 1983.*
3   *Gollwitzer: 1975.*
4   *Strunk: 1986*, p. 124.
5   *Haarbeck: 1986*, p. 29.
6   Ibid. p. 24.
7   *Strunk: 1986*, p. 124.

personal reality,"[8] or even a "stabilization of the state church"[9]—all of them interpretations which had nothing to do with our intention.

In view of this confusion it is understandable that some critics pointed out that the significance of this approach "should not be regarded as so important as it seems to be in the *Theology of Church Development*."[10] Nevertheless, I would decidedly contradict this statement. I am now more convinced than ever that the bipolar approach is essential for a theological understanding of church growth; and it is definitely the theological key for understanding what natural church development is all about.

As I said, some of the expressions we used in our book may have been ambiguous[11]—and I thank all the critics who have pointed this out—but the *issue* that this concept aimed to clarify remains essential. I hope that the following pages can explain more clearly than previous publications why the bipolar ecclesiology is of fundamental importance for anyone who is interested in a theological reflection of church growth.[12]

---

8   *Strunk: 1986*, p. 125.
9   *Weth: 1986*, p. 149.
10   *Herbst: 1987*, p. 303.
11   I would like to correct the terminology we used in the *Theology of Church Development* in six areas. *First*, it is not exegetically correct to assign the New Testament term *ekklesia* only to the "organic" pole of the church. The New Testament concept of the church includes "both the expression of its life and its permanent structures" (*Weber: 1964*, p. 275). *Second*, the term "institution" in our book is not meant to describe only the institutional forms of the state church. However, as the book drew largely on our experience in the state church, it could give the impression that we were dealing with problems that arise in just one denomination. We did not express clearly enough that we were talking about a theological paradigm with interdenominational significance. *Third*, I now regard our description of *ekklesia* as an "end in itself" as problematical. As a contrast to the characterization of the institution as a "means to an end" the term has a limited justification, but in its traditional use, "end in itself" has so many associations that do not correspond to the New Testament concept of *ekklesia* that it would be better to do without the word. *Fourth*, in spite of our attempts at clarification, the concept of "institution" in the *Theology of Church Development* remains too vague. Sometimes the term is used for the forms and structures of the church (as distinct from the people), and sometimes it is used as an overall term for the church (including the people). This is one of the causes of the misunderstandings apparent in reactions to the book. *Fifth*, with hindsight, I would still say that it was right in 1984 to lay so much emphasis on the *distinction* between "organization" and "organism." But it was easy to overlook our real intention, which was to use this distinction as a logical precondition for describing the constructive *interrelationship* of these two elements. *Sixth*, in many ways, the methods we used to explain this distinction in the *Theology of Church Development* appear to me now as too static—and a number of concepts are, without doubt, still too technocratic. The specific biotic categories which have been exceedingly fruitful in theoretical and practical work on church growth were not yet available to us. The current book aims to do justice to the present state of development in these areas.
12   For the sake of clarity, I would like to state categorically what is *not* meant by the distinction between organization and organism. With this terminology, I am *not* drawing a distinction between state church and free church, visible church and invisible church, sinful church and perfect church, born-again Christians and nominal Christians,

The Dynamic and the Static

The nature of the church is made up of two elements: a dynamic pole (organism) and a static pole (organization).[13] Both are necessary for church development, and both poles are implied in the New Testament concept of *ekklesia*.[14]

The dynamic pole is mainly found in New Testament statements which describe the church in biological, organic terms and therefore emphasize the aspect of "growth." The prime example is the way the church is characterized as the "body of Christ," and the individual Christians as "parts of the body."[15] The static element is found in statements which describe the church in terms of architectural and technical metaphors and consequently emphasize the aspect of "church building." The prime example is the way the apostle Paul characterizes himself as a "wise architect" who laid the "foundation" on which others "build."[16] In the New Testament, both approaches are present, and they are in no way in competition with each other.

There are even a number of passages in which the two aspects are so closely intertwined in a single statement that the resulting picture—judged by standards of linear logic—seems contradictory.[17] Examples are such phrases as "living (organic metaphor) stones (technical metaphor),"[18] "growing (organic metaphor) into a temple (technical metaphor),"[19] the description of the Corinthians as "God's field (organic metaphor) and God's building (technical metaphor),"[20] or "that the body of Christ (organic metaphor) may be built up (technical metaphor)."[21]

---

manifest church and latent church, and I am not talking about the concept of the *ecclesiola in ecclesia*. This note is necessary because, in different contributions to the debate, the distinction between organization and organism has been confused with all of these concepts. For more detail, see *Schwarz/Schwarz: 1987*, p. 50ff.

13   With the word "static" I am *not* referring to the pathological phenomenon of institutional or dogmatic inflexibility. What I mean is a protective, preserving structure of the church, comparable to the load-bearing structure of a building.

14   Rudolph Weth correctly points this out in his constructive criticism of the *Theology of Church Development:* "We are dealing with a basic distinction and classification, and *both elements* belong to the full concept of *ekklesia* and church development (by contrast to the position taken by Schwarz): organism and organization, the work of the Spirit and human action, spiritual gifts and institutions, the 'present working' of Jesus Christ through the Holy Spirit, which cannot be planned and must be prayed for (Barmen III, basic premise) and the corresponding acts of obedience of the church and its institutions (consequence)" (*Weth: 1986*, p. 150f).

15   Romans 12:3-8; 1 Corinthians 12:12-31.

16   1 Corinthians 3:10f.

17   A rhetorical device which was quite common in classical antiquity, cf. the article on *oikodomeo* by Otto Michel (*Michel: 1954*, p. 143).

18   1 Peter 2:4-8.

19   Ephesians 2:19-22.

20   1 Corinthians 3:9.

21   Ephesians 4:12; cf. also v. 16: "the whole body . . . *grows* and *builds itself up* in love."

Dynamic pole	Static pole
organic grow freedom "all by itself"	technical build order human-made

Fig. 1: The distinction between the church as an organization and the church as an organism.

Each of these two poles can be assigned to a number of opposing concepts, as I have done in figure 1. This polarity expresses the distinction between the church as an organization and the church as an organism. Before I go into more detail concerning the distinction between these two poles and their practical interdependence, it seems sensible to take a closer look at the nature of both the static and the dynamic element.

The Nature of the Dynamic Pole

In the ecumenical discussion, there is a large measure of agreement on what needs to happen in a church so that it can be called a church in the *theological* sense: faith, fellowship, and service.[22] These central concepts cannot be taken for granted wherever a church as an institution exists; they need to become reality again and again. That is what church development is all about.

---

22 In every secular institution it is taken for granted that the organization lives on the three elements of inspiration, communication, and action, which can be regarded as the secular counterparts of faith, fellowship, and service. In the discussion of church growth in the United States, the concept of the "three priorities" propounded by Raymond Ortlund (commitment to Christ, commitment to the body of Christ, commitment to the world) has gained great influence (*Ortlund: 1983*, pp. 11, 119, etc.). In the ecumenical discussion, the formula *kerygma, koinonia, diakonia*, which was introduced by Johannes Christiaan Hoekendijk, has become generally accepted (*Hoekendijk: 1950*, p. 171f). I can agree to this formula, but I find it more consistent to speak of the threefold effect that results from the *kerygma*. In several discussions in the past it has been suggested that this concentration on the effect is a shift to a subjectivist approach. On the following pages it will become clearly apparent that my own position has nothing to do with subjectivism. But—by contrast with an abstract objectivism—I do emphasize the subjective effect of the *kerygma* (i.e., the effect it has on the subject).

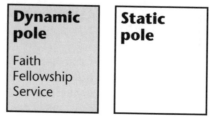

Fig. 2: Concepts that describe the church as an organism.

Wherever the concepts of faith, fellowship, and service are used to describe the church as an organism, critics point out—as a counter-claim—the "objective" *notae ecclesiae* which, in the Lutheran tradition, for example, are defined as "correct proclamation and administration of the sacraments."[23] But here we can see what happens if we do not distinguish clearly between organization and organism. Both preaching (in the Lutheran context largely understood as the pastor's pulpit lecture) and administration of the sacraments are part of the organizational side of the church. They are institutional elements which are meant to help (and in countless cases *have* helped) the organic pole of the church to develop. They must never be regarded as a substitute for faith, fellowship, and service. Rather, they need to be placed in a functional relationship to these three elements, as will be developed in more detail later on.

The reduction of the *notae ecclesiae* to "word and sacrament" must be seen historically as an offer of unity in the context of the conflict of the Reformation churches with the Roman Catholic Church. "For the precise definition of the fellowship of believers, however, this phrase is not enough. Although the word and the sacrament constitute the fellowship, this fellowship itself must also be emphasized in mutual sharing and commitment."[24] In other words, whenever faith, fellowship, and service—or just one of these elements—are missing or neglected in an institution, we should not regard this institution as "true church."

Perhaps a simple illustration will help to clarify this discussion. If we deduce from the mere existence of certain organizational features that the church as an organism is guaranteed, the structure of our thinking is similar to a soccer fan who deduces from the mere presence of a soccer field, a ball, soccer boots, and a referee's whistle that a soccer match must be in progress. That is not necessarily so. The existence of this "standard equipment," however basic it may be for a soccer match, is no *substitute* for a real game with 22 players, one referee, and two

---

23   Here, however, we must not overlook the fact that the two *notae* in the *Confessio Augustana* are only one of many attempts in the Christian world to set up criteria for the "true church."

24   *Moltmann: 1975*, p. 341f.

45-minute sessions of completely unforeseeable action. In the same way, the church must come into action as an organism before we can call it a church. Institutions on their own—even such essential ones as proclamation and the sacraments—do not guarantee the presence of the church as an organism, in the same way as the existence of a soccer *field* does not guarantee that a soccer *game* is being played.

The Nature of the Static Pole

The above explanation also makes it plain that the distinction between organization and organism in no way devalues the institutional side of the church. Church as an organism can never find expression in a vacuum, free of all institutions. From the beginning, the church had legal statutes. In the understanding of the church, evident in the New Testament, "spirit" and "order" do not exclude, but rather *include* each other. [25]

There was a plausible reason for the creation of legally ordered institutions. Numerous false teachings threatened to overcome the young church. For example, the Gnostics appealed in the same way as the church "to the Spirit speaking and working within them." [26] Thus, three institutional elements arose early on which proved to be helpful in this critical situation: the biblical canon, the rules of faith, and the episcopalian hierarchy. Beside the dynamic element there was now a static one, the adherence to formal authority and tradition. It remains to be shown how, in each of the three areas of faith, fellowship, and service, a multitude of institutional elements arose, accompanied by the desire for the protection, preservation, and stimulation of the church as an organism.

Dynamic pole	**Static pole**
Faith	Doctrine
Fellowship	Sacraments
Service	Office

Fig. 3: Concepts that describe the organizational pole of the church.

The creation of these institutional elements makes sense, but they cannot *guarantee* the church as an organism. At best, institutions can be *useful* for

---

25 Cf. the classical work of Eduard Schweizer on the New Testament church (*Schweizer: 1949*).

26 *Käsemann: 1960*, p. 129.

the development of the organic pole. But they can also be a hindrance to its development. They are theologically legitimate in as far as they prove their usefulness. Demonstrating the doctrinal implications of this statement is one of the tasks of this book.

The Relationship Between Organization and Organism

The approach outlined here shows that "organization" and "organism" are in a twofold relationship to each other. On the one hand, the development of the church as an organism inevitably leads to the creation of institutions. On the other hand, the aim of these institutions is to be useful in stimulating the development of the church as an organism.

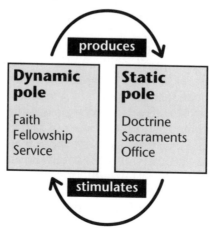

Fig. 4: The (ideal) relationship between organization and organism.

As long as this reciprocal flow is intact, the relationship between organization and organism is harmonious (see fig. 4). It would be completely misleading to speak here of a "dialectic tension" or a "paradoxical identity." [27] Tension only arises when this relationship is interrupted, and paradox thought patterns are only necessary when this unhealthy condition must be justified theologically. In healthy churches, we can study a relatively harmonious functioning of this interrelationship.

Let me make an important distinction that will become highly relevant when we come to consider the practical side of church develop-

---

27   Concepts such as "dualism" and "dichotomy," if they are used to describe the relationship between organization and organism, also take us in a completely wrong direction. There certainly are dualism and dichotomy—as we will see—between the institutionalistic paradigm and its spiritualistic counterpart, but not between organization and organism.

ment. The church as an organization can be "manufactured" by humans; the church as an organism cannot. We can have control over the organization, but never over the organism. The well-trodden discussion about whether we can "make" a church grow is hindered by the fact that these two levels are usually not distinguished.[28] In natural church development, all we can do—to present my thesis briefly from the outset—is subject the elements we *can* influence to the criterion of functionality in such a way that the elements that are beyond our control may take place. We do not make them; rather they happen "all by themselves."

The importance of linking the institutional with the personal, the organizational with the organic, the static with the dynamic, is repeatedly underlined when our institute carries out scientific studies of local churches. In these analyses we have discovered eight quality characteristics which are measurably more developed in growing churches than in stagnant and declining ones.[29] For each of these eight quality characteristics, the organizational level and the organic level are functionally related to each other.[30]

1. Empowering leadership
2. Gift-oriented ministry
3. Passionate spirituality
4. Functional structures
5. Inspiring worship service
6. Holistic small groups
7. Need-oriented evangelism
8. Loving relationships

These quality characteristics are not meant to be normative in a dogmatic sense. Rather, they are tried and tested instruments to ascertain how *healthy* a church is. But they certainly have a doctrinal relevance, and they must be reflected from a doctrinal point of view. In later chapters we will discuss the relationship between *health* and *truth*, and the influence that both have on *growth*. I wish to treat the eight quality characteristics as practical illustrations within the theological paradigm of natural church development at the point at which they play a doctrinal role in the overall system.[31]

---

28 For a more detailed treatment, see pages 252-263.
29 Cf. *Schwarz: 1996.*
30 For further details see pages 221ff.
31 "Empowering leadership" and "gift-oriented ministry" will be treated in the context of our discussion of spiritual gifts and office (p. 186), "passionate spirituality" in the context of doctrine and Scripture (p. 124), "functional structures" in the context of traditions and change (p. 159), "inspiring worship service" in the context of baptism and communion (p. 149), "holistic small groups" in the context of church planting and cooperation (p. 171), "need-oriented evangelism" in the context of evangelism and conversion (p. 211), and "loving relationships" in the context of Christian ethics (p. 134).

Dangers to the Right and to the Left

This mutual interrelationship of the organizational and the organic poles of the church is a description of an ideal condition, which is only rarely to be found in practice. The statements above are not facts that we should *believe*—and then project onto a reality that is completely different. They are a goal that we should strive for by adopting practical measures. In many cases, the relationship between the static and the dynamic poles is sadly out of balance.

It can go astray in one of two directions: *to the left*, towards a dualistic subjectivism, which is anti-institutional out of conviction (and which on the following pages will be labelled as "spiritualistic paradigm")[32]; *to the right*, towards a monistic objectivism, which deduces from the very existence of certain institutions that the body of Christ is a reality in a given situation (on the following pages, this position will be labelled as "institutionalistic paradigm").[33]

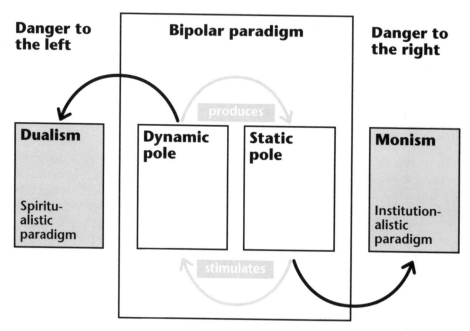

Fig. 5: The "true church" and the dangers to the right and to the left.

Every institution (static pole) is in danger of developing into a monistic institutionalism; in the same way, every spiritual experience (dynamic

---

32   For a more detailed discussion of this concept, see pages 32-38.
33   For a more detailed discussion of this concept, see pages 24-31.

pole) brings with it the danger of moving towards a dualistic spiritual-ism. It can be demonstrated that major parts of church history are charac-terized by a conflict between subjectivism and objectivism, spiritualism and institutionalism, dualism and monism, mysticism and magic—in other words, by a conflict between two misunderstandings of the Chris-tian faith. Renewal movements such as the Reformation and the evan-gelical revivals had to fight on two fronts—in that they had to set them-selves apart from both of these misunderstandings. And it is precisely at this point that they were most misunderstood themselves.

Even today, these two extremes, with their "either-or" logic, seem to be more prevalent than a functional relationship between organization and organism, as it is characteristic of the bipolar paradigm. In this situ-ation it is not surprising that the subject of church growth does not really get off the ground. In the next two chapters I aim to show why it is sim-ply not possible for advocates of both the spiritualistic and the institu-tionalistic paradigms to find a positive relationship to natural church de-velopment.

2
Danger to the Right: The Institutionalistic Misconception

The mistake of the institutionalistic misconception is that it identifies the "organization" with the "organism." This paradigm is based on a monistic thought pattern. Instead of evaluating the institutional side of the church from a functional point of view, institutions are assumed to have an almost magical quality: wherever certain institutions are present, the church of Jesus Christ is guaranteed.

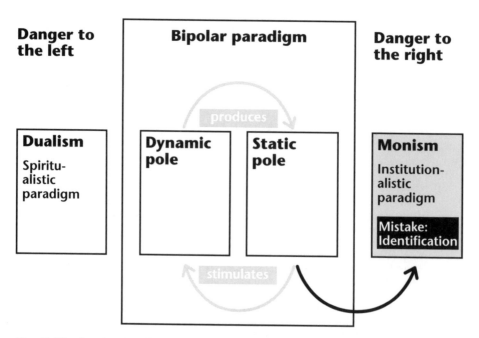

Fig. 6: The institutionalistic misunderstanding: organization and organism are identified with each other.

A faith in this sort of automatic relationship is a mark of all forms of magical thinking. The magician is convinced: If I only speak the magic formula, the result will automatically come about. We can find analogous thought structures within the church: "If I speak the words of consecration, the earthly elements will automatically be changed into divine medicine." "If I am correctly ordained, I automatically have the Holy Spirit." "If I am in the apostolic succession, I automatically have spiritual authority." "If I hold a worship service in accordance with a certain pattern, the church of Jesus Christ is automatically a reality." All these—and many other—methods have, in the sense outlined above, a magical structure.

This misconception occurs in a variety of ways, and only rarely in its pure form. Therefore it is sometimes not easy to detect the institutionalistic structure behind certain theological positions. The following five characteristics are typical of the pure form of the institutionalistic misconception.

Characteristic 1: Objectivism

Objectivism arises out of an understandable human drive for security.[1] People are not content with the *certitudo* of faith; rather, they seek the *securitas* which always tries to reassure itself with guarantees. Whatever version of the institutionalistic misconception is involved—fundamentalism, sacramentalism, dogmatism, traditionalism, clericalism, and so forth—the basic urge for security can always be clearly seen.[2]

A theology that offers this sort of security fulfills the felt needs of many people, so that even in a secularized age, proponents of this paradigm can expect to find a certain number of followers. It is noticeable that this way of thinking is present in almost all religions—with similarities even in the most surprising details.

Proponents of the objectivist misconception are usually really concerned to further the church of Jesus Christ. Their mistake is that they cannot see the function of institutions as being merely useful to *stimulate* the organic side of the church. They want more: they want the church to

---

1   In his book *Discipleship*, Dietrich Bonhoeffer describes in a classical way that this security mentality is a contradiction of the nature of the Christian faith. He sees the "content of discipleship" as being basically a "stepping out": "The disciple is cast out of the relative securities of life into complete unsecurity (i.e., in reality into the absolute certainty and security of the fellowship of Jesus); out of the comprehensible and predictable (i.e., in reality the unpredictable) into the totally unpredictable and random (i.e., in reality, into the only path that is necessary and predictable); out of the sphere of finite possibilities (i.e., in reality, of endless possibilities) into the sphere of the boundless possibilities (i.e., in reality, the only way to liberty)" *(Bonhoeffer: 1981*, p. 29f).

2   Alfred Jäger is right when he comments on fundamentalism: "It wants to give security, security in the inner behavior of the student, security around the biblical word . . . Large areas of fundamentalism are, in fact, a theology of fear" *(Jäger: 1983*, p. 21f).

be *guaranteed*. The result of this (often well-meaning) concern for security is that, in many cases, they achieve the exact opposite of what was originally intended. The church as an organism becomes simply unnecessary. It needs no longer find expression, because it is (so it is believed) already present, if only we have the right institutions! Even where it cannot be seen, adherents of the institutionalistic paradigm are not embarrassed. They simply appropriate in faith what is not visible. In their imagination, biblical statements are projected onto a reality that is completely different—and they begin to live in a world of make believe. This is probably the highest level of institutionalistic thinking, and it is interesting that it comes close to a radical spiritualistic position.[3]

Not everything about the objectivist misconception is actually wrong. It is no mistake when objectivists remind us that we cannot equate God's revelation with our own pious feelings. The mistake lies in the wish "that revelation should be secured—in such a way that in reality the church secures itself."[4]

Characteristic 2: Heteronomism

The security-mentality of the institutionalistic paradigm inevitably leads to a heteronomic concept of the church and the faith. There is a longing for a legalistic, manageable authority. One example, which is a typically Protestant variety, is the orthodox teaching that Scripture is an axiomatic authority. Or, in the Roman Catholic variety of heteronomism, it can be the doctrine of the infallibility of the Pope. There are numerous other versions which are far more subtle. The common element is that God becomes an authoritative postulate, a philosophical axiom. Proponents of this kind of heteronomism fight passionately to preserve God as part of the cultural identity of an increasingly secularized society—with greater passion than they invest in winning others for a personal *relationship* with this God.

Heteronomism means that the *gramma* again takes the place of the *pneuma*.[5] The archetype of this concept of "faith" is the law. Legal precepts and institutions take the place that should be occupied only by Christ. In this way, Christ is replaced. What need is there for a personal relationship with Christ if the acceptance of doctrinal statements, the adherence to a moral code, or the subjection to ecclesiastical authority is sufficient?

---

3   As will be shown, however mutually exclusive the two positions of "spiritualism" and "institutionalism" seem to be on the surface, they are both based on an unhistorical concept of revelation. Therefore it is not surprising that, although they normally regard each other as enemies, in their more radical forms they do, in fact, have certain similarities.

4   *Weber: 1964*, p. 202.

5   2 Corinthians 3.

In the more radical versions of the heteronomic paradigm, it is only consistent to emphasize a strict external order, a hierarchical leadership, and an uncompromising discipline—as a means of protecting the immutable Christian truth from all sorts of heretical deviation. A particularly consistent expression of this concept of faith was the Inquisition. Similar patterns of thought, however, can still be observed in various Christian groups today, in which people follow the illusion that faith can be secured by the use of force or authority.[6]

Characteristic 3: Formalism

Objectivists fight—understandably, from their point of view—against all forms of compromise and decay. But they are blind to the danger that is lurking—figuratively speaking—at the other end of the scale: paralysis. It is like a frozen waterfall; the shape of the movement can still be seen, but all movement has long ceased.

This is where the often quoted phrase, "dead orthodoxy," has a certain justification. Formalism is a flight into *necrophilia.* Life is replaced by a multitude of rituals, which can assume a number of forms, depending on the basic theological position and the devotional style. The magical use of the rosary, holy water, and amulets is one version; the illusion that outmoded, antiquated, "sacred" linguistic forms and thought patterns can be used to reach modern men and women is a more rationalistic variety. Basically, both varieties represent a formalistic externalizing of the faith.

As formalism becomes stronger, the question of the content is becoming less and less important. When, for example, the "Brotherhood of the 11,000 virgins" in Cologne, Germany, demanded that novice nuns recite 11,000 "Our Fathers" and "Ave Marias,"[7] the very formalism—in this case quantitative—ensured that the exercise would have nothing whatever to do with worship and piety.

This example from the Middle Ages shows the effects of a thoroughly consistent formalistic premise. But even in modern Christianity, we can trace innumerable formalistic elements, albeit not as dramatic as

---

6 The following observation is particularly interesting. The more "tolerant" proponents of the institutionalistic paradigm are (in order to absorb as many positions as possible), the more unyielding and even fanatic they can become when they are faced with positions that touch what they consider to be the heart of their institutionalistic security. For example, many European state church ideologists, who otherwise show an incredible amount of tolerance and broad-mindedness (absorbing both faith and unbelief with equal ease), suddenly display an almost inquisitorial intolerance when the real *articuli stantis et cadentis ecclesiae* are called into question: infant baptism, church taxes, the parochial structure. This is a symptom of the deep heteronomic character of an institution which emphasizes, in other areas, "autonomy" and "freedom" so much.

7 Cf. *Schmidt: 1960,* p. 261.

the example quoted. For instance, in the training of pastors in some churches, the emphasis is placed exclusively on rational standards of knowledge, not on the necessary spiritual gifts of the candidates. Or some church services always follow a static pattern, and no one ever asks how effective it is. Or some Christians believe that their spiritual power increases if they use certain words in prayer. In all these cases, we see the consequences of a formalistic externalizing of the faith. Viewed through the bipolar paradigm, this formalism can easily be recognized as a dangerous influence. Against the background of the institutionalistic paradigm, however, it is not only understandable to think like this—it is inevitable.

Characteristic 4: Rationalism

Rationalism is, in a sense, a form of institutionalism on the level of philosophical reflection. Theological rationalism, at least in its more radical forms, is a rejection of all forms of religious "experience." The shift of the concept of faith from the personal, spiritual level to the abstract, intellectual level aims to make faith manageable beyond the dimension of experience. This misconception makes the church the object of faith, and even places theological value on the premise that the *communio sanctorum* has nothing to do with experience. This position is, in fact, *intellectual pelagianism*. As Rudolf Bultmann rightly pointed out, there is no difference between "security on the basis of good works" and "security that is mediated by objective knowledge."[8]

Rationalism prefers the language of abstraction. It works on the principle: the greater the abstraction, the more active the spirit.[9] There is a predominantly linear logic with a static pattern of cause and effect—a danger, incidentally, which has not spared parts of the church growth movement, as we will see.

Characteristic 5: Magic

Our familiarity with the theological debate on the sacraments can help us to characterize the basic structure that lies behind the institutionalistic misconception as a whole. The term *ex opere operato* expresses the conviction of sacramentalists that merely performing the sacrament automatically guarantees its effectiveness due to its integral qualities.

---

8   *Bultmann: 1964*, p. 100.
9   Although it is not the *degree* of abstraction I take issue with, but, as will be shown later, the increasing shift away from a functional perspective which frequently (although not necessarily) goes hand in hand with the increasing degree of abstraction.

Emil Brunner describes this mechanism as follows: "Human beings are accustomed and have a striving to build everything they have no control over, and which by its very nature cannot be controlled, such as divine grace and truth, into a system of human security. The sacrament which the Lord gave to his church and in which he gives his presence to believers and feeds and strengthens their faith was already in early times reinterpreted in such a way that a free gift of God, an event intended to express the freely given and now present grace, became a priestly sacrifice which human beings took into their own hands: the presence and grace of God, managed by man. By speaking the words of consecration, the priest transubstantiates the bread and wine into the body and blood of the Lord, thus creating the means of redemption like a heavenly medicine—*pharmakon athanasias*, as it was described as early as the second century; he may not do so, but *per nefas* he is able to perform the miracle of transubstantiation whenever and wherever he will. The means of salvation is in the hands of the priest—or at least in the power of the church."[10]

This structure of thought and action which seeks to bring God within our grasp is manifested in a parallel manner in other areas apart from the sacraments. Whether in traditionalism, clericalism, dogmatism—everywhere we encounter the same thought pattern: by maintaining certain traditions (for their own sake), the preservation of the faith is assured *ex opere operato*; by the institution of a bishop or pastor, the church of Jesus Christ is guaranteed *ex opere operato*; when a person rationally assents to certain doctrinal facts, personal commitment is guaranteed *ex opere operato*. It strikes me that it is not disrespectful to suggest that in the three examples mentioned, the phrase *ex opere operato* could be replaced by the words *hocus pocus fidibus*.[11] This parallel seems to me rather to put its finger on the decisive theological point, i.e., the magical character of the institutionalistic paradigm.

The magical pattern of this thinking can be illustrated particularly well by referring to the faith in relics found in the old church and the Middle Ages. The bodies of martyrs were cut up, and the parts were circulated as sources of supernatural power. Many theologians claimed that the smallest of relics had the same effectiveness as whole bodies: a divided body, but undivided grace! Other theologians postulated a certain hierarchy of relics. They distinguished between capital parts *(reliquiae insignes)*, i.e., whole bodies or main limbs such as heads, arms, legs, from the less important relics, the *reliquiae non insignes*. In these relics, a further distinction was made between significant relics *(notabiles)*, such as hands and feet, and the lesser relict *(exiguae)*, such as fingers and teeth.[12]

---

10 *Brunner: 1984*, p. 73.
11 Interestingly enough, the actual words *hocus pocus* originally come from the Eucharist liturgy: *hoc est corpus meum*—a malicious manipulation of the words in the polemic propaganda of reformed dogmatics.
12 Cf. *Pfister: 1912*, p. 323.

As the demand for these magical souvenirs was far greater than the supply, the church proceeded to manufacture artificial relics. These were brought into contact with the remains of martyrs, and by this means, people believed they too became bearers of divine power. From the fourth century onwards, the church mass-produced and exported cloth relics.[13] In the sixth century, Pope Gregory I declared that the cloths laid down by the graves of martyrs received the same efficacy as the elements of the Eucharist in consecration. Pope Leo the Great, Gregory claimed, had once cut such a cloth to convince doubters of the miraculous power of these artificial relics. Blood had flowed from the cut.[14]

I deliberately quote these extreme examples in this context because they express in a particularly graphic way the same magical thought pattern that lies behind the more subtle, hidden forms of the institutionalistic paradigm. The dimension of the personal encounter with Christ and with our brothers and sisters is replaced by the touching of *theophorous* objects.

Parallel thought patterns may be hidden behind relatively "harmless" sounding phrases. For example, some people declare with a great deal of conviction that a certain church building (or musical work, church structure, or whatever) was created to "give glory to God." That is magical thinking, even if in this case the underlying magical thought pattern is not so obvious as for the relic worship outlined above. Buildings (or music or structures) cannot give glory to God. They can merely be *useful* (or a hindrance) for *people* to give glory to God. This distinction, as this book will show, is not just a play on words and concepts. Wherever people try to substitute material objects for the personal element, the magical misconception is apparent.

Albert Schweitzer reported one episode from his jungle experience in Lambarene which graphically illustrates the essence of magical thinking. When he wrote a medical prescription for the natives, it often happened that they ate it up before his eyes. They were obviously convinced that a prescription for good medicine itself had healing power. Anecdotes like that make us, as enlightened western Christians, smile; but they should not blind us to the fact that the same magical thought pattern—the identification of symbol and object—is also widespread in our culture.

Who Advocates This Position?

Institutionalism is not the same as the presence of institutions. Rather, the term describes a pathological condition, an illness which consists in a refusal to understand institutions from a functional point of view. A radi-

---

13   Cf. *Lucius: 1904,* p. 195.
14   Ibid.

cal examination of the usefulness of structures is felt by adherents of this position to be an "affront to the institution."

In the course of this book it will become clearer how strongly the institutionalistic paradigm influences the thought and—perhaps more importantly—the emotions of countless people even today. It can be traced especially in the Roman Catholic Church, which legitimates itself with arguments largely based on the five points mentioned. The Reformers turned away from all five characteristics of the institutionalistic misconception, but, as will be shown later on, in many areas remained trapped in what we could call a "modified institutionalistic paradigm."[15]

When I make such general statements, I must, of course, emphasize that there are countless Roman Catholic Christians and churches which are hardly influenced by the institutionalistic misconception. Some of these groups have a model function for church development—but they represent, at least in most cases, an alternative model to the prevailing paradigm of their surrounding.

On the other hand, there are Christians and churches in a radical reformed tradition that have *formally* freed themselves from all traces of the Roman institutionalistic misconception, but in their practice, all five characteristics of the institutionalistic paradigm play a prominent role (for example, among some sorts of "fundamentalists"). And it is certainly true that we can learn much, even from Christians who advocate a clearly institutionalistic position. The fact that they live in a wrong thought paradigm does not mean that everything they think and do is wrong. We should not, however, let them teach us the principles of church development.

There is a certain irony in the fact that among those who have accused the church growth movement—rightly or wrongly—of being technocratic, we often find some of the greatest "technocrats." The differences among a magical, object-based sacramentalism, a heteronomic fundamentalism, and a technocratic input-output logic with regard to church growth are, in terms of the underlying thought patterns, negligible. Recite a certain formula (as a correctly ordained servant of God)—and the Holy Spirit will come on you. Demand that people affirm the historical inerrancy of the Bible—and their hearts will turn to the living God. Use a certain church growth program—and your church will start to grow and blossom. Sacramentalism, fundamentalism, and church growth technocracy all have the same root—a strange alliance of enemies united only by their unadmitted monistic thought structures.

When I speak of the institutionalistic paradigm[16] in the course of this book, I am referring to the understanding of "institutionalism" outlined on the previous pages. I shall always use the term as an abbreviation for a system of thought that is made up of the five concepts explained in this chapter.

---

15   Cf. pp. 83-88.
16   In my book "Natural Church Development" *(Schwarz: 1996)* I call it the "technocratic paradigm."

3
Danger to the Left: The Spiritualistic Misconception

From the beginning of church history there has been a dualistic countermovement to set against the monistic tendencies of what we have called the "institutionalistic paradigm": the spiritualistic paradigm. Whereas the mistake of institutionalism is to *identify* the organization with the organism, the mistake of spiritualism lies in the *separation* of these two poles—a mistaken view with equally serious results.

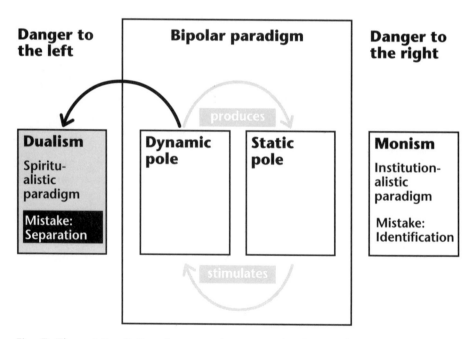

Fig. 7: The spiritualistic misconception: organization and organism are separated.

Thus, spiritualism can be understood on the one hand as a countermovement to the paralysis and formalism of orthodoxy, fundamentalism, dogmatism, and other forms of the institutionalistic misconception (in the same way as the institutionalistic position is partly a conscious countermovement to spiritualistic tendencies).[1] On the other hand, the spiritualistic paradigm also has its genuine roots in a dualistic world view which is antagonistic to institutions as a matter of principle. This position largely corresponds to the phenomenon known in theological discussion as the "enthusiasts."[2]

Characteristic 1: Subjectivism

Proponents of the institutionalistic paradigm are right when they insist that faith must appeal to an objective element. Their mistake is that, for them, this objective element is not Jesus Christ, but the institution. Thus, they are in danger of substituting the *organization* for Christ.

In the same way, proponents of the spiritualistic paradigm are right when they turn away from this objectivism and emphasize that faith must be appropriated subjectively. Their mistake is that, under the surface, they make religious experience the standard by which everything else is judged. Thus, they are in danger of substituting *human beings* for Christ.

We identified the psychological motivation behind the institutionalistic misconception in a security-mentality. The spiritualistic misconception

---

1   In such reciprocal relationships it is fairly futile to ask what is cause and what is effect—in fact, the static logic of cause and effect is the main weakness of a technocratic understanding of history, which is unable to do justice to complex historical processes. See also p. 240ff.

2   It seems to me problematical, however, to see everybody who is labeled "enthusiast" (*Schwärmer*) in church history as belonging to the spiritualistic paradigm. This applies especially to some adherents of the "left wing of the Reformation," who, in some aspects, touched the heart of what we today would call church development more consistently than the "orthodox" Reformers. I agree with the comment made by Emil Brunner on the Anabaptist movement: "When the Reformers, Luther as well as Calvin and Zwingli, fought against the Anabaptist movement and called its adherents 'enthusiasts' and 'rabble rousers,' today, with historical hindsight, we can understand both their bias towards the old tradition of the compulsory church (*i.e., the institutionalistic, heteronomic paradigm—the author*) and their resulting lack of understanding of the Anabaptist cause, and also the historical inevitability of the accusations they made . . . The accusation of being 'enthusiasts,' i.e., of subjectivism and illusionism, that was voiced by all the Reformers does not, at any rate, apply to the beginnings of the Anabaptist movement. Rather, the historical sources paint the picture of a sober faith in Christ, based on the teaching of the New Testament as its only authority, which had, in fact, a large measure of agreement with the faith of the Reformers . . . The Anabaptist movement had to pay the price of being ahead of its time: it was forced to go underground or into a revolutionary opposition, and there it did, in fact, go off course in ways that were sometimes dangerous" (*Brunner: 1960 c,* p. 98ff).

is a counter-tendency which is fed by the drive—which is perhaps even more basic—for unconditional freedom and spontaneity. Radical subjectivists allow nothing to have a binding value. They trust, as they say, only in the freely flowing Spirit of God, who inspires them as and when he will. This inspiration occurs moment by moment, without any rules or standards. It is, in fact (in the opinion of spiritualists), a hallmark of the Holy Spirit that he generally works in contrast to all rules.

Characteristic 2: Autonomism

As objectivism provokes subjectivism, the heteronomism of the institutionalistic paradigm provokes the counter-reaction of spiritualistic autonomism. Spiritualists answer heteronomism by emphasizing the direct experience of the Spirit. "Everything that is defined and fixed, every doctrine, every ordained office, every church ordinance or institution, even the fixing of God's word in the canon of the Scripture is in itself a distortion and a fossilization."[3] The degree of this autonomism, in other words the radicalness with which spiritualists advocate the principle of "directness," can vary a great deal. But the central aspect is always the desire to establish the autonomy of the individual.

We can see a prototype of radical autonomism in Thomas Müntzer, one of Luther's early followers and later opponents. He rejected all baptisms (not only infant baptism) and applied his dualistic thinking especially to the relationship between "Spirit and letter" in the Bible. Scripture as a book, he said, was no more than paper and ink. "Bible, Babel, Bubble," he proclaimed. Luther countered that the letter without the Spirit was undoubtedly dead, but that the two could no more be separated than body and soul.[4]

In the less radical forms of the spiritualistic misconception, the historical revelation and the validity of Holy Scripture are not denied, but the direct contact between the spiritualist and God is, at least, equally valid.[5]

Characteristic 3: Dualism

The spiritualist opposes the formalism of the institutionalistic paradigm with a tendency to other-worldliness. This position is sometimes manifested in a dualism between spirit and matter, in which the spirit is given absolute priority, while the material world is, at best, regarded as unimportant and, at worst, as evil. The theological justification for this posi-

---

3   *Brunner: 1984*, p. 77.
4   Cf. *Bainton: 1983*, p. 268.
5   Cf. *Richter: 1960*, p. 1238.

tion can vary. Either God the Creator (as *demiourgos)* is separated from God the Savior, for example by Marcion; or—in a version that is more widespread today—creation is primarily regarded as "fallen" so that, although it is still postulated as the work of the one God, it can no longer be understood as a positive entity.

Both hypotheses have the same results, which have fatal consequences not only for church development: the created world is devalued in favor of what is regarded as "spiritual." Rudolf Bohren rightly warns: "A theology and proclamation which forgot the Creator and the fact that we are created beings was not troubled by the pollution of our water and our air, nor by the poisoning of the earth . . . If the Trinity is neglected, the humanity of Christ is spiritualized and creation is reduced to a merely emotional experience."[6]

The prototype of this kind of dualism is gnosticism, in which life on earth was sometimes called a "catastrophe" and even identified with hell. *Soma sema,* "The body (is) the tomb (of the soul)"—a statement attributed to Plato and taken over by the Gnostics—was the shortest watchword for this anti-materialistic way of thinking.[7] The striving of the Gnostics was thus directed to escaping the sphere of influence of the world, and thus, the sphere of evil.

Gnostic dualism almost inevitably leads to a *docetic* way of thinking. This does not necessarily involve accepting the Christological theory of docetism, namely that the divine Christ was pure spirit and his human nature was merely an appearance *(dokesis).* The modern Gnostic can come to terms with "orthodox" formulas which hold to the full incarnation of Christ. But his or her whole thinking shows that the significance of what incarnation means has not really been understood. Dualistic thinking locates the spiritual manifestations, not in the events of history, but beyond them on a different level.

Thus, spiritualists are in danger of coming into conflict with historical events of any sort. Culture, art, and science are almost entirely regarded as negative, or at best indifferent. Luther's warning at this point reflects an accurate observation: "If someone despises music, as all enthusiasts do, I am not content with him. For music is a gift and present from God,"[8] the Reformer argued against his spiritualistic opponents. This statement did not arise because the musician in Luther got the better of the theologian—on the contrary. Luther the theologian had accurately observed that a contempt for music can be a symptom of a far more deep-rooted problem, namely a contempt for God's creation. For good theological reasons, he wanted to have nothing to do with the hostility to culture shown by the *iconoclasts* of his time.

---

6   *Bohren: 1975,* p. 50f.
7   *Plato,* Gorgias, 493 A.
8   Weimar Edition 6, p. 7034.

The dualism of their paradigm explains why spiritualists have difficulty in understanding the strategical implications of church development. Anyone who is influenced by *soma sema* thinking can't see any spiritual meaning in empirical concepts such as "church analysis." Terms like "planning," "strategy," or "principles" are anathema. Whether the underlying thinking is *soma sema*, "Mere humans can't contribute anything to church development," or "Bible-Babel-Bubble"—all of these phrases are just different ways of expressing the same spiritualistic premise.

Characteristic 4: Irrationality

The spiritualistic counterpart to the rationalism of the institutionalistic misconception is an overestimation of religious feelings. This approach can lead, in extreme cases, to irrationality.

The mistake of the spiritualists is not in reminding us that reality can never be explained completely in rational terms. The danger is that spiritualists tend to regard the irrational as being more spiritual than things that can be explained rationally. They do not understand that rationality (not rationalism!) is a gift of God. For the spiritualist, because of the paradigm in which he or she thinks, rationality and rationalism are synonyms.

Insights gained in church growth research by sociological, psychological, or statistical methods are, for people influenced by this paradigm, not really "spiritual." The only things that are "spiritual," and therefore "from God," are occurrences that cannot be explained rationally. Because of their paradigm, spiritualists cannot see that, in the end, this approach means that God constantly needs to overrule his own principles. For them, these principles are not God's principles at all, they are creations of human beings, if not of the devil.

Characteristic 5: Mysticism

The spiritualistic paradigm has a strong affinity to mysticism. For the mystic, the true spiritual reality is the *unio mystica*, which cannot be described in words. It is this anti-empirical approach which gives mysticism its name. The Greek word *myein* simply means "closing your eyes." It is a synonym for the rejection of the world of the senses, empirical reality, and logical thinking.

This view is not merely a reaction to the institutionalistic misconception. Rather, it directly springs from the spiritualist's dualistic paradigm. The mystic not only opposes the pathological phenomenon of institutionalism—he or she is against *institutions in themselves*.[9] Institutions are part of

---

9   Cf. *Ozment: 1973*, p. 163.

the created material world which adherents of this thought pattern view skeptically as a matter of principle. Therefore, spiritualists cannot examine them without prejudice, and to consider their functionality is unthinkable. The mystic believes that the freedom of the Spirit forbids commitment to any sort of external form. In some cases, this anti-institutional attitude can develop into a general animosity towards churches. In other cases, the mystic comes to terms with the inevitability of institutions. He or she does not fight against them, but they are seen as spiritually meaningless. This is one of the underlying reasons why many Christian groups today regard all structural questions related to the church as being spiritually irrelevant.

It is no accident that mysticism is a form of theology that is mainly defined in terms of negatives. The mystic is right in rejecting the magical structure with the underlying presumption that we can guarantee the presence of the Spirit. But he or she is in danger of being caught in a string of negatives: anti-clericalistic (i.e., individualistic), anti-sacramentalist (i.e., spiritualistic), anti-monopolistic (i.e., separatist). Mystics are not wrong in rejecting the things they reject. But the alternative position that they have to offer does no more justice to the biblical revelation than the institutionalistic misconception.

Much of spiritualism draws its identity from the fact that it is a protest movement against its opponent. Thus it is more closely related to the institutionalistic paradigm than appears at first sight, as we will see in more detail later. Particularly in the sometimes rather immature revolt against the institutional side of the church, spiritualism turns out to be the child of institutionalism. It is like the baker's son who stubbornly refuses to become a baker. There is the danger that he will spend his whole life thinking of himself as a *non-baker*. The picture of his father—even if it is a negative one—continues to influence all his decisions. Thus, even in his rebellion he remains dependent on his father, a danger typical for escapist positions of any kind.

Who Advocates This Position?

When I speak in this book of the spiritualistic paradigm, the term is always meant in the way I have outlined here. The same applies when I use the nouns "spiritualist" or "spiritualism."

Spiritualism is even more difficult than the institutionalistic misconception to press into a uniform scheme. There are numerous forms of spiritualism, and not all of the five characteristics outlined above apply to all spiritualistic positions. It is in the nature of spiritualism that it resists classification, even classification in an anti-church-growth paradigm.

The examples given in this chapter—docetism, gnosticism, "Bible-Babel-Bubble," and so forth—clearly betray the anti-biblical nature of this position. But there are many versions of the same misconception which are more subtle because they hide behind orthodox terminology. For example, I know numerous groups that have replaced any strategic work on church development with a nebulous expectancy of "revival." The principles of church development may in their view have a limited validity (at least, for the more moderate adherents—radical advocates can do entirely without churches). But the *real* thing will be "the revival" (although, characteristically, no one is able to say exactly what it is). When revival comes, then . . .

What then? Then, church development will more than ever be the need of the hour. Then we would be wise to prepare ourselves now by planned, specific action. Then, more than ever, we will need to be better informed, to question our comfortable thought patterns, mercilessly to analyze the (often pitiful) state of our churches, to uncover the hindrances to church development that we carry within ourselves, and to set about the difficult task of overcoming them.

People who have substituted their revival expectancy for the task of working for church development will see things differently. For them, all the terms set out here are unimportant, unspiritual, and presumptuous. They advocate the position typical of dualistically oriented spiritualists, i.e., that the *only* thing we can do is to ask God for revival (and, of course, to hold on to a strong belief that he will grant our request).

This position, like so much of what spiritualists advocate, is unbiblical. It is correct that church growth cannot flourish without committed prayer. But as the Bible clearly shows us, prayer is certainly not the only thing we can do, nor is it the only thing God wants us to do. If we examine this position more closely—the deliberately woolly goals, the devaluation of human action, the dualistic contrast between Spirit and principles, the passive, lethargic attitude which claims to be the precondition for God to act, and so forth—then we discover behind the mask of revival expectancy, which on the surface seems to be so attractive, none other than the spiritualistic paradigm.

To avoid misunderstanding, let me say that these Christians, like the adherents of the institutionalistic misconception, are usually honest, well-meaning people who often have a lot of constructive things to say on theological and practical issues. But they are blind to *one* fact: that they are influenced, often despite their intention, by a disastrous theological paradigm. The spiritualistic paradigm undermines the foundation on which revival can flourish, as we will see in detail later.[10] Here, the same applies as for the institutionalistic paradigm: not everything that spiritualists advocate is wrong simply because they are spiritualists. Many of the experiences they make can be an inspiration to other Christians. Especially with regard to forms of practical spirituality we can learn—not always, but in numerous instances—a lot from them. But we must add here, too, that we should not let them teach us the principles of church development.

---

10   Cf. pp. 259-263.

4

The Fight Between Spiritualism and Institutionalism

In the way we have described the two positions of "spiritualism" and "institutionalism," I must add that I have not portrayed them as they perceive themselves, but rather I have given a *typology*.[1] In reality, there are probably very few positions which are pure forms of the thought patterns described. The boundaries are in a constant state of flux.

If we apply the concepts developed here, we will find that there are theologians who adopt an institutionalistic position in some areas and a spiritualistic position in others. Other people, whose thinking is basically a model of the bipolar approach of natural church development, may show spiritualistic tendencies in some strands of their argument and institutionalistic tendencies in others. And there are typical advocates of spiritualism who surprisingly take over certain positions of the bipolar paradigm; in the same way, this occurs in representatives of the institutionalistic paradigm.

These facts do not negate the relevance of our typology, for it remains the argument of this book that spiritualistic and institutionalistic *tendencies* should be overcome, no matter where they occur (and irrespective of whether it is Martin Luther, C. Peter Wagner, John Smith, or Joan Jones who shows these tendencies). But careful differentiation will help us to avoid the risk of using the theological paradigm of natural church development as a sort of black-and-white yardstick—and thus misusing it as an ideology.

In real life, dangers to the right and to the left (i.e., towards institutionalism and spiritualism) are unavoidable. Even in churches that obviously have a healthy basic structure and can serve as models for natural church development, we can sometimes identify spiritualistic or

---

1   This typology is not 100 percent identical with the conventional use of the words "spiritualism" and "institutionalism." Especially, *spiritualism* (as used in this book) should not be confused with *spiritism*.

institutionalistic tendencies. In practice, church development is not possible if we make it dependent on a sterile freedom from every "disease." That would inevitably take us from the infectious climate of everyday church life into the artificial climate of the laboratory in which illnesses are successfully prevented, but organic church development is prevented as well. Just as a healthy organism goes through times when it is attacked by illness, the church also goes through such times. But the more the bipolar paradigm of natural church development is integrated into the life of the church, the higher, metaphorically, is its level of immunity to disease, and the better it will be able to resist such infections.

There is only one place where all spiritualistic and institutionalistic tendencies can be radically eliminated: the quietness of the study, where we can carefully formulate theological definitions and typologies of what is right and what is wrong. I am not against such abstractions (in some ways this book is an example of them), but I reject the illusion that theological formulas can give an adequate description of the pulsating complexity of life. In the reality of the situation, we are repeatedly faced with the task of identifying institutionalistic and spiritualistic tendencies which, in varying degrees, affect us all, and overcoming them as far as possible.

for summary

Who Is a Christian?

Depending on whether a person is more influenced by spiritualistic and institutionalistic tendencies or by the bipolar paradigm, the concept of what he or she understands as the nature of Christianity will also vary. Here, I have learned much from Paul Hiebert, who described with his distinction between *bounded set* and *centered set* exactly the same issue I have characterized in terms of the "institutionalistic" and "bipolar" paradigms.[2]

How is being a Christian understood within the institutionalistic paradigm? Representatives of this thought pattern work with what Paul Hiebert calls the bounded set. First of all, a boundary is defined. In figure 8 (right hand picture), this boundary is represented by a circle, with the dots representing individual people. Specific characteristics or behaviors are defined which are deemed to be constitutive. Whether a person is a Christian depends on whether he or she fulfills these criteria. Anyone who does not fulfill them is outside the circle.

---

2   Cf. *Hiebert: 1979*, pp. 217-227. The following section draws on Hiebert's representation. Hiebert, however, only compares two positions: the *bounded set* (institutionalistic paradigm) and the *centered set* (bipolar paradigm). I have supplemented this exposition with a representation of the spiritualistic position.

Spiritualism:
Only the dynamic
movement counts

Bipolar position:
The direction shows
where the boundary is

Institutionalism:
Only the static
boundary counts

 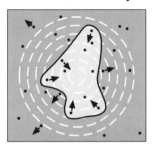 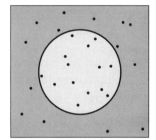

*Fig. 8: A graphical representation of the thought patterns of the spiritualis-
tic and institutionalistic paradigms; the bipolar position (centered set)
provides a third alternative.*

It is characteristic for this way of thinking that the boundary line is
drawn *first*, and *then* it is decided who is inside the circle and who is
outside: "If you think and act in a certain way, then you are a Christian."
For some groups, this boundary is the affirmation of the doctrine of the
Trinity, for others it is the performance of infant baptism, for still others it
may be the struggle against racism and nuclear weapons.

Once the boundary line has been drawn, it does not change; it is static.
According to this model, being a Christian can be defined as a system of
different qualities that every believer must display at all times (e.g., right
doctrine plus right behavior plus right political views). This thought structure is to be found both in circles we would regard as being "legalistic"
and in groups in which the demands placed on a Christian have declined
to an absolute minimum (e.g., infant baptism and church taxes, as in many
European state churches), and which are therefore most noted for their
liberalism. The actual theology may differ significantly from one group to
another, but the underlying paradigm remains the same.

It is interesting that this type of thinking is currently especially
prominent within two groups: on the one hand, among fundamentalists,
on the other hand among Christians who have committed themselves primarily to social and political questions. Although these groups are radically different in the subjects they place on their agenda, both work on
the model of the bounded set. Both start by setting up rigid boundaries,
and then decide who is a Christian and who isn't. People in one group
may say, "Anyone who smokes and drinks cannot be a Christian." People
in the other group may say, "Anyone who approves of atomic power stations cannot be a Christian." In one group, conversion means believing in
Jesus Christ and renouncing tobacco and alcohol. In the other group, conversion means believing in Jesus Christ and fighting against atomic

power stations.[3] In both cases, whether someone is a Christian or not depends on their adherence to moral criteria.

In the spiritualistic paradigm, as we can see in figure 8 (left hand picture), this boundary line is completely absent. Everything is in flux, in movement. Some people are moving towards the center, others away from it. The position can change from one moment to the next. For spiritualists, only the movement is decisive; they categorically reject boundary lines of any sort. Doubtless the spiritualists, like most representatives of the institutionalistic paradigm, are concerned to further genuine Christianity. However, the spiritualist's statements about who is and who isn't a Christian are unclear, vague, and nebulous. That is not an accident; it is a logical consequence of the spiritualistic paradigm.

How can this question be seen from the perspective of the bipolar paradigm? We follow on from what Paul Hiebert calls a *centered set*, which is shown in the middle part of figure 8. The main point of attention is not the boundary line but the center, Jesus Christ. It is not the fulfillment of certain doctrinal or ethical requirements that makes a person a Christian, but the relationship he or she has to Jesus.

In this approach, the first concern is not the definition of the border—like in the bounded set—rather, it is the center.[4] As can be seen in figure 8, some people are relatively far from the center but are moving towards it. Others may be much closer to the center, but they are moving away from it. The way the boundary line is drawn shows that in this model, only those people are "included" who are moving towards the center.

It should be noted that in the centered set there is also a boundary line; there is a definite distinction between Christians and non-Christians. But this boundary is not based on a catalog of qualities that people must display. It is only drawn *after* it has been discovered in which direction the person's life is moving. The most important thing about being a Christian is not conformity to certain doctrinal and ethical standards, but the relationship to Christ.

In this model, conversion is understood—in keeping with the New Testament word *epistrepho*—as being a real "turning around." A person's

---

3   Cf. C. Peter Wagner's description of the thought patterns of Jim Wallis (whose social *concerns* Wagner fully shares): "Reading Jim Wallis' *Agenda for Biblical People*, for example, I find a book-length boundary game. Boundaries between biblical Christians and others include such things as 'the consumptive mentality,' 'the will to power and domination,' 'oppression of race, sex and class,' 'arrogance of national destiny,' 'economic imperialism,' and 'military aggression.' Christians who have different social views are frequently accused of 'idolatry,' and it must be assumed that Wallis believes that idolators will not inherit the kingdom of God (1 Cor. 6:9-10). His boundaries have excluded his opponents" *(Wagner: 1981,* p. 160).

4   Cf. Paul Hiebert's descriptions of what he regards as the centered set: "It is created by defining a center and the relationship of things to that center. Some things may be far from the center, but they are moving *toward* the center; therefore they are part of the centered set" *(Hiebert: 1980,* p. 95).

life (the arrow in the illustration) is literally changing its direction. Instead of moving away from Christ, from now on the person moves constantly closer to Christ. The original conversion is only the beginning of a lifelong process. It is not possible to be converted and then to remain at the same point for the rest of one's life.

The Ideological Nature of Spiritualism and Institutionalism

There is one thing that the spiritualistic and institutionalistic paradigms definitely have in common: Both are ideological positions. This becomes clear when we relate both systems of thought to different dogmatic issues. We then get the following pairs of concepts:

Dualism	**Monism**
Spiritu-alistic paradigm	Institution-alistic paradigm
Relativism	Dogmatism
Eclecticism	Fundamentalism
Libertinism	Legalism
Spiritualism	Sacramentalism
Docetism	Traditionalism
Separatism	Monopolism
Individualism	Clericalism
Anarchism	Conservatism
Quietism	Universalism

Fig. 9: The effects of spiritualism and institutionalism on dogmatically relevant issues.

At first sight, the concepts in the right hand column express the opposite of the equivalents in the left hand column. But they have at least one thing in common—they are all "-isms." Every "-ism"—"communism" as well as "capitalism" and "spiritualism"—gives us an indication of the ideological background of the concept.[5]

5　The fact that both paradigms are ideological and thus not acceptable does not mean that they do not "work." God can use people whose thinking is caught up in the institutionalistic or spiritualistic paradigm, and he can even pour his blessings on them. But I find it problematical—in this and other areas—to draw conclusions

Unfortunately, theological debate does not maintain clear distinctions in this area. Concepts such as "spiritual" and "spiritualistic," "traditional" and "traditionalistic," "rational" and "rationalistic," "personal" and "personalistic," "institutional" and "institutionalistic," "sacramental" and "sacramentalist" are largely regarded as synonymous. But not everything which is called an "-ism" is really ideological. In the course of this book, I will keep strictly to the following linguistic convention: I will only use the suffix "-ism" when I am referring to the perverted ideological form. The term "sacramental," for instance, refers to the legitimate use of "sacraments" as a means to encourage and strengthen faith. By contrast, I use the terms "sacramentalism" and "sacramentalist" to describe the illegitimate attempt to assign to the sacraments a beneficial function in their own right, irrespective of the faith of the person involved. The same applies by analogy to the other "-isms."[6]

Institutionalism and spiritualism—like all ideological positions—are motivated by strong interests, which reflect basic psychological needs. On the one hand (institutionalism), there is the need for security and order; on the other hand (spiritualism), the need for freedom and spontaneity. But both paradigms do not justify themselves as advocates of a particular interest group. They claim—typically for ideologies—that they are the defenders of the absolute, universally valid truth: their position is right, everyone else is wrong.

The same, of course, could also be said about the bipolar paradigm of natural church development, which still remains to be defined more clearly. Is it not also motivated by a special interest, the interest of stimulating the organic life of the church? Of course it is. This interest really is the "filter" through which it views reality. Does this, then, mean that this paradigm is just another sort of ideology?

We need to differentiate carefully here. There are points at which we must say that proponents of church development are at risk of being ideological. This applies, for example, where a success-oriented mentality, which cannot be justified from Scripture, is regarded as the key to theological understanding—numerical growth as a proof of the theological integrity of those who experience this growth.

But we should be careful not to oversimplify when accusing someone of being ideological. The mere existence of an interest does not, in itself, prove that a position is ideological. Theologically, we need to distinguish between legitimate and illegitimate interests. It remains to be

---

about the theological legitimation of the position advocated on the basis of this blessing. The fact that God blesses people does not mean that they are right in all they say and do.

6   In most of the Indo-European languages, the distinction between the original word and the ideologic "-ism" can be made relatively consistently. Exceptions to this rule are only those "-isms" which have nothing to do with ideology (e.g., methodist, criticism, evangelism).

demonstrated why natural church development describes a theologically legitimate and necessary interest (in that it is consistent with the interest of the biblical revelation), whereas both the institutionalistic and the spiritualistic positions set up illegitimate, particularistic interests as the standard by which everything should be judged. The bipolar paradigm therefore implies a stance that is deliberately critical of ideologies.

The Struggle Between Ideological Paradigms

Where different ideologies meet, a struggle ensues. In consequence, large parts of church history can be interpreted as a conflict between the spiritualistic and institutionalistic misconceptions—a statement which will be developed extensively in part 2 of this book.

Many people who examine closely the actual disputes between advocates of these two positions will find that they have a certain sympathy for *both* sides. Let us remind ourselves what the arguments of the spiritualists are directed against: traditionalism, monopolism, dogmatism (and all the other "-isms" in the right hand column of fig. 9). Who among us would not agree with the spiritualists in this conflict? All of these features of institutionalism *are* to be rejected. They are false interpretations of the Christian faith against which we—together with the spiritualists—could stand up and fight.

Let us then look at the target of the arguments of the proponents of the institutionalistic paradigm. We will probably find that, here too, we feel sympathy for their concern. They oppose docetism, separatism, relativism (and all the other "-isms" in the left hand column of fig. 9). Who would not support them in this struggle? All these forms of spiritualism *are* to be rejected. They are false interpretations of the Christian faith against which we—together with the institutionalists—could stand up and fight.

The issue is confusing, to say the least. Must we conclude that spiritualism and institutionalism are *both* right? But if we regard the questions we have cited as areas where we agree with both sides, we are in danger of being left in no-man's-land.

Things become surprisingly clear if we look at the way both positions regard the bipolar position—the position represented in figure 10 (p. 46) by the functional combination of the two boxes in the center. The problem is that advocates of the spiritualistic and institutionalistic paradigms—since they only think in terms of "either-or"—do not even perceive the existence of this middle position.

How does a spiritualist regard the bipolar approach? Being against institutions on principle, he or she cannot distinguish it from the institutionalistic paradigm. This is why proponents of church development are unjustly accused by advocates of the spiritualistic paradigm of being "hooked" on methods or on the illusion of technocracy (typical signs of the institutionalistic position). In vain they claim that these accusations do not apply to them, that there is a wide difference between their position and the institutionalistic paradigm. Spiritualists are unable to see any distinction. For them, to put it in simplified form, everything that is institutional, principle-oriented, and strategic is by definition evil. The functional attitude to institutions in natural church development and the formalism of the institutionalistic paradigm are, for spiritualists, both an unacceptable commitment to institutions.

The same phenomenon becomes apparent when we examine the way institutionalistic thinkers regard natural church development: as an affront to the institution. On the basis of their paradigm, they are unable to distinguish between the bipolar position and the spiritualistic misconception. Both paradigms refuse to accept institutions as ends in themselves (although for different reasons)—and this information is sufficient to lump the two positions together and fight against both. This is why proponents of natural church development can be accused of being anti-institutional, although their words give no justification for this accusation.

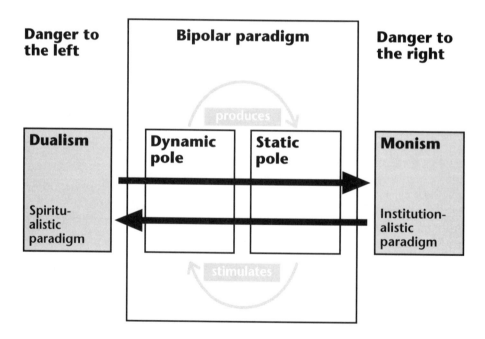

Fig. 10: The struggle between spiritualism and institutionalism: it comes about because the middle position (bipolar paradigm) cannot be perceived.

Depending upon the group I was with at the time, I have sometimes been accused of having a "spiritualistic" position, sometimes of being "institutionalistic," or even a "technocrat." Until recently I did not understand these reactions, and I usually replied with a certain irritation, "Have you been listening to what I have said? Can you quote one sentence I have said that justifies that accusation? You won't find any."

When I said that I was undoubtedly right—seen from the perspective of my own thought paradigm. But I overlooked the fact that, in terms of the paradigms of my audience, they had not been so inconsistent as it seemed. Of course I could be sure of my own ground and outraged at the way these people had "lost touch with reality." But if we make the effort to examine the issues from the point of view of the spiritualistic and institutionalistic paradigms, we will realize that this "loss of reality" is almost inevitable (in fact, it is a general hallmark of ideologies that they have a clouded relationship to empirical reality).

Proponents of both the spiritualistic and the institutionalistic paradigms are acting perfectly consistently in terms of their own philosophical premises when they identify natural church development with their (institutionalistic or spiritualistic) opponents. When I first realized this, I suddenly saw why most discussions about this subject are so futile. It cannot be any other way as long as we speak from one paradigm into another.

The spiritualistic and institutionalistic positions are both right to reject each other. Consequently, we should not argue against this intention, but only against the thought paradigms which do not permit this intention to be implemented. Both positions are wrong insofar as they are unable to distinguish between their opposite paradigm and the bipolar paradigm of natural church development. This is precisely the danger of ideological thought patterns. Both are right in their struggle against each other—and church development can be left out completely.

For a spiritualist, planned work for church development may be inconceivable because the church as an organism will come into being sometime and somewhere, as it pleases God—if only invisibly, as a sort of *civitas Platonica*. Institutionalistic thinkers can develop a similar attitude (although for different reasons). For them, the church is always present *ex opere operato* wherever there are certain institutions—even if it is without the Holy Spirit, without love, without people. Here, the opposing positions are surprisingly united—another indication of their shared ideological nature.

We could try to resolve the dilemma by seeking a compromise between spiritualism and institutionalism, subjectivism and objectivism, dualism and monism, mysticism and magic. Yet nothing could be more destructive! We can never seek for a synthesis of two heresies, only for an *alternative* to overcome both misunderstandings. The alternative to the autonomism of the spiritualistic and the heteronomism of the institutionalistic paradigm is, to quote Paul Tillich's wonderfully accurate phrase, *theonomy*.[7] In heteronomism, as we have seen, there is a danger that the institution takes the place of God; in autonomism it is the individual. But a theologically legitimate paradigm would be one in which *God* takes the place that is due to him.

In part 3 of this book[8] I will examine what the practical consequences are if tendencies of both ideological paradigms become mixed with each other. In the present context, we could ask how it is possible for such a mixture to take place in view of the irreconcilability of the two positions. But it can be demonstrated that both paradigms spring from a common root: a view of God in which the biblical basis is obscured by non-biblical influences.

---

7   Cf. *Tillich: 1962 b*, p. 65.
8   See p. 216ff.

5

The Root of the Misconceptions: The Impersonal God

A theological justification of church development cannot, in my opinion, consist simply of a comparison of New Testament passages that mention *ekklesia* or *oikodome*, a discussion of these passages with reference to approved commentaries, and an illustration of the dynamics of numerical growth with examples from church history. This sort of procedure, which is the basis of some writings, can easily give the impression that church growth is a question of exegetic detail (or detail of church history or practical methodology) on which some experts have one opinion and others take a different view.

This approach does not go far enough. The theological hindrances to church development are, to put it metaphorically, not like a localized ulcer or an organ that is not working well; rather, they are like a contamination of the blood which has a detrimental effect, sometimes hidden, on all parts of the body. Therefore, we must not remain at the extremities when we deal with this issue—we must penetrate to the heart of the matter. This heart is the revelation of God, whose nature is nowhere expressed more plainly than in the incarnation of Jesus Christ. It is only from this point of view that we can frame a justification of church development that is—in the original sense of the word—*theo*logical.

This chapter will explain why the real hindrances to church development are not due to differences in ecclesiological or denominational opinions. I am in no doubt that a wrong (e.g., institutionalistic or spiritualistic) ecclesiology certainly can lead to hindrances towards church development, but they are not the *causes*, they are merely *symptoms* of a far more deep-seated defect: a wrong view of God. And where we do not understand the nature of God, however conscientiously we phrase the details of our ecclesiology, we cannot really understand the nature of the church. That is where I believe the problem lies.

The Influence of Hellenism

In theological discussions it is no new insight that the character of the Christian faith was radically altered by Greek culture. Otto Weber summarizes the process as follows: "The doctrine of God in the old church, in the Middle Ages, and in the orthodox period is a strange mixture of Greek, especially neo-Platonic, and biblical thinking."[1]

It was not for nothing that one of the main concerns of the Reformation was to eliminate these tendencies, which in many areas contradict biblical thought. Martin Luther traced the destructive effects of Scholastics in the Middle Ages to the mixture of theology and Aristotelian metaphysics. Especially the metaphysical concept of reality, with its emphasis on ontology, made people blind to "the new dimension of history, which the Reformation had brought to light."[2]

In his pamphlet *To the Christian Nobility of the German Nation*, Luther criticized the fact that at the universities, "only the blind heathen master Aristotle" ruled. He advised people to get rid of the books of Aristotle with which "so much valuable time and so many souls have been burdened in vain." He added, "It is painful to me in my heart that the damned, arrogant, devious heathen has misled and made fools of so many of the best Christians with his false words."[3]

This radical verdict was theologically well justified, but it was not adhered to for long. Melanchthon felt unable to manage without Aristotle in his reorganization of Protestant education, and certainly by the time Lutheran orthodoxy developed, the "damned heathen" again exercised his influence on Christian theology. The phenomenon known by the term "Hellenization of Christianity"[4] is thus not merely a subject of the past. In both the spiritualistic and the institutionalistic paradigms of today—so I suggest—the Greek visitor celebrates a belated triumph.

What is the main danger of Hellenization? At the risk of oversimplification, it is a view of God which completely differs from the Christian faith, but is projected onto biblical statements and threatens to engulf them. God is seen as the *absolute*, the *original principle*, the *summum bonum*, an ontological, metaphysical category of thinking. Whatever the concepts used, we can clearly see the difference from the personal, his-

---

1   *Weber: 1964*, p. 439.
2   *Wallmann: 1973*, p. 107.
3   *Luther: 1983*, p. 225.
4   When I speak of Hellenism, I must, of course, emphasize that it is by no means a uniform concept. In the context of this book, the term does not so much refer to the historical phenomenon—much of what I refer to as "typically Hellenist" is only partly applicable to the historical phenomenon of Hellenism—rather, I use the term largely in the sense of a basic religious position: a paradigm of perception of the world which is of significance far beyond the historical epoch of Hellenism.

torical, event-based view of God in the Bible. The God of the philosophers is not the God of Abraham, Isaac, and Jacob!

At this point we must be fair. The Hellenization of Christianity had good historical reasons. In the world the Christians lived in, people thought, spoke, and lived largely "Hellenistically," and it was a legitimate concern of the church to express its faith in the language and the thought categories of its age.[5] The problem is not in this inevitable contextualization (with all the risks that such endeavor involves in any age). The problem is that these historically rooted decisions became dogmatized, then liturgically and legally canonized. The process of Hellenization, which was originally meant as a contextualization, has become a traditionalistic convention. It should be plain, however, that *contextualization* and *traditionalism* are mutually exclusive concepts.[6]

I would like to illustrate the effect Hellenistic thinking had on the biblical understanding of the faith by reference to two especially central passages: John 1:14 and Exodus 3:14.

"The Word Became Flesh"

The prolog of John's Gospel presents a prime example of the actualization of the gospel, speaking of the *logos*, of which it is said that it was with God from the beginning.[7] The non-Christian Greeks had clear ideas about the *logos*—for them, it was the eternal, unchangeable principle of the world. But there follows a phrase which must have been a shock to adherents of the Hellenistic concept of the logos: *Ho logos sarx egeneto*, "The Word became flesh."[8] For the Greeks, unless they had become Christians, it was totally unacceptable to believe that the *logos* could become flesh. But that is the revolutionary concept in the New Testament that goes beyond the Old Testament: the incarnation of the Word, the presence of God in the person of his Son. That is why the term *logos* can be described in the first letter of John as "that which we have—not only heard, but seen, looked at, touched with our hands."[9]

This clearly shows that "the Word" is not the same as what we usually understand by the term "word." Jesus Christ himself is *the* Word. It is

---

5   Cf. Eberhard Jüngel: "The problem is not the fact that the Christian faith made use of the language of the metaphysical tradition. Faith must speak the language of the world if it does not want to be at a loss for words. Therefore, from the early days of Christianity it had to speak the language of metaphysics, the language of the thought of its time, if it did not want to decay into thoughtlessness. This involved, however, the danger that faith would become dominated by metaphysics, instead of *critically* using its language" (Jüngel: 1977, p. 49).
6   In more detail on pp. 152-155.
7   John 1:1-3.
8   John 1:14.
9   1 John 1:1.

surely no accident that the Gospel of John, which begins with the concept of the *logos*, mentions this term only in the prolog, and then no more. The use of the term does not imply that Jesus is the *logos* (and thus, the starting point for the typically Hellenistic *logos* speculations); rather, it implies that the *logos* is really Jesus—the end of all speculation.

But early on, Christian apologists turned the real point of these words around. They took the word *logos* as a means of explaining the nature of Jesus Christ, and projected a variety of heathen, Hellenistic *logos* concepts onto the Son of God. Thus the very words which express the historical dimension of the gospel in an unparalleled way could become the starting point for an a-historical, metaphysical doctrine of absolutes.

"I Am Who I Am"

This shift in the Christian understanding of truth and revelation began early. It not only affected the New Testament (which was written in Greek, but largely Hebrew or Aramaic in thought), it also affected the reception of the Old Testament (Hebrew both in thought and language).

In the only place where the Old Testament itself offers an explanation of the name "Yahweh," the divine self-explanation is: *ehyeh asher ehyeh*, "I am who I am."[10] This text would probably be better translated, "I will show myself as the one I will show myself as," or "I will happen as I will happen."[11] However we formulate our translation in order to transport the tremendous variety of the verb *hayah* into our more static language, we can be sure that it is a refusal to lock the nature of God into the cage of an ontological definition.[12] Hans-Joachim Kraus correctly observes: "If the question about the name was aimed at . . . finding ways to gain access to his power, then the formulation in Exodus 3:14 is all too obviously a gesture of refusal."[13]

When this completely un-Hellenistic statement was translated into Greek in Alexandrian Hellenism, a translation was produced which changed the real point of the sentence into its opposite: *ego eimi ho on*, "I am the being one" was the translation in the Septuagint. In a typically Greek manner, the verbal structure was changed into a noun participle.[14]

This, though, is far more than simply a difference of grammar. Here we see two completely different systems of thought in conflict. The Septuagint made of Exodus 3:14 precisely what the Hebrew text was meant

---

10   Exodus 3:14.
11   This formulation should not, however, be interpreted in terms of the content attributed to it by "process theology."
12   Cf. *Zimmerli: 1982*, p. 15.
13   *Kraus: 1983*, p. 145.
14   Cf. *Zimmerli: 1982*, p. 14.

to prevent. Behind the phrase "I am the being one" in the Septuagint is the concept of absolute being in philosophical speculation. The one whose nature is to show himself as he wishes to show himself is transformed into *the being one*, or even *being* itself. The one who is undefinable is made into an ontological definition.

Through influences like that, which can be demonstrated in a wide variety of areas, a view of God that is in conflict with the biblical message became more and more embedded in Christian theology: unhistorical, transcendent, neutristic, deterministic—the living God became an abstract concept of truth. It remains to be demonstrated how these concepts of God that are foreign to the biblical revelation of necessity lead either to the spiritualistic or institutionalistic paradigm. An understanding of the personal and historical categories that play such an important role in the paradigm of natural church development is, given this unbiblical view of God, all but impossible.

The Unhistorical Tendency

The God of the Bible is a historical God, the God of Hellenistic philosophical speculation is not. He is a trans-historical, timeless, self-sufficient being. The God of the philosophers has no bearing on history. Incarnation, and thus subjection to the conditions of existence in history, is unthinkable from the point of view of an abstract doctrine of absolutes.

Incarnation involves a radical rejection of all forms of unhistorical views. In John 1:14 we do not simply read that the *logos* became human *(anthropos)*, but that he became flesh *(sarx)*. The term *sarx* is, in the thinking of John, the epitome of that which is "earthly, of the lower sphere."[15] The interpretation of incarnation as an *insecularization* of God, although easy to misunderstand, therefore has some justification.[16] This "insecularized" God does not build his kingdom without reference to history—he does so in and through history.

Anyone who starts from an unhistorical view of God cannot understand the concept that God becomes reality in our time, that he "happens" (Exodus 3:14). Therefore, such a person also has difficulty with the notion that the church has to "happen." This person prefers a trans-historical view[17] in which the life of the church as an organism need not become manifest, at least not in any empirically observable way. In his or her imagination many things may happen, but this fits in with the unhistorical starting point: away from tangible historical fact towards the

---

15   *Schweizer: 1964*, p. 139.
16   Cf. *Pöhlmann: 1980*, p. 139f. The interpretation of incarnation as an insecularization should not be confused with pantheism.
17   Cf. *Thielicke: 1978*, p. 268.

abstraction of thought (in the institutionalistic paradigm) or the inner world of feelings (in the spiritualistic paradigm).

The fact that both misconceptions are just different manifestations of one and the same illness, the illness of unhistorical thinking, is not accidental; it is inevitable. Where mysticism and magic begin, history ends.[18]

The Transcendental Tendency

The concept of the transcendence of God, when seen in opposition to the attempt to understand God's nature as purely immanent (e.g., in nature), has a certain justification; perhaps it is even necessary as a means to resist all sorts of *pantheism* or *theologia naturalis*. But as a description of what is characteristic of the biblical concept of God, it is just as unsuited as the concept of immanence.

The God of the Bible is neither transcendent nor immanent. If we must have a concept of this type, he is a God of *condescendence*. He came down from transcendence into immanence, he humbled himself and took a step towards us. "God is transcendent in the midst of our life,"[19] as Dietrich Bonhoeffer wrote in his attempt to characterize the unique combination of transcendence and immanence in the biblical concept of God.

The Greek view of God did not have any concept of condescendence. For the Greeks, God was exclusively transcendent. The God of the Bible wishes to be recognized as God, but for Zeus it is unimportant whether we recognize him or not. The God of the Bible is passionately concerned that human beings should accept his offer of love, whereas Zeus goes on his eternal odyssey over the archway of heaven without taking any notice of what happens around or beneath him.

The danger now is that, using the concept of transcendence, this Hellenistic view of transcendence, which is in conflict with the biblical faith, creeps into the Christian doctrine of God. That is exactly what has happened. The traces can be found wherever Christian theology concentrates more on God's nature *in itself* than on the *relationship* between God and us humans.

What is meant by the term condescendence applies not only to the New Testament. Even Old Testament faith did not see God "in a transcendent self-existence, but rather in his move to Israel and the world."[20] Thus, Israel first recognized God as *their* God, then as the creator of the world—

---

18   Here, one particular interpretation has proved disastrous which implicitly or explicitly regards the historicity of mankind and its life under the conditions of space and time as a consequence of the fall. The Bible does not contain this concept. The historical existence of humans is overshadowed by the expulsion from the garden of Eden, but historicity itself is never described as a consequence of the fall.

19   *Bonhoeffer: 1952*, p. 182.

20   *Zimmerli: 1982*, p. 123.

and not the other way around. That was not accidental, it was an inner necessity. "Anyone who speaks of God can only do so by speaking of his relationship to humans,"[21] says Helmut Thielicke. "The sentence 'God is' is not a required climax for theological statements, rather it is merely a variation of the sentence 'You are.' This expression in the second person is its original form."[22]

What applies for the doctrine of God affects Christology in the same way. Philipp Melanchthon described this relationship in the classical words, "Knowing Christ means knowing his good deeds."[23] Only because Christ has acted for my good, only by his *beneficia* can I know his godhood.

This new understanding—away from speculation about God's nature *as such* towards a recognition of his deeds *for us*—was the so-called "tower experience" which Martin Luther himself described as the trigger for the changes that led to the Reformation. Luther was meditating about the concept of the "righteousness of God,"[24] which greatly troubled him. Everything began with something that seems to be a purely philological discovery, but which gave the words of the biblical text a completely new direction.

Luther understood anew the meaning of the genitive case—*God's* righteousness. God's righteousness is not the quality which characterizes God himself *(genitivus subjectivus)*, but a quality which he gives to someone else *(genitivus objectivus)*. Hardly had Luther realized that when he remembered a multitude of other biblical expressions which can all be understood in a similar way. "Work of God" comes to mean, "what God works in us"; "power of God" comes to mean, "what God uses to make us strong"; the same applies to the wisdom of God, the salvation of God, the glory of God, and so forth. It is understandable that the Reformer was euphoric in his description of this discovery: "I had the feeling that I had been born anew and had entered paradise through open gates. The whole of Scripture showed itself to me in a new light."[25] A classic example of a paradigm shift!

---

21 *Thielicke: 1968*, p. XII.
22 Ibid. p. 232. It is important not to confuse such a statement with the subjectivist, spiritualistic misconception. The difference becomes clear in what Thielicke says next: "The expression in this form assumes that the encounter has taken place, assumes the new existence and thus makes apparent that the sentence has its place *within* the relationship between God and the self, God and the self-awareness, and not *before* this relationship. But ontologically, as cannot be emphasized strongly enough, the sentence 'God is' comes before any relationship, exists independently of it, and would even apply and remain true if the silence of ancient days were to return, if the sun were eclipsed in a new hardening of the heart and if no more relationships between God and humans would come about, but only the stones would cry out . . ." (Ibid.).
23 *"Hoc est Christum cognoscere, beneficia ejus cognoscere"* (*Ph. Melanchthon*, Loci theologici, Introduction).
24 Romans 1:17; 3:21ff.
25 *Luther: 1983*, p. 23.

God reveals himself in the Bible as the one who longs for fellowship with us humans.[26] Real fellowship involves two sides: we must agree to it just as much as God. Appropriating what God has done for us in Christ is part of the revelation. "The objective event and the subjective acceptance both belong to the act of revelation," writes Paul Tillich as a summary of the biblical understanding of revelation.[27]

Anyone who starts out from the Greek transcendent view of God does not need to worry much about the acceptance of the Christian faith. Depending on whether this person tends more to the institutionalistic or the spiritualistic paradigm, he or she will either play down this question spiritualistically (fellowship with God as an esoteric mystery), or will identify it with objectivistic assent to the divinity of God, affiliation to a church, acceptance of a Christian world view, and so forth. But in either case, the question need not be the subject of empirical research or planned action. From both the spiritualistic and the institutionalistic paradigms, such attempts are regarded as improper interference in God's affairs—a logical consequence of a transcendent view of God.

The Neutristic Tendency

The God we are dealing with in the Bible is not an "it," not a substance, not an object of thought, not a "being existing-for-itself-in-itself,"[28] but the "subject that speaks of himself as 'I' and addresses us as 'you.'"[29] In other words, God is a personality who speaks, acts, and communicates himself and his will. This difference between the divine *it* and *you* is of fundamental importance for the Christian doctrine of God; it is the difference between a *neutristic* and a *personal* understanding of God.

It is interesting that in the Old Testament there are almost one hundred verses, and in the New Testament more than two hundred, which speak of the *name* of God. "The concept of the 'name of God' has this outstanding importance . . . because it summarizes in a simple way that everyone can understand a decisive aspect of revelation: we are face to face with God, and he is face to face with us. God is not an object, he is a person who speaks to us. He reveals himself by his self-revelation so that we can call on him and have fellowship with him."[30]

---

26 It was the protest against the *theologia gloriae* of medieval metaphysics that made the Reformers warn against speculation about a *deus apud se* and only allow the view of God as the *deus erga nos*. "I know of no God other than the one who became man; and I will accept no other," as Luther replied in Marburg to Oekolampad (quoted in *Köhler: 1929*, p. 27).
27 *Tillich: 1964*, p. 135.
28 *Biedermann: 1884*, p. 534.
29 *Brunner: 1960 a*, p. 142.
30 Ibid. p. 124.

The concept of the "name" of God unmistakably expresses the fact that he is a person. Telling someone your name means that you establish a personal relationship. "God's self-revelation is the act in which God steps out of his self-glory and self-sufficiency by becoming the one-for-us rather than the one-for-himself."[31]

In the relationship of God to human beings, we are dealing with a personal relationship, not a relationship between substance and substance or nature and nature. Greek thought, on the other hand, understood God and humanity mainly in categories of "substances." Paul Tillich correctly emphasizes that the doctrine of the "two natures" of Christ is "correct in its formulation of the question, but not in the application of the terminological tools." The basic mistake lies in the concept of "nature," which is "ambiguous" when applied to humans and simply "wrong" when applied to God.[32] Emil Brunner expresses the difference between a personal and a neutristic, substance-oriented view even more plainly: "You may philosophically refine the concept of substance as you will; it is and it remains the concept of the object. It was a real tragedy that this fatal concept was taken into the creed."[33]

Whether the term is "nature," "substance," or *summum bonum,* whether it is the "divine," the "transcendent," the "absolute"—all of these neuter forms are not only neutral, they also leave us neutral. If I am a rationalist, I can develop a thought relationship with a neutral concept. As a sacramentalist, I can make sure that I come into contact with theophorous material. As a spiritualist I can try to come into the sphere of influence of divine power. But in none of these cases the central event of the biblical understanding of revelation has to occur: the personal encounter between God and human beings.

The Deterministic Tendency

As long as God is understood neutristically, the transfer of deterministic categories of one sort or another to our view of God is almost inevitable: a timeless God, unaffected by the events of the world, having effects on the world but not being in a reciprocal relationship with it. In this concept, God becomes an "unmoved mover," a programmer who determines the machinery of the world. The *personal* relationship between God and human beings becomes a *causal* relationship. God is the cause, humans are the effect.

It is typical that on the basis of deterministic views of God, the wildest speculations about the power of God could flourish. Wherever the categories of *personality* and *encounter* are replaced by a mechanical determinism,

---

31 *Brunner: 1960 a,* p. 128.
32 *Tillich: 1984,* p. 154.
33 *Brunner: 1960 a,* p. 243.

this also has an effect on the understanding of God's power. The center of attention is then not his actual power over the universe, but rather the abstract, theoretical question of what God is able to do *(omnipotentia).*[34]

On this foundation all those theoretical, hairsplitting, tongue-in-cheek questions could develop which we find, for example, in the works of Thomas of Aquinus. "Could God make the past not happen?" "Could God do what he does not do?" "Could God make what he does better?"[35] The whole structure of these questions has no relation to the biblical concept of the God of heaven and earth. The starting point for these considerations is no set of real, existential concerns which seek an answer, but theoretical reflection as an end in itself, which finally makes a farce of itself.

A deterministic view of God, of course, also has an effect on soteriology, which becomes deterministic as well. Concepts such as *predestination* or *apocatastasis* are classical examples of static, deterministic thought patterns.[36] In a deterministic view of omnipotence, however, God is no longer really free—at least, he no longer has any power over the things he once has determined. But the biblical God is someone who shows his boundless freedom in doing things that have no place in a deterministic world view. He gives human beings the freedom to decide for or against him. In an unhistorical, abstract concept of God's omnipotence, it is only possible to imagine God's omnipotence as being something that limits human freedom and independence. Instead, we must note that "the decisively biblical element in the knowledge of God is that, together with God's power over the universe, the freedom of the creature is also guaranteed, and every temptation to reduce the freedom of the creature in order to increase the omnipotence of God is rejected."[37]

The practical consequences of a deterministic view of God are easily evident. The test case is prayer. Either, as is typical for large areas of mysticism, it degenerates to pure meditation and thus in the last resort to self-reflection,[38] or it becomes a formalistic incantation (as a sort of magical key to overcome the determinism in God's world computer by break-

---

34 Cf. *Brunner: 1960 a*, p. 253f: "The thought of the *omnipotentia* . . . is grounded in the idea of the *posse,* the being able to, which is completely absent from the biblical concept. That is not accidental, but a necessary result from the speculative, ontological premise, 'God equals being.' An exact analysis of its content would show that it is a compromise between the neo-Platonic, Areopagistic concept of Being and the Christian concept of God, a sort of product of the attempt to start from the speculative idea of the all-being and the all-being-one, the all-one, and to find a link to the contrasting doctrine of God in the Bible."

35 *Thomas of Aquinus,* Summa theologica I, p. 157ff.

36 For a more detailed examination of such universalistic concepts, see pp. 199-207.

37 *Brunner: 1984,* p. 96.

38 Genuine mystics do not pray, but meditate in the ground of their soul in order to reach a state in which they know themselves one with eternal reality, and feel accordingly.

ing the code). Here, there is no insight into what prayer really means—a personal encounter between God and us humans, with all its ups and downs and all the incalculable elements that go with any love relationship.

Again we must say that, from the point of view of an impersonal concept of God, such concepts of prayer are not even illogical. But this view cannot make appeal to the God of the Bible—only to the God of Aristotle, who was described by a critic as follows: "The poor Aristotelian God! He is a *roi fainéant,* a God with nothing to do. 'The king reigns, but he doesn't rule.' No wonder the British love Aristotle so much: his God is obviously a copy of their king."[39]

An Abstract Concept of Truth

Like the view of God, the biblical understanding of truth[40] is not theoretical, abstract, and neutristic; it is historical, specific, and personal. In the Bible we read that the truth *came,*[41] and we are instructed to *do* the truth.[42] But a truth that *comes* and that we *do* is, for people trained in the Greek understanding of truth, unthinkable. In their way of thinking (both in its philosophical, rationalistic form and in its mystic variety), truth is that which is timeless, the eternal "ground of our being." But in the Bible, a different concept of truth is fundamental: "Truth is what happens, what God does."[43]

When the communist writer Bertold Brecht said that truth is always "specific," this concept was, perhaps unintentionally, closer to the biblical understanding than, for instance, an unhistorical fundamentalism that appeals vehemently to the Bible, but can be regarded as a prime example of an abstract, impersonal and thus unbiblical concept of truth.

The biblical understanding of truth is so fundamentally different from the concept of truth in Greek thinking that this difference also affects epistemology. "Knowing" in the Bible is not an abstract, theoretical act but a deeply personal occurrence. "Knowing God" is synonymous

---

39   *Durant: 1945,* p. 61.
40   Emil Brunner is right to point out that the question of the "understanding of truth" is never explicitly treated in the Bible. "If we collected all biblical passages in which the word *truth* occurs and analyzed them exegetically, we would be hardly one step closer to the goal of our study. Just as Scripture hardly presents explicit doctrine of the concept of Scripture and hardly enlarges on the 'doctrine of the Word of God,' so we would also search in vain for a 'doctrine of truth.' The more formal a theological concept is, the less it can be deduced directly from Scripture itself, or 'proven' by Scripture. Formal theological concepts are attempts to hold fast, as it were, the hidden premises behind the content of the Bible, the 'structure' of what is characteristic of the biblical revelation" *(Brunner: 1984,* p. 87).
41   John 1:17.
42   John 3:21.
43   *Brunner: 1984,* p. 154.

with having fellowship with God. This is especially well illustrated in the fact that the Hebrew word for knowing *(yada')* is also used for the consummation of the marriage relationship,[44] "that deeply human partnership which, both in the Old and the New Testament, mirrors the relationship between the God of the covenant and his covenant people."[45]

From the perspective of this concept of truth, the debate about the absolute claims of Jesus receives a new dimension which has often been overlooked in discussion. When Jesus says, "I am the truth,"[46] this statement undoubtedly expresses an absolute claim. But it is an absolute claim of its own kind, and not to be confused with the abstract absoluteness which could manifest itself in assent to an orthodox doctrine. The absolute truth is not a *doctrine* about Jesus—that would bring us back to ideology—but the *person* of Jesus. Therefore, assent to even the most orthodox Jesus dogma is not what leads us into truth, but only a personal relationship with the one who said of himself that he is the truth.

Consequences for Anthropology

The effect of the neutristic, substance-oriented way of thinking proves to be particularly destructive with regard to the doctrine of sin. On the basis of the Greek philosophical approach it is only logical that sin is also understood as neutristic and substantial.

In the Bible, sin is a personal event. It is no more nor less than a breach of fellowship arising out of mistrust and rebellion against God. The deepest root of sin in the biblical view is not sensuousness—which can be no more than the immediate cause—but lack of faith, disobedience, emancipation from God. Each individual sin is in itself avoidable; what is unavoidable is our status as sinners, as beings separated from fellowship with God.

But neutristic, abstract thinking causes sin to be removed from the level of relationships and understood as substantial, almost by analogy to an organic infection. Thus, the Augustine doctrine teaches that after the "fall" of Adam, sin was transmitted to all following generations, and the method (here this doctrine irretrievably leaves the biblical revelation) is by the act of reproduction![47] This combination of sin and reproduction

---

44   As early as Genesis 4:1, and frequently from then on.
45   *Weber: 1964*, p. 215. Cf. also Rudolf Bultmann: "The concept of knowledge in the OT is not determined by the thought that the reality of that which is known is most purely perceived if the personal relationship between the one knowing and the object of that knowledge is eliminated and knowing is reduced to a viewing from a distance. The very opposite is true: knowledge takes place if the meaning and claim of the object of knowledge is perceived and made effective" *(Bultmann: 1953*, p. 697).
46   John 14:6.
47   What, for Augustine, was the heart of his argument, the *in quo omnes peccaverunt* (Rom. 5:12) in the Vulgate, is a wrong translation. Here the word "because" in the

led to a teaching that has continued up to the present day, the doctrine of "original sin."[48] This teaching makes sin into a biological, natural destiny. In the Bible it is nothing of the sort.

The theological concern behind the doctrine of original sin—to emphasize the inevitability and universality of sin in the face of Pelagian teachings—is highly legitimate, even necessary. Again it is the terminological form which appears more than unsuited, because it became the starting point for false teachings which contradict the biblical, personal concept of sin. That Pelagianism was rejected by means of the teaching of original sin is something we can be thankful for; the fact that theologians fell into the equally fatal alternative of a moral determinism—and, despite all claims to the contrary, the doctrine of original sin can be understood no other way—was disastrous.[49]

As long as sin is regarded as a tragic inheritance, we must indulge in a highly paradoxical strain of thought to preserve the responsibility of the individual—a quest that has never yet been satisfactorily solved. Neither can it succeed. If we make sin into a biological, substantial fate, we need not be surprised if people have difficulty in facing up to their moral responsibility. Emil Brunner is right: "If we believe, as has happened frequently, particularly in Protestant theology, that we should glorify God by minimizing the independence and freedom of human creatures, or by removing it altogether in determinism, then we are not serving the God who reveals himself to us in the Holy Scripture, but instead an abstract, philosophical concept of God."[50]

Greek original was replaced by the fateful "in whom" (equals Adam). Correctly translated, this text expresses the fact that every person becomes a sinner by their own action—thus having a share in the death of Adam. This text says not a single word about the inheritance of sin by the means of natural reproduction or the sexual intercourse of our ancestors.

48 This idea is based on the assumption that sensuousness is the source of all evil—a concept that cannot be reconciled with the biblical faith in the Creator. This is the same root that led to the denigration of human sexuality—again, a grossly unbiblical idea which still flourishes and causes havoc within Christianity.

49 Emil Brunner accurately summarizes the dangers of Augustine's doctrine of original sin: "1. His doctrine of original sin made sin into a natural calamity and shifted the concept of sin from the sphere of responsibility into the sphere of nature. 2. His doctrine of original sin was directly connected with his teaching that sexual desire was the root of all sin, and sexual conception the reason for the sin of every human being, especially the new-born child. 3. His concept of *inherited* sin darkened the understanding of the nature of sin as disobedience to God. 4. His argument from infant baptism replaced the biblical, personal understanding of sin with extraneous motives" (Brunner: 1960 b, p. 127).

50 *Brunner: 1984*, p. 93.

Spiritualism and Institutionalism
as Consequences

It has already been mentioned that, on the basis of the impersonal view of God described here, two different paths can be trodden with equal logical justification: the path to spiritualism and the path to institutionalism. Which of these paths a person chooses largely depends on whether he or she has a greater longing for "freedom" or for "order"—a scale of values which can, and in fact, does, change in the course of our lives. Thus it can be demonstrated that there are movements which began by being "spiritualistic," only to end up being "institutionalistic" (whereas a development in the opposite direction is much more rare).

The common root of the two false paradigms gives us an answer—at least provisionally—to the question why these apparently contradictory tendencies are, in reality, sometimes strongly, almost inextricably, linked together. One example of this is, yet again, the Roman Catholic Church, in which both spiritualistic and institutionalistic, subjectivistic and objectivistic, mystical and magical tendencies are so manifest that it is often difficult to know which paradigm is the dominating one.

The overall understanding of the Roman Catholic Church (not to be confused with the understanding of individual Roman Catholic Christians!) is without question deeply institutionalistic (to examine this issue, the five characteristics of the institutionalistic paradigm described on pages 30–39 can be used as a checklist). But wherever a renewal movement arises in the Roman Catholic Church—often as a protest movement against the "establishment"—this usually occurs in terms of the spiritualistic paradigm. The path to strategic church development, with all its consequences for structures, is only trodden rarely or halfheartedly. The Christian life is exhausted—typically for spiritualism—in prayer meetings, fellowships, communities, or even in a completely individualistic form of devotion.

Now comes the real irony. A church dominated by institutionalism finds it easier to deal with these spiritualistic forms than with the bipolar paradigm of natural church development. Spiritualism, at least in its non-revolutionary variety, can, if necessary, be integrated into the institutionalistic paradigm. Natural church development cannot.

The same interrelationship of spiritualism and institutionalism can be demonstrated in almost every church. Many Christians concerned about revitalizing the church remain dominated by spiritualistic thinking, often against their own theological intention. Intuitively they sense that, as long as they restrict themselves to the non-aggressive variety of the spiritualistic paradigm with the motto, "After all, institutions are not what really matters," their church can afford to allow them a certain amount of freedom. But this freedom would vanish if they began to understand faith as radically *personal* and institutions as radically *functional*—that view can no longer be integrated in a church dominated by institutionalism.

Thus, many Christians are on a spiritualistic path, not because they are particularly enamored by the impersonal view of God in spiritualism (which they basically reject), but because they see in this procedure their only chance of survival in an institutionalistic church.

In reality, then, matters are far more complex than our typology would, at first sight, make them appear. Many Christians, whose thought and actions are demonstrably marked by the spiritualistic or institutionalistic paradigm, are, in fact, deeply and actively concerned about a biblical, and thus personal, view of God. They have no greater longing than that people should encounter Jesus and come to a personal relationship with him. To simply accuse them of having a Platonic or Aristotelian view of God would not do justice to their intention nor to the facts.

This phenomenon, which apparently contradicts the argument so far, can be explained as follows: for themselves, these Christians reject an impersonal view of God. Their problem is that they have taken over paradigms which demonstrably originated from an impersonal view of God, and which, in fact, are in conflict with the actual intentions of these Christians. The impersonal view of God is not necessarily to be found in their *person*, but rather in the *tradition* that surrounds them, which they have taken over far too uncritically.

These remarks are necessary to prevent the paradigm presented in this book from being interpreted simplistically, along the lines: I identify spiritualistic or institutionalistic tendencies in a fellow Christian, and then automatically accuse him or her of displaying all characteristics of these paradigms described in this book (including the impersonal view of God). This simplistic method would turn the actual intention of the bipolar approach into its opposite. A paradigm that is meant to contribute to the destruction of ideology in theological positions would itself become an ideology—a pattern that no longer helps us to perceive reality more clearly, but instead distorts reality in favor of a dogma. In this way, what was meant as an aid to perception could become a hindrance to perceiving reality accurately.

Both the spiritualistic and the institutionalistic paradigms are closed systems of thought. But life is far too complex for a Christian's thinking to move only within the boundaries of a single system. In most theological positions, whether propounded by theologians or by non-theologians, we can find divergent and sometimes completely incompatible influences.

The typology presented here is meant to help us to unravel the complex "knots" of theological concepts we encounter in reality (and, not least, within ourselves). It is meant to show the real causes of the theological concepts which we sense in our practical work to be a hindrance to church development. It is meant to help to unmask certain positions, which are only "sanctified" by their wide acceptance and frequent reiteration, so that they can be seen for what they really are: unbiblical influences which, in the last resort, not only block us for church growth, but—far worse—draw us away from the God of the Bible.

6
Functionality as a Theological Criterion?

In many of the theological debates about church growth (and other practically relevant subjects) a strange understanding of theology can be observed. It has its deepest roots in a static, unhistorical concept of truth. Advocates of this concept regard it as a threat to the academic character of theology when it is seen as a servant of practical work for church development.[1] Behind this concern, they suspect an untheological pragmatism, and they tend to regard the question of functionality in general (e.g., the functionality of structures) as plain utilitarianism.

This conception of theology almost inevitably leads to a schizophrenic relationship between theology and practice. "What is theologically correct can be wrong in practice"—in a number of variations, this sentence occurs in large parts of theological literature.[2] Such statements, which at times are regarded as an especially deep wisdom (the favorite word here is "dialectics"), are a symptom of the general failure to integrate systematic and practical theology. If what is accepted as theologically correct is wrong in practice (i.e., obviously has destructive consequences), then we should at least be allowed to ask if the "theological correctness," which is postulated with such *pathos*, is really as correct as is claimed. Often, the practical test is an unambiguous sign that there is something basically wrong with the theology.

The real dilemma is that, although it is not voiced in many cases, a theological question is generally felt to be the opposite of a practical question. But what is the real opposite of the term "theological"? Surely, it is not "practical," but "untheological." By surreptitiously declaring "practical" to

---

1   Cf. Rudolf Bohren: "As if the question 'how to do it' were not a theological question. Basically, practical theology is here fighting the person who conceived it (Friedrich Schleiermacher). It must prove its academic respectability by preserving its theoretical character. It best preserves its theoretical character by resisting what is practicable . . ." (*Bohren: 1975*, p. 181).

2   Cf. for example *Fritzsche: 1982*, p. 74, where the author calls this problem "the tension between the question of truth and the question of appropriation" and then continues, "We seem to lose the one to the extent that we gain the other. Both are necessary, but it seems that we can only achieve one at the expense of the other."

be the opposite of "theological," it is not surprising that in many circles, "practical" is seen as a synonym of "untheological"—an unreflected and theologically untenable equation.[3]

But what is a theological question, and what is an untheological question? The question of whether God can do what he can do even if he does not want to do it is certainly not a theological question (because it is not theologically legitimate).[4] But the question of whether I use technocratic or biotic methods in my practical work for church development is not an untheological question but a very theological one (because it is theologically legitimate and necessary).

The problem is that the term "theological" is often identified with a static, ideological concept of truth. To justify a church form theologically is taken by many people to mean that this particular form is *the* theologically correct one (and other forms are wrong). To ask about the functionality of this form in its specific context ("Is it effective?") is not regarded as a theological question, but merely as a practical one, or it is even disqualified completely as theologically illegitimate. But in fact (as this chapter will argue), to ask about the (practically demonstrable) functionality of church structures is an eminently theological concern. I would even say that a *functional* understanding of the church as an organization is the only legitimate way to justify the institutional side of the church theologically.

The functional approach, however, is outside both the institutionalistic and spiritualistic paradigms, and everything that is outside of ideologically dominated thought patterns cannot be adequately evaluated from within these paradigms. This is perfectly normal. We are all accustomed to study theology within a specific thought pattern and to accept as "theological" everything that conforms to the boundaries of our own paradigm. Anything that is outside we see as either "untheological" or "wrong."

In this chapter I propose to demonstrate that the concepts of *truth* and *functionality* (understood as usefulness for church development) are theologically closer together than appears in conventional discussion. People who argue for the "true church" usually do so in the context of a conscious rejection of attempts to justify ecclesiastical forms with regard to their usefulness. But the opposite of the "true church" is not the useful church, but rather the untrue, false church. What is a "false church"? My thesis is that it is a church whose structures have not been justified in terms of how useful they are for effective church development.

---

3   Cf. the statements Peter Singer makes on ethics. In Singer's opinion, ethics is "not an ideal system, which is very noble in theory but unsuitable in practice. The opposite is closer to the truth; an ethical judgement that is no use for practice must also have a theoretical defect, for the purpose of moral judgements is to guide action" *(Singer: 1984,* p. 10).

4   At least, this applies as long as we are dealing with a *Christian* concept of theology and thus the God of the biblical revelation.

Functionality in the Bible

The *word* "functionality" does not occur in the Bible. But only people who adopt a grossly biblicistic position (and thus actually cloud over the true nature of the Christian revelation) will find that sufficient reason to reject the *content* of the word out of hand. Theologically, our concern can never be to justify a concept by looking up in a concordance the number of biblical references. The question must rather be whether the content that is behind the word illuminates or obscures a biblical concern.

These remarks are necessary because the church growth movement uses a whole host of terms which are not found in the Bible, terms which it has either created itself or taken over from other disciplines.[5] It has been criticized for this practice by biblicists (and not only by them). People are afraid that this procedure will lead to an alienation of biblical contents by unbiblical categories.

This is doubtless a real danger. But it is no solution to this problem if we start to use only "biblical terms," because they, too, can easily become gateways for non-biblical and even anti-biblical thinking, as the Hellenization of Christianity shows. The only solution is to ask to what extent certain terms (whether they are "biblical" or not) reflect biblical concerns, views, and principles. The decisive question, then, cannot be how often the word "functionality" occurs in the Old and New Testaments, but whether the Bible as a whole teaches functional principles. The answer to the first question is negative, but the answer to the second question is an emphatic "Yes."

Asking the functional question means asking about the fruit and the effect. What comes out of it? The nature of many things cannot be understood without evaluating this question. For example, how can we expect to understand the nature of radium if we do not find out about its effect, radioactivity? It is only by learning what radioactivity is that we can understand the nature of radium. And it is only by studying the demonstrable effect of church structures (or dogmas, traditions, and so forth) that we can understand their nature. Nature and function are not contradictory concepts; rather they interpret each other.

Christology, insofar as it developed Christological statements in relation to soteriology, has expressed this relationship between nature and function well. Every sentence about the incarnation, the mission, passion, death, and resurrection of Christ corresponds to a sentence of soteriology expressing the intention, goal, and purpose of the history of Christ.[6] The salvation function of Christ is explained in more detail by

---

5   Examples of such concepts in the American church growth movement are *homogeneous units, hyper-cooperativism,* and *St. John's syndrome.* Examples of concepts I have introduced into the discussion are *quality index, minimum factor,* and *biotic principles.*

6   Cf. *Stauffer: 1950,* pp. 324-334.

the Christological titles. "The original Christology is totally functional, not substantial. We could say that it is verbal, not nominal. It is a question of what Jesus *does* as the Christ. From that perspective we can then say what and who he *is*."[7]

I quote these statements merely as one illustration—which could be replaced by many others—of the central theological significance of the concept of functionality. In asking this question, we are not balancing somewhere on the edge of the legitimate range of theological reflection; we are right at the center of the revelation. Jesus Christ himself, the incarnate Word of God who died and rose again for us, is the prototype of a valid theological treatment of what we call "functionality."

It is noticeable how much Jesus attempted, according to the witness of the New Testament, to impress the "functional question" on his hearers. The prime model for this new, functional view is the Sermon On the Mount, in which Jesus redefines the relationship between men and women on the one hand, and the law on the other in an unsurpassed way. Again, these passages are not *adiaphora*; rather, they take us straight to the center of Jesus' teachings.

Dietrich von Oppen comments that the Sermon On the Mount offers "with the norms and forms of behavior it names under the heading of the 'law' more than just a reference to the Jewish law; it takes issue with institutional human life as such, and draws a picture of it that has lasting validity."[8] Oppen sees the new approach in the Sermon On the Mount as being an "overthrowing of the institution, the old, sacred, traditional, axiomatic order."[9] In our terms, we would need to speak more precisely of the overthrowing of an *institutionalistic* institution and the old, *sacralistic, traditionalistic* axiomatic order. The "law" is here the synonym for an order which is regarded as an end in itself.[10]

But what is to take the place of a legalistically understood order (i.e., an order that exists for its own sake)? This is the uncompromising question of the meaning, the function and thus the effect of the order. Jesus rejects all formalism. In place of legalism he places the category of personal responsibility.[11] We only need to think of the numerous conflicts about healing on the Sabbath in which the question arises in a number of variations whether man is made for the Sabbath or the Sabbath for man.

The functional understanding of the Sabbath (and the law) does not do away with the law; instead, it reveals its deepest meaning. Therefore Jesus could say in the Sermon On the Mount: "Do not think that I have

7   *Brunner: 1960 a,* p. 213.
8   *Oppen: 1960,* p. 17f.
9   Ibid. p. 19.
10   At this point we should mention that this, of course, was not the original purpose of the law, but a symptom of the increasing legalistic inflexibility in Judaism of antiquity.
11   Cf. *Pokorny: 1969,* p. 42.

come to abolish the Law or the Prophets; I have not come to abolish them but to fulfill them."[12] To *fulfill* means "to make it complete, to give it the whole fullness, the whole content, the whole depth and breadth that it was designed for."[13]

If we transpose this to institutions, it means, "The sense and purpose of the Sermon On the Mount is not to abolish the institution in favor of a purely personal behavior, but to achieve both at the same time, their parallel existence and interrelationship."[14] Jesus did not abolish institutional elements, but he relativized their significance by questioning their function. We should not forget that the conflicts that resulted from this approach eventually took him to the cross. An institution that exists for its own sake cannot tolerate being relativized and thus demythologized by questions about its function—that applied to Judaism in the time of Jesus just as much as it does to institutionalistic thinking in the church 2,000 years later.

The *locus classicus* of a functionality seen in terms of church development is 1 Corinthians 10:23: "Everything is permissible—but not everything is beneficial *(sympherei)*. Everything is permissible—but not everything is constructive *(oikodomei)*."[15] In these words it is clear what the aim of the functional criterion is. As it is not accidental that the verse is phrased by analogy with the Hebrew *parallelismus membrorum*, it can only be taken that the two concepts *sympherei* and *oikodomei* are to interpret each other. This means that those things are regarded as beneficial that serve the building up *(oikodomei)* of the church.

Konrad Weiss comments on Paul's use of the term *sympherein* that the benefit involved describes, on the one hand, "the individual spiritual existence, the connection of the individual Christian with the Lord and of the Lord with him."[16] But the second "point of view, which (for Paul) was most prominent in the foreground" for the determination of what is beneficial, was the following: "*symperon* is what builds the church."[17] For his own and other Christians' behavior, Paul knew "no greater benefit than that which serves to build the *ekklesia tou theou*."[18]

---

12 Matthew 5:17.
13 *Oppen: 1960*, p. 26.
14 Ibid. p. 29.
15 Cf. also the similarly constructed passage in 1 Corinthians 6:12: "Everything is permissible for me—but not everything is beneficial *(sympherei)*. Everything is permissible for me—but I will not be mastered *(exousiasthesomai)* by anything."
16 *Weiss: 1973*, p. 78f.
17 Ibid. p. 79.
18 Ibid.

Functionality as a Question of the Holy Spirit

In his book *Holy Spirit*,[19] Eduard Schweizer points out that from the beginning of church history there had been two misconceptions of the Holy Spirit and his manifestations: on the one hand the tendency to cement the working of the Holy Spirit in institutional forms; and on the other hand the opposite tendency to identify the working of the Holy Spirit solely in that which is spontaneous, ecstatic, extraordinary, and unplanned.

The prototype of the first tendency (which, in our terminology, we could call institutionalistic) was the Council of Trient, in which the Roman Catholic Church set itself apart from the Reformation. "Through holy ordination . . . grace is conferred" we read there.[20] Thus, "the bishops, who follow after the place of the apostles, . . . are appointed by the Holy Spirit to rule the church of God," and "if anyone says that the Holy Spirit is not conferred by holy ordination . . . let him be cursed."[21]

But also on the side of the Reformation, says Schweizer, a guarantee for the presence of the Holy Spirit had been sought in order to judge where the Holy Spirit is and where not. "On the Catholic side, the guarantee was sought in spiritual office, on the Protestant side in the Bible; in both cases the aim was to secure the Holy Spirit so that man could control him either because of being ordained to a holy office or because of being trained in the interpretation of Scripture."[22] Schweizer refers to this concept as "canning" the Holy Spirit.[23]

The exact opposite of this approach can also be observed from the beginning of church history. In our terminology, again, we could refer to it as the spiritualistic paradigm. "In an early church order we hear of wandering prophets who spoke as they were driven by the Spirit, and whom others were under no circumstances permitted to criticize or interrupt; that would be the unforgivable sin against the Holy Spirit."[24] As proponents of this line, Schweizer mentions Montanus, Joachim von Fiore, the Zwickau prophets, Thomas Müntzer, Jan Matthys, Jan Bockelsen, but also much quieter people such as Valentin Weigel or Jakob Böhme.

The relationship between the two tendencies was this one: "The more the official teachers regulated the Holy Spirit and strove to confine him in their systems, the more strongly those strange figures arose out of the underground, who were not approved, but who for that reason did not allow themselves to be controlled by others and reminded of their limitations, but fascinated all the more people for that."[25]

---

19   *Schweizer: 1978.*
20   Quoted as in *Schweizer: 1978*, p. 10.
21   Ibid.
22   Ibid. p. 12.
23   Ibid.
24   Ibid.
25   Ibid. p. 46f.

Schweizer makes it clear that both lines were, in fact, misunderstandings of the Holy Spirit. Paul emphasized that all manifestations of the Holy Spirit must be judged by whether Jesus is lifted up as Lord and the church is built.[26] In other words, "The Holy Spirit is revealed wherever God becomes manifest on our earth and in our presence."[27] Translated into our terminology, it means that the Holy Spirit is the one who produces what we—within our bipolar paradigm—call "functionality." He makes sure that God is manifested among us and that the church as an organism becomes a reality. Conversely, the fact that God becomes manifest and the church as an organism becomes a reality is a sign that the Holy Spirit is working. Our understanding of functionality, then, is so closely linked with the workings of the Holy Spirit that we could speak of a *pneumatic functionality*.

In figure 11, this dynamic is illustrated. In this case, the circle linking the organization and the organism together is the decisive factor. This circular movement is a visible manifestation of the work of the Holy Spirit. Where it is intact, the church grows in the power of the Spirit. Where it is disturbed, the initiative may pass to the misconceptions to the right and left, which may vehemently appeal to the Holy Spirit but have little in common with the biblical understanding of the Spirit.

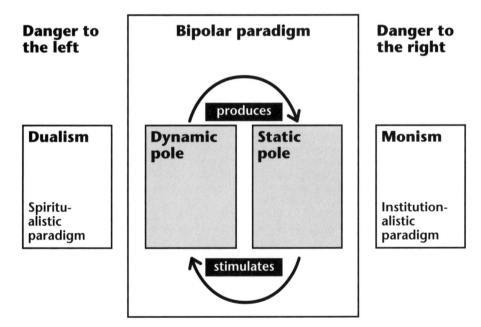

Fig. 11: The Holy Spirit gives life to the church as an organism. He guards the church from the dangers of spiritualism and institutionalism.

---

26   Cf. 1 Corinthians 12:3, 7; 14:1-5.
27   *Schweizer: 1978*, p. 15.

I assume that this understanding of functionality is also what is meant by the church growth movement when it speaks quite uninhibitedly of "pragmatism."[28] However, I feel that this choice of terminology is extremely unfortunate, as "pragmatism" is a term for a philosophical direction which has certain (outer) similarities with the functional approach described here, but at the decisive point, its theological qualification and spiritual goals, it differs considerably from the concept of pneumatic functionality. Above all, the word "pragmatic" is associated with a non-principle-oriented approach, whereas, as we will yet see, natural church development, which aims to put into practice the concept of pneumatic functionality, is characterized by its orientation to clearly definable principles.[29]

Functionality as an Ecumenical Category

The remarks to this point should have made clear that the practical theological question of functional structures for church development cannot be separated from the systematic theological question of the "true church." The "true church" is not a static institutional structure (or lack of structure) which is defined for all time and situations; rather, it can assume many different forms according to the time, the culture, the target group, and so forth. Against the standards of a static, unhistorical concept of truth, these forms may sometimes even be felt to be contradictory. Much (if by no means all) of what seems contradictory from the point of view of an abstract concept of truth can be understood from a historical perspective as an extremely harmonious addition.

This argument is in no way intended to suggest that church forms are a "random" matter.[30] Rather, I am concerned about a theologically

---

28 Cf. C. Peter Wagner: "Since God's goal is clear, church growth people approach the task of accomplishing it in a fairly pragmatic way. The word 'pragmatic,' however, has drawn some criticism. Perhaps it is not the best word, but since it is being used, it should be explained. My dictionary defines pragmatic as 'concerned with practical consequences or values.' This is the way church growth understands the term. It does not mean the kind of pragmatism that treats people as objects and dehumanizes them. It does not mean pragmatism that will compromise the doctrinal and ethical principles of God, the Bible, and the kingdom. But it does mean pragmatism as far as value-neutral methodologies are concerned" (*Wagner: 1981*, p. 71).

29 For a more extensive treatment, cf. *Schwarz: 1996*, p. 100ff. I have myself contributed to misunderstandings in this area by, in the past, speaking of a "theologically reflected pragmatism." With this phrase, I *meant* the same thing as what I call "pneumatic functionality" in this book, but the terminology I selected seems to me to be poorly suited to communicate this concern.

30 The third rejection statement of the *Barmer Theological Declaration* of 1934 (in which the "Confessing Church" declared its position in Nazi Germany) rightly criticizes such indifference. But it is surprising that in the discussion, advocates of church development, of all people, are implicitly accused of regarding ordinances and structures as indifferent. This seems to me to be only possible on the basis of an institutionalistic

reflected standard which does justice to the differences between people, cultures, mentalities, and styles of devotion, but which holds on to the commission that applies to all churches at all time to build up the church of Jesus Christ. The criterion for all churches should be whether faith, fellowship, and service become a reality; whether God becomes manifest in them; whether the Holy Spirit works in them; whether their many forms and structures are such that love is facilitated and encouraged. In other words, the criterion for every institution should be how *useful* it is for building up the body of Christ. To the extent that it fulfills this criterion, it is a "true church."

This standard provides us with a helpful criterion for *constructive* criticism of the church. In the current discussion, everyone who voices criticism towards the church is liable to be classed as "destructive." But the question of whether criticism is constructive or destructive depends on its purpose. The purpose of the criticism that I wish to express of a wide variety of church forms is the development of the organic pole of the church (not to be confused with "inward edification," "numerical growth," or other terms that do not describe natural church development sufficiently). I consider this sort of church criticism to be extremely constructive.

Advocates of the spiritualistic and institutionalistic paradigms do not need to worry about the functionality of institutions. Spiritualists do not need to do so because, in their creed, structures are spiritually indifferent (if not evil) anyway; institutionalists need not be concerned with this question as the mere presence of certain forms (in their opinion) contains the corresponding effect almost "substantially" within itself.

We would be far more advanced in our discussion about the church for tomorrow if all churches would at least accept the functional principle. Our energies should not be taken up by the discussion about *whether* a church should see its institutional side functionally; rather, it should be devoted to the really complicated question of *how* this functionality can be worked out in an actual situation. Here, the field is wide open for fruitful—and controversial—discussions. If only we could spend more time on *that* sort of controversy!

The more radically a church examines its structures from a functional point of view, the closer it will come to what we could call the "true church." The more helpful the answers it finds to such questions, the greater potential it has for growth. Growth is then in no way guaranteed—as the magical, technocratic misconception would suggest—but there is a high probability that the all-too-human, ideologically justified hindrances to growth will be largely removed. And where that has happened, numerous churches have already had the experience of seeing

---

understanding of ordinances, so that the bipolar approach is regarded as equivalent to the spiritualistic paradigm (for which ordinances really are indifferent).

God do what he has promised: *He* gives the growth.[31] This is the way that the principle works which we, with our imperfect words, have called pneumatic functionality.[32]

When, in the rest of this book, I use the term "functionality," I am not referring to what is generally understood by words such as pragmatism, functionalism, or utilitarianism. Instead, I am always referring to the understanding of functionality[33] within our bipolar paradigm: How useful is the organizational (static) pole of the church to help stimulate the organic (dynamic) pole?

---

31   Cf. 1 Corinthians 3:6.
32   In our practical tools on natural church development, we refer to the same dynamics as the "all-by-itself principle."
33   I will explain in more detail the important distinction between *technocratic* and *biotic* functionality in part 3 (p. 223ff).

7
The Interdenominational Approach

Probably all of us have a certain tendency to regard ourselves as the center of the universe. Even if we deny that this statement applies to us, it still contains an element of truth for every human being. God seems to have deliberately placed *our* eyes in the middle of *our* universe. For example, the eyes with which I view the world are not located on the moon or in Los Angeles or Calcutta—for about fifty percent of my working time, they are located in the office of an interdenominational institute in the north of Germany. That is where I look at the world from, just as other Christians look at the world from wherever they happen to be.

Our location naturally influences our view of the world. If my eyes were currently in Calcutta, I would not spend my time looking at the books, manuscripts, church analyses, and tape recordings that at present fill my office. These different views of the world have a significant effect on what we have called our theological paradigm.

In view of the subject of this book, I feel that these personal remarks are important. Theology is never conceived in a vacuum; it is always set in specific circumstances, in a personal context. Theology developed in a vacuum would surely be unhistorical, and therefore false theology. Problems arise because too few authors give information about their own formative influences, their interests, intentions, and experiences. Sometimes they convey the impression that their theology has come out of a vacuum—or directly from the moon.

Anyone who defends Lutheran theology today usually doesn't do so because he or she has tested all other viewpoints—from Pentecostal to Roman Catholic—and *subsequently* decided to be molded by the Lutheran church, the best of all churches. That would be a strange, unreal, unhistorical way of setting about things. People who today defend Lutheran theology do it because the Lutheran church is their home, and in some ways the center of *their* universe. The same applies to Episcopalians, Baptists, Methodists, Catholics, and Pentecostals. And it also applies to people who—like me—attempt to develop an interdenominational theology. We do it first of all because interdenominational work is our home, and thus, in some ways, the center of *our* universe.

Karl Marx was undoubtedly right when he emphasized that our existence molds our consciousness. The situation in which we live *does* have an effect on our consciousness, and conversely—as Marx chose not to recognize—our consciousness has an effect on our existence. The relationship is reciprocal. The circumstances of our life (and not only the economic ones) have an effect on our theology, and that in turn (so we hope) has an effect on what we are and what we do.

So we see that theology is always "theory between practice and practice."[1] This also applies to those theological theories that reject this understanding and consistently deny their practical consequences. They *are* determined by practice—even if only the practice of the quiet study room—and they *do* have an effect on practice—even if it is unintended or destructive.

If I am consciously trying to present an interdenominational position in this book, this has something to do with the circumstances in which I have worked for the last twelve years. I regularly hold seminars in many different countries in which I work with very different Christians and denominations: state church and free church people, Pentecostals and Baptists, charismatics and anti-charismatics, denominational and independent groups, newly planted churches and churches with a long tradition. I try to help all of these groups with their practical steps towards church development.

I cannot, of course, say that I feel equally at home in all these groups and understand them equally well, but it is a significant part of my job to get to understand them better so that I can present the principles of church development, as far as possible, in a way that is helpful for them. My experiences with these brothers and sisters in the context of the practical quest for church development have, of course, deeply affected my theological thinking.

The Ecumenical Nature of the Church

These personal experiences, however, are not in themselves sufficient reasons to call the paradigm outlined in this book an interdenominational pattern. Beyond this personal position, my encounters with so many Christians of different traditions in different countries have convinced me that the basic thought patterns (and thus also the blockages) concerning the subject of church development are the same throughout all denominations.

But there is even a more important reason why I emphasize the interdenominational approach. In the last few years I have learned that the theological paradigm behind natural church development can form a bridge between widely differing Christian groups. None of the groups I

---

1   *Gollwitzer: 1978*, p. 38.

have dealt with is interested in a vague ecumenism which combines different church confessions to make an extract that does not contradict any of their positions. But almost all of them have a growing longing for unity. They are keen to learn from Christians with different traditions— not least, in order to become more effective in their own ministry.

I am convinced that the bipolar paradigm as presented in this book can be a helpful theological foundation for *that* type of ecumenical relationships. This approach is broad enough to include widely differing churches, but it is "narrow" enough not to lose sight of the central goal— that the church of Jesus Christ should develop, grow, and multiply.

Wolfgang Huber is right to emphasize: "Theology is not only ecumenical in its appendix—it is ecumenical through and through. A theology which neglects or forgets this basic dimension opts out of the time we live in. It opts out of the question of the future of Christianity, because this future will be ecumenical."[2] Even if the local churches necessarily (and fortunately) express themselves in a specific denominational and devotional style, this is no alibi for denominational provincialism. In its very nature, *ekklesia* is an ecumenical family, "that means a family that is spread over the whole world and, by definition, spans the whole globe."[3]

The "Both-And" Position

In this area I learned a lot from Donald McGavran, the "patriarch" of the church growth movement who died in 1990. In 1988 he wrote me a letter that included the following paragraph: "Mankind is a gigantic mosaic that is made up of countless pieces. Whereas the essentials of the gospel are eternally true for all people, at the same time, from the point of view of effective evangelism, we must select different forms for each piece of the mosaic . . . I am writing to you, my friend, to endorse most cordially your concept that we need different kinds of evangelism to bring people into different forms of the Church, different parts of the body of Christ. As long as these branches of the universal Church believe in Jesus Christ as God and only Savior, as long as they believe in the triune God, as long as they accept the Bible as God's perfect revelation, they are parts of the body of Christ. They will of course differ on certain convictions. Some will believe that unconscious infants should be baptized. Some will believe that the only baptism is of repentant, mature persons by immersion. Some will believe that any real Christian speaks in tongues. Some will not. Some will believe that the Church is ruled by the Pope. Others will consider that the idea of the Pope is non-Biblical. Such differences of

---

2   *Huber: 1980,* p. 48.
3   *Brunner: 1960 c,* p. 51.

opinion exist today, and will continue tomorrow. Nevertheless, all branches of the universal Church are parts of the body of Christ." [4] McGavran made it clear in his letter that an answer to all these questions, however important they may be, cannot be made a precondition for energetically advancing with the gospel.

Wherever I have quoted these words, I have met clearly articulated opposition. The position that McGavran tried to advocate is regarded in many circles as "selling out theology." That seems to me to be linked to the phenomenon described in the previous chapter [5] that we only accept statements as "theological" if they are compatible with our own thought paradigm. It is characteristic that almost everyone who argues strictly denominationalistically, [6] and thus demonstrably ideologically, can claim to be speaking theologically. People may not agree with his or her arguments, but even opponents will generally not question the fact that the argument is theological (because even the statements that people disagree with are conceived within the rules that also apply to their own, ideologically molded paradigm).

But an interdenominational position which breaks out of the conventional paradigms is liable to be disqualified from the discussion as being "untheological." This understanding of theology, which I feel is inadequately reflected, seems to me to be a major hindrance that an interdenominational approach has to deal with.

I am not saying that every Christian should sign the statements I have quoted from McGavran. I personally could not. But I am convinced that it would do every Christian good to understand the *concern* behind these statements. The church growth movement consciously tries to take up a "both-and" position in many of the contentious issues that concern Christians because it regards the variety in the body of Christ as basically positive. It wishes to enable advocates of different churches to apply the principles of church growth without denying their own theological traditions. [7]

It may be that church growth sometimes goes too far with this "both-and" position and really gets involved in theologically questionable compromises (just as denominationalistic narrowness can also be theologically questionable). Therefore, I am not saying that a "both-and" position is theologically legitimate in every case (that must be carefully examined for each individual case). My concern is merely to protest against the line of thinking that the "both-and" position is of necessity untheological, and thus irrelevant.

---

4   From a letter of Donald McGavran of March 4th, 1988.
5   Cf. p. 65ff.
6   Please note that *denominationalistic* and *denominational* are not the same.
7   Cf. *Herbst*: 1987, p. 256ff., although his evaluation of McGavran and the American church growth movement is not always fair due to the extremely limited source material he uses.

The Necessity of Denominational Application

It would be a misunderstanding of my argument for the interdenominational approach if the consequence were to advocate predominantly interdenominational positions in our work on the local level. For church development it would surely not be helpful if several positions, all of which have some degree of justification, were advocated in the same church at the same time: both infant baptism and believers' baptism, both charismatic and noncharismatic, both parochial and church planting. A local church needs a clear identity. It does not have to cover all possibilities; rather it should passionately advocate the segment it stands for.[8] Although a "both-and" position may be right from a wider point of view, this does not usually apply on the level of the local church.

"Think interdenominationally, act denominationally" would be a way to summarize the principle that I mean here. People who think interdenominationally and imagine they can act interdenominationally overlook the fact that local churches are molded denominationally.[9] They will talk at cross purposes with the churches and achieve little. People, on the other hand, who restrict themselves to thinking and acting within their denominational framework are in danger of becoming provincial. As they refuse to integrate the segment they cover into the larger picture, it can easily happen that their work, in spite of their good intentions, is actually counterproductive for what God plans for the region or the nation.[10]

To be fair, I must add at this point that the sentence, "Think interdenominationally, act denominationally," is a typical example of a theological formula which indicates a correct goal, but is often difficult to put into practice. I myself am exposed to the tension between the interdenominational approach and the denominational application almost every week when I travel to different churches to hold seminars on natural church development. As my concern in these seminars is not primarily to hold lectures on church growth, but rather (as far as is possible in one weekend) to help the churches to *apply* the interdenominational principles of church development in practice (which always means: in the framework of a given denomination), I am well acquainted with the difficulties that this attempt involves.

---

8   Our research, in any case, indicates that a specific church identity and a clear positioning are positive growth factors.

9   By the phrase "denominational," I do not mean the so-called "denominations" themselves, but the type of specific shape which gives each church its own identity. Even (especially!) churches that adopt a consciously "anti-denominational" stance (toward other denominations) themselves have an easily identifiable "denominational" identity.

10   Within natural church development, we emphasize the biotic principle of *symbiosis*, i.e., the coexistence of different organisms (groups, churches) for the mutual good. Cf. p. 245f.

Some Christians cannot understand—to quote one example—why I hold different seminars on spiritual gifts in a Pentecostal church on the one hand and a noncharismatic church on the other. The principles[11] I advocate are the same in both cases (and I do not ask whether the respective groups like them or not), but the forms with which I try to communicate them, the examples I use, the subjects I emphasize (or omit), the style in which I try to encourage the churches to put the principles into practice differ widely from one situation to another. However, in all cases, I try to apply the *same* theological principle, the principle of functionality.

If in the course of such a seminar a doctrinal question is asked which I would answer in a somewhat different way from the church leadership, I usually ask someone from the church leadership to deal with the point. I have made it a principle in my work as a visiting speaker that for the duration of such a seminar I place myself under the leadership of the church involved—and thus, their doctrinal position. I would, of course, not do this if I thought their doctrine were pure heresy!

I have written so extensively about my own background at this point because I am convinced that the tension between interdenominational thinking and denominational action cannot be resolved by abstract theological formulas, but only by constantly new attempts to put it into practice. Here, each Christian must find his or her own calling and style. In the kingdom of God, we need both—Christians who consciously understand their work interdenominationally and Christians who commit themselves, with all the passion they are capable of, to a specific church, denomination, or model. These two approaches should not be played off against each other.

Limits of the Interdenominational Approach

This book is written to answer the question of where the theological roots of natural church development are to be found. As we will see later, I frequently refer to what I labeled "the reformation principle." This term refers to the Reformation in the 16th century to which all Protestant churches worldwide, in the final analysis, can trace their existence. It also refers back to the Pietistic renewal (second reformation), which began in the 17th century, and since then has had a profound effect on the devotional practice of—at least—the evangelical sector of Christianity.

Even though I regard it as important to present our theological paradigm in an interdenominational way, I assume that the achievements that the Reformation and the Pietistic renewal have contributed to Christendom worldwide are not just special insights of a few churches. Rather, they are achievements that the whole body of Christ has benefitted from,

---

11   For a more extensive treatment, see p. 238ff.

and can continue to benefit from in the future. From both movements we can learn, above all, what we have defined as the functional approach.

But this reference to the prior reformations also expresses where the limits of our interdenominational approach are. It will only appeal to churches which have already accepted the first two reformations. Those who do not share in the achievements of the first reformation (e.g., the Roman Catholic Church and the Orthodox churches) will not appreciate the paradigm presented here. This also applies to people who deny the center of the second reformation, the emphasis on a personal relationship with Christ (for example, some of the church groups that are lumped together under the imprecise term "liberal").

In my experience, adherents of the Orthodox churches find the functional approach of church development even more difficult to accept than Roman Catholics. It became abundantly clear to me that we live and think in completely different paradigms when I asked the leaders of the 13 largest denominations in Germany what their plans for the third millennium are, and what they would change in their own churches to achieve these aims. Twelve of the thirteen church leaders sent answers which were more or less informative. The only person who saw himself unable to answer the question was, characteristically, the Greek Orthodox representative, Augoustinos, the metropolitan of Germany and exarch of Central Europe.

He arranged for his office to write to me as follows: "We regret that His Eminence is not able to answer your questions. This is because of the questions . . . You should consider that the church is not a commercial enterprise and that the bishops and priests are not managers whom you can ask about future plans, changes in the management, and obstacles that may be in the way . . . According to orthodox belief, the church is the body of Christ in the sense of the New Testament, the church of the saints, God's new people. It is the place where its crucified, risen and glorified Lord Jesus Christ works in the world through his Holy Spirit to save it. That happens today as in the days of the apostles, as in the first and second centuries, and it will continue to happen in all coming ages up to the moment when Christ returns and the world is perfected. The task of the church is not to make plans, to implement changes and make 'improvements' or to prepare a special contribution for the third millennium, but rather to fulfill the task given by its Lord." For me, our question and the (officially rejected, but nevertheless given) answer is a typical example of the clash between the bipolar and institutionalistic paradigms. Meaningful communication is simply no longer possible.

I do not doubt that there are ways to communicate natural church development even to such churches. But I personally do not have enough imagination for the task. I am sure, though, that God has prepared other Christians who will be able to translate the message in the right way.

8
Three Reformations

C hurch growth is interdenominational, but it can never be atheolo-
gical—here I differ from proponents of the American church
growth movement.[1] It is more than a value-neutral method; there
is a definite *theological* paradigm behind it. We must assume that this paradigm even applies to some of those advocates of the church growth movement who so passionately refuse to be identified with a specific paradigm.

Where are the theological roots[2] of this paradigm? It can be demonstrated that the functional criterion which characterizes our approach is
largely identical with what we could call the *reformation principle:* The
existing forms of a church are not accepted as sacrosanct, but radically
questioned in terms of their *meaning* and their *effect.* That's a hallmark of
any reformation movement.

I propose to illustrate the reformation principle by describing two
examples of movements that have had a lasting effect on the Christian
church: the *Reformation* of the 16th century and *Pietism* in the 17th century. Both movements fought against the apparently overwhelming su-
premacy of the surrounding "orthodoxy"; both had to struggle against
an institutionalistic paradigm (in one instance in its sacramentalist form,
in the other instance in a more dogmatistic form); both had to face up to

---

1   Thus, for example, C. Peter Wagner writes: "Donald McGavran, though his theologi-
     cal roots are in the Restoration Movement . . . has assiduously attempted not to allow
     church growth teaching to identify itself with any particular paradigm of systematic
     theology. Church growth principles have intentionally been kept as atheological as
     possible, on the assumption that they can be adapted to fit into virtually any system-
     atic theological tradition . . . My impression is that church growth cannot reasonably
     be labeled as Reformed or Wesleyan or Lutheran or Calvinistic or Pietistic or Pela-
     gian or Arminian. It can, however, be labeled as evangelical. But, I repeat, this is a
     subject for further research and awaits much enlightenment" *(Wagner: 1981,* p. 83).
2   The church growth movement has repeatedly been criticized for not facing up to
     this question. Thus, for example, Charles van Engen writes in his thorough study of
     the ecclesiology of church growth theory: "It is far beyond the scope of this work,
     though a very urgent task, that the Church Growth Movement should strive to elu-
     cidate its theological roots. These would include, historically, the Roman Catholic
     monastic missionary movements prior to the Reformation and the Protestant Refor-
     mation, refashioned through European Pietism, English and subsequent New En-
     glish Puritanism, and twentieth century American Evangelicalism" *(Engen: 1981,*
     p. 240).

their own spiritualistic extremes and thus to fight on two fronts; both achieved a significance in church history which goes far beyond their own churches.

These remarks are not meant to imply that I regard Reformation and Pietism as prime examples of church growth—the following pages will show that this is simply not true. In some areas, they remained entangled in the institutionalistic paradigm, and where they overcame it, they often moved towards spiritualism. But we can show that both of them, compared with their historical predecessors (i.e., Roman Catholic and Protestant orthodoxy), expressed central aspects of what our activities for church development can (and should!) be based on.

It is well worth examining both movements more clearly to see to what extent they reformed the following three aspects of the church: *theology*, *spirituality*, and *structures*.[3] This perspective will explain why our work for church development today, as much as it stands in the tradition of the two preceding reformations, will have a different emphasis at some points.

The First Reformation:
Luther and His Companions

When Martin Luther[4] drew up his 95 theses, he had neither a plan nor a program for the reformation of the church. The radical changes in the Reformation began with the *theological*—or, to be more precise, exegetical—discovery of what Luther himself called the "justification of the sinner" by faith alone.[5]

But the more time progressed and the more Luther and his companions thought through the consequences of this insight for all areas of church life, the clearer it became that this discovery would leave hardly anything unchanged. The theological discovery had set off a development which had a dynamic of its own and directly led into the Reformation.

In a gradual process, the Reformer successively freed himself from the institutionalistic, sacramentalist approach of the Roman Catholic

---

3 I deliberately refer here to central, well-known and largely accepted contributions made by Reformation and Pietism, even at the risk that they may have the effect of being regarded as mere clichés. Of course, the same features could be demonstrated by more sophisticated observations as well. But first, that would go beyond the scope of this book, and second, it could obscure the fact that the questions dealt with in this book are always concerned with the *center* of Christian theology.

4 The fact that I concentrate mainly on Luther in my outline of the Reformation does not mean that the Reformation of Calvin or Zwingli is less relevant to church development (the opposite is probably true); the reason is rather in the fact that the other streams of the Reformation (including what we call its "left wing") are historically dependent on Luther.

5 Cf. p. 55.

Church and became more and more skeptical towards the abstract meta-physics and scholastic theology that legitimized Catholicism. Eventually, a Reformation movement developed, whose several streams were all dependent on Luther, but yet took different directions: from the anti-papal princely churchmanship of the Lutheran tradition via the theocratically biased attempts in Zurich and Geneva to the "radical Reformers," whom Luther called *enthusiasts* ("Schwärmer"), who in modern study of church history are more neutrally called the "left wing of the Reformation."[6]

Even though these streams very soon became involved in a bitter struggle with each other, there was one concern which, without doubt, they all shared: their rejection of the clericalistic theology of the Roman Catholic Church. They were united in believing *that* the institutionalistic paradigm was to be rejected—their argument was merely what the proper alternative should be like.

It is no accident that the question of the sale of indulgences was the external incident that triggered the Reformation. The practice of indulgences in the late Middle Ages was a typical expression of the institutionalistic teaching of the Roman Catholic Church. The "excess good works" of the pious were, in the official doctrine, a (substantial) treasure which could be transferred to the sinners who were in arrears in their "account" *(objectivism)*. The transfer of this "credit" was performed by the church, and especially by the Pope, who, as the successor of Peter, held the keys for binding and releasing *(heteronomism)*. Indulgences could be acquired by paying money or undertaking certain exercises for which there were clearly defined rules *(formalism)*. The efficacy was independent of any subjective experience *(rationalism)*. They came into effect through the fulfillment of the conditions laid down *(magic)*. By means of this practice, so said Luther's accusation, the institution assumed an authority which was only rightly due to Christ. In other words, the practice of indulgences combined all those elements that are consequences of an institutionalistic understanding of the church. Here, we have more than just one of a number of reformable errors.

When Luther, in the course of his conflicts with the Roman Catholic Church, eventually came to call the Pope "anti-Christ," this was not an example of the tendency he sometimes displayed to use rough, exaggerated personal insults. Here, the word "anti-Christ" expressed precisely his actual theological intention.

Whereas critics of the papacy in the late Middle Ages—Fraticelli, the Wyclifites, the Hussites—called individual Popes "anti-Christ" because of their evil lives, for Luther, this term had a different, programmatic significance. He saw *every* Pope as an anti-Christ, even if he lived an exemplary life. For Luther, the term was a symbol of a system, an institu-

---

6   This term was coined by Roland Bainton *(Bainton: 1941)*.

tion which falsified the truth by putting itself in the place of Christ.[7] That is precisely the danger of the institutionalistic paradigm: the institution that originally intended to safeguard Christ's authority eventually puts itself in his place. The Greek word *anti* can mean "instead of" as well as "against." In the context of the institutionalistic paradigm, these two meanings become synonymous.

The fact that the fight of the Reformers was not an argument with individual errors but a question of a new theological paradigm is shown in the particularly symbolic events of those years. When, on December 10th, 1520, Luther threw not only the papal bull, but also a canonical book of the law into the fire, this was not a symptom of unreflected reactions in emotionally heated confrontations. The "holy law of the church"—which is what the canonical books of the law stood for—was the epitome of a heteronomic, clericalistic doctrine. With the canonical book of the law, metaphorically speaking, the whole institutionalistic paradigm of Roman Catholic orthodoxy went up in flames!

The contrast between the heteronomic paradigm of the Roman Catholic Church and the *personal* concept of truth, became clear in the confrontation between Luther and the Habsburg Emperor Charles V at the Diet of Worms. Luther refused to recant and declared that, if he were not convinced by the witness of Scripture or clear reasoning—for he did not believe the Pope and the Council as they had often been wrong and contradicted each other—then he was overcome in his conscience by the Holy Scripture. "And as my conscience is caught in the words of God, I can and will recant nothing because it is dangerous and impossible to do anything against the conscience."[8] The famous additional remark, "Here I stand, I can do no other" is not historically confirmed, but it is not an unfitting expression of the point of Luther's concept of truth in his fight against Roman Catholic heteronomism. "Reason," "conscience," and the "Holy Scripture"—these are the three central concepts in Luther's argument (which is neither autonomist nor heteronomic: it is *theonomic*).

The answer given by the Habsburg Emperor a day later is characteristic of the formal, objectivistic concept of truth of the Roman Catholic Church. He pointed out that he was descended from the most Christian emperors of the German nation, from the Catholic kings of Spain, the archdukes of Austria and the dukes of Burgundy. All of them, he declared, had been faithful to the church of Rome until their death. They had defended the Catholic faith, the holy ceremonies, edicts, ordinances and the holy customs to the glory of God. Therefore he was determined to follow in their footsteps. "For it is certain that a single brother is in error if he stands against the opinion of the whole of Christendom, as otherwise Christendom would have erred for a thousand years or more."[9]

---

7 Cf. *Bainton: 1983*, p. 104.
8 *Luther: 1983*, p. 269.
9 German Reichstag Archives 1893-1935, vol. II, p. 595f.

Anyone who thinks in terms of a non-formalistic paradigm will ask themselves in surprise, "What do the things Charles appealed to have to do with the question of truth?" Within the institutionalistic paradigm, however, the words of the emperor are a classical "proof." Two differing paradigms could not clash more dramatically!

The Emphasis:
Reformation of Theology

If we now examine the effect the first reformation had on the three areas of theology, spirituality, and structures, we find that Luther's emphasis, even according to his own estimation of the contribution he made, was primarily in the area of *theological teaching*. His central theological achievement was his rejection of Roman Catholic objectivism, which permeated every area of theology, from the doctrine of God and anthropology right through to ecclesiology. In almost all questions Luther dealt with, personal values replaced the objectivist categories.[10] He understood that faith is not the obedient assent to a doctrine, but rather an encounter with Christ, who is present in his word and his Spirit. Erich Seeberg aptly summarizes this insight of Luther: "Christ becomes 'our Christ' precisely 'by faith.' Faith gives us what Christ has done. It makes Christ real for us. Without faith, Christ remains dumb, and his deeds remain fruitless. The objective is only effective in the subjective."[11]

But if we look for a reformation of *spirituality* (and this area really must not be regarded as identical with theology!), we must agree with the critics who express their regret that, in this area, Luther stopped half way. Walter Nigg writes, "It was disappointing, painful, and depressing that no reformation of *life* took place in the Reformation."[12]

We should not pretend—as some "edifying" books would have us believe[13]—that the Reformation was a time of spiritual "revival." Of course we can report a number of very moving instances of deeply felt encounters with Christ from this period (among others, Luther himself), but that also applies to every other period of church history. For the large majority of the population, the spiritual effect of the Reformation was that millions of nominal Catholics became millions of nominal Protestants.[14] They thus

---

10 Cf. *Lohse: 1983,* p. 165.
11 *Seeberg: 1950,* p. 91.
12 *Nigg: 1959,* p. 67.
13 Cf. for example *Cho: 1988,* p. 9f.
14 When I use the word *nominal* in this context, I do not mean that religion was unimportant to these people—the opposite is more likely to be true. But I would doubt whether this type of religion was really a personal faith on the lines described in the New Testament. This era can only be regarded as a "time of blossoming for the Christian faith" by people whose thinking is caught in the institutionalistic paradigm and

came under the influence of Reformation theology—which can perhaps be regarded as progress—but the idea that this meant an upsurge of spiritual life is one of those popular legends we would do well to lay aside.

Even in his own lifetime, Luther was criticized by some of his original companions because the reformation of life largely did not occur. Kaspar Schwenckfeld summarized this criticism as follows: "Doctor Martin has led us out of Egypt through the Red Sea into the desert; there he now lets us remain and wander, lost, on unleveled paths, but he wants to convince everyone that we are already in the Promised Land."[15] How true that was!

The same inconsistency showed itself—especially—in the area of the reformation of *structures*. It is not true that Luther regarded the question of structures as being irrelevant. In principle, he was very much interested in what we today would call a functional concept of structures, because this was the logical consequence of his basic theological convictions. He was even close to the point—astoundingly close for his time—of conceiving church structures from the perspective of the task of church development, as his frequently quoted words in the *Prolog to the German Mass*[16] demonstrate. But especially in his view of the church, there was such a mixture of numerous mutually incompatible influences to be reconciled[17]—from grossly sacramentalist elements to purely personal categories—that this underdeveloped ecclesiology just could not bring forth a structural reform geared to church development.

In particular, it was Luther's conflict with the religious "enthusiasts" which in his later years—presumably against his original theological intentions—drove him back into the institutionalistic paradigm (although it was no longer the Roman Catholic form, but now a Lutheran variety). He undoubtedly said much about the enthusiasts that was right and necessary—the parallel with our criticism of the spiritualistic paradigm springs to mind—but Luther did not have a well developed capacity to differentiate between spiritualism and genuine efforts for building up the church. This ability decreased almost from year to year in the older Luther, as can be seen in his writings.

---

who thus cannot differentiate between a heteronomic concept of faith and a personal, theonomic concept.

15 Quoted out of *Ecke: 1978*, p. 33.

16 Weimar Edition 19, pp. 72-78. Characteristic of Luther's deficits in the reformation of *spirituality* and *structures* is his remark that for his concept of the church he did "not yet have the people and persons." Why did he not try to win these people with the gospel? It is not productive to pursue this question further with regard to the Reformation. However, it is hard to believe that now, half a millennium after these remarks, a lot of churches still complain that they do not have the people. Perhaps, in this quotation, they even "delete the hopeful word 'yet' and do not even notice how grotesque it is that the church of the priesthood of all believers has made no more progress with this statement since 1525 than to delete the word 'yet'" (*Bohren: 1979*, p. 52).

17 Cf. *Bainton: 1983*, p. 322.

The inconsistencies in the areas of spirituality and structures also—inevitably—had a negative effect on the further development of theological teaching, which was unable to develop consistently in keeping with the heart of the Reformation approach. This evaluation is not criticism of Luther himself or other Reformers and their decisions. It would be unhistorical to express such criticism from our modern perspective. It may be that the Reformers of those days, in the very compromises they made, had a "providential" eye for what could historically be achieved in their actual situation.

Rather, my criticism is directed at modern "Lutherans" (or advocates of other denominations) who think they owe it to Luther or other Reformers to remain bound by such inconsistencies in a completely different situation. Wherever the reformation principle changes into reformation nostalgia and traditionalism, the institutionalistic paradigm has won the day. Thus by using Lutheran *formulations* Luther's *intentions* can be prevented from being carried out.

The Second Reformation: Pietism

The Pietistic reform—"the most significant religious renewal movement in Protestantism since the Reformation"[18]—took its identity from the program of the Reformation, which it consciously aimed to "take up and continue."[19] By contrast with the first reformation, however, it is not so easy to identify it with a particular person or to regard it as a development of a uniform basic precept. It founded no church of its own and formulated no confession of faith.[20] The comment made by Kurt Aland, "*The* Pietism never existed"[21] therefore cannot be denied.

If I nevertheless speak of "Pietism" in the following remarks, I am thus referring to a multifarious movement which ranges from the classical Pietism of the baroque period at the end of the 17th century, via the revival movements at the beginning of the 19th century and the fellowship movement of the 20th century down to the evangelical movement of our time.[22] Even parts of what is labelled today as "charismatic move-

---

18   *Wallmann: 1986*, p. VII.
19   *Kantzenbach: 1966*, p. 132.
20   Cf. *Egelkraut: 1983*, p. 214.
21   *Aland: 1960*, p. 545.
22   Cf. *Busch: 1978*, p. 12. Johannes Wallmann places German Pietism "in the context of a devotional movement in the whole of Europe which in the 17th century included Anglo-Saxon Puritanism, Precisism in the Netherlands, Jansenism and Quietism in France, and finally also the Jewish Chassidism of Eastern Europe" (*Wallmann: 1973*, p. 136).

ment" can be classified, as far as the central intention is concerned, within the overall scope of the Pietistic renewal.[23]

Pietism began with a concern it shared with the Enlightenment[24]—a critical approach to the formalism of Protestant orthodoxy.[25] In contrast to the original intention of Luther, theology had again become a collection of absolute doctrinal statements, an orthodoxy, a *scholastic* system, "which was in no way less strict than the scholastics of the Middle Ages."[26] In almost all areas of theology, orthodoxy had "replaced the dynamism of the Reformation with a static system."[27] Lutheran theology had once more been linked with the unhistorical thought patterns of Aristotelian metaphysics, which Luther himself had regarded as basically flawed and aimed to abolish from theology once and for all.[28]

Many years of studying the writings of Luther, especially the younger Luther, convinced Philipp Jakob Spener of the "gap between the original intentions of the Reformation and that which has become of it in orthodox scholastics and the hierarchically governed state church."[29] In his concept, Luther had firmly linked the personal assurance of salvation "with an objective foundation of this salvation outside of the subject of faith,"[30] but of these poles, which for Luther inextricably belonged together, Lutheran orthodoxy had "so emphasized the objective ground of salvation that it became almost isolated."[31] This was the point at which Pietism saw its calling: it was concerned with the *appropriation* of personal salvation.

---

23 This connection is pointed out by the work of the Lutheran theologian C. Lindberg, "The Third Reformation? Charismatic Movements and the Lutheran Tradition" *(Lindberg: 1983)*. This book discusses the question whether the charismatic movement can be considered as a "third Reformation" after Luther and Pietism. Lindberg's answer is a little ambiguous, but tends to the negative—hence the question mark in the title.

24 Apart from the content relationship between the Enlightenment and Pietism, this link was also symbolized in personal relationships. Leibniz, the "father of the Enlightenment," and Spener, the "father of Pietism," were close friends in Spener's Frankfurt years (cf. *Wallmann: 1973*, p. 160). "They share their rejection of the argumentativeness of orthodoxy and of Aristotelian scholastics, they jointly seek new, strong foundations for a spiritual reconstruction in Germany . . ." (Ibid.). The difference between Pietism and the Enlightenment is also shown in these two characters: "Spener turns away from worldly wisdom to overcome godlessness *(impietas)* by godliness *(pietas)* . . . It is the rationalistic trait, with its trust in reason, which separates Leibniz from Pietism and brings him close to Western European Enlightenment" *(Wallmann: 1973*, p. 161).

25 Cf. *Weber: 1964*, p. 146. We must note, however, that Pietism did not only meet opposition within orthodoxy, but also had a positive echo.

26 *Lohse: 1983*, p. 218.

27 Ibid.

28 Cf. p. 50.

29 *Wallmann: 1973*, p. 137.

30 *Schmidt: 1960*, p. 415.

31 Ibid.

The Emphasis:
Reformation of Spirituality

Pietism emphasized *praxis pietatis,* the devotion of the heart, a new relationship to the Bible, regeneration, assurance of salvation, evangelism, and sanctification. These terms in themselves show where the emphasis of Pietism lay: it was a reform of spiritual life. Spener appealed to Luther's *Prolog to the German Mass* when he founded his *collegia pietatis* in Frankfurt, "edification meetings" he regarded as *ecclesiola in ecclesia.* Whereas Luther complained that he did not have the people to put into practice the program described in the *Prolog,* Spener went a step further and gathered around him the people with whom he wanted to "be serious about being Christians."

In terms of *theology,* Pietism did not bring much that was new—and deliberately so. Here, it consciously followed on from Luther and the other Reformers. It was not concerned with a new theology but with the practical application of what the Reformers had formulated theologically. In his program, the *Pia Desideria* of 1675, Spener deliberately claims Luther as a witness of biblical theology. As Luther had fought against the scholastic theology of the Middle Ages, so Spener fought against Lutheran scholastic theology which had been "admitted back into the Protestant church through the back door."[32]

How did Pietism fare in the reformation of *structures?* At this point, apart from a few remarkable exceptions, we again find a worrying halfheartedness which meant that the actual concern of Pietism—the living faith—did not find a suitable vessel. So Pietism was a faith movement, and in some ways also a fellowship movement, but it was certainly not a church growth movement.[33]

The evident reticence with regard to a radical reformation of structures has a number of reasons. On the one hand, there were doubtless mystical, spiritualistic influences which formed some proponents of Pietism and caused them not to give the structural question the importance it deserves from a theological and spiritual point of view. In the context of Pietism, we normally do not speak of spiritualists, but rather of the "quiet ones in the land." But their individualistic, quietistic devotional style, which is deliberately set apart from the world, shows many characteristics of the spiritualistic paradigm.

A second motive for devaluating the structural question may have been the fear of what at the time was called "separatism." Would an insis-

---

32 *Kantzenbach: 1966,* p. 142.
33 Doubtless, the Herrnhut Brethren church of Count Zinzendorf takes a special position here, the "only lasting specially founded church to be brought forth by Pietism" (*Wallmann: 1973,* p. 151). Characteristically, this was a movement which proceeded to plant daughter churches modeled on the Herrnhut pattern in Germany and abroad.

tence on functional structures not easily have led to the formation of a new church? Because Pietistic proponents did not want that to happen under any circumstances, they were more ready to accept structural hindrances than to be suspected of being separatist and thus becoming a "sect."

Third, those Pietistic groups that did emigrate out of the state church all too often remained in an attitude of protest in the structures that they themselves created, so that an unprejudiced, functional understanding of structures was well nigh impossible. A lot of them were too much dominated by ideology. Furthermore, the mystic, spiritualistic influence was particularly strong in precisely these groups.

To sum up: however much Pietism attempted to return to the theology of the Reformers and to fight against Protestant orthodoxy, however revolutionary its achievements were with regard to the practice of spirituality, it remained largely bound by the spiritualistic or institutionalistic paradigm when it came to the structural question. The advocates of Pietism did not see clearly enough that this would have negative effects on their spirituality, and thus eventually on their theology (which had to justify the wrong practice).

The Third Reformation:
Our Task Today

This is the reason why, today, no less than a third reformation is needed. I do not believe that we need to develop new theological formulas—what the Reformers rediscovered in terms of biblical theology is, to a large extent, already formulated in classical form. I also do not believe that we need to look out for a completely new spirituality—what Pietism and the related devotional movements have demanded and begun to live seems to me to be exactly what is needed today.

Our problem, however, is that the wonderful insights of Reformation and Pietism are largely smothered in the mire of unsuitable structures.[34] In the third reformation we need to create structures which will

---

34 A prime example of the surprisingly halfhearted view of the structural question even today is the "Conference of Confessing Fellowships in the Protestant Churches" in Germany, whose leadership met in 1989 to discuss the structural question (which can be regarded as a progress in itself). But the result of the conference remained completely on the usual Pietistic lines: "The fellowships combined in the conference unanimously rejected this thought (of planting their own confessing church with its own leadership—*author's note*). Formal structural changes are not the requirement of the hour. The groups faithful to the Bible and the creed set out a good 20 years ago 'in order to resist, as far as possible, the distortion of the message, and with the aim of the inner revival and renewal of their churches'" *(Hauschildt: 1989,* p. 19). It is understandable that Wolfram Kopfermann comments on these words: "Whoever wants something other than what the Confession Movement has fought against for over 20 years, needs a new church!" *(Kopfermann: 1991,* p. 189).

be suitable vessels so that what the first two reformations demanded can be *put into practice.*

Therefore it seems to me to be completely legitimate that the church growth movement in our times, at least in the early years, devoted so much attention to the question of structures. The movement, which was founded by Donald McGavran and was later on largely influenced by C. Peter Wagner, has taught us to examine all institutions, doctrines, and programs (including church growth programs!) relentlessly and critically to find out what contribution they make to the growth of the church.

I have already pointed out that the opponents of the church growth movement (and other related reform movements) are mainly to be found among those we could call "orthodox." This is where history repeats itself. Whereas the first reformation set out to fight against Roman Catholic orthodoxy, before long it became orthodoxy itself. Then Pietism stood up against Lutheran and Reformed orthodoxy—and soon itself became orthodoxy. Reform movements in our days must, therefore, expect resistance to come from evangelical orthodoxy. It would be surprising if this did not happen!

Thus, whoever tries to put the principles of church development into practice, has to face a battle on two fronts simultaneously. On the one hand, some people (proponents of the spiritualistic paradigm) accuse them of a manipulative, technocratic mentality and a lack of trust in the Holy Spirit; the others (proponents of the institutionalistic paradigm) accuse them of spiritualistic, separatist, and enthusiastic tendencies. At this point, we merely experience the repetition of the same arguments that have dominated the whole of church history.

Church growth is not trying, as Kent Hunter puts it, to "reform the theology of the Reformation," rather, "it is based on it."[35] The fact that this basis also applies to those advocates of church growth who, as we have seen, refuse to be identified with a particular theological school, is shown by the fact that they have made as good as no contact to the Roman Catholic rank and file—which is surprising in face of their interdenominational approach and their emphasis on "pragmatism." If church growth were really just a growth-oriented method, that would be perplexing. But there is more to it than that: the center is, at least in my understanding, the consistent application of the reformation principle.

The second reformation is also implicitly assumed by prominent proponents of the church growth movement, for example when C. Peter Wagner passionately (and, in my opinion, rightly) refuses to assign church

---

35   *Hunter: 1983,* p. 16. Kent Hunter writes: "Whereas Martin Luther and the Reformers of the 16th century brought about a reformation of theology, many people today believe that the Church Growth Movement is bringing about a reformation in practice. If this is correct, the church today is in the midst of another reformation ... Church growth puts into practice the great truths of Scripture which were emphasized by Luther and the reformers" (Ibid.).

growth to any denominational label, but then states that the label "evangelical" would not be inaccurate.[36] But what does "evangelical" signify if not groups that are in the tradition of the two previous reformations?

The Emphasis:
Reformation of Structures

If we lay a certain emphasis on the structural question, this does not mean that this is considered to be more important than the question of theology or spirituality. Nothing could be farther from the truth! The reason is rather that, in the past, this area has not been treated consistently enough.

One exception to this thesis—although only an apparent one—is the work of the Ecumenical Council, which has been working on the subject "evangelism as a structural principle" since 1961.[37] Much that has been produced by this group seems to be in agreement with the demands raised in this book: the insight that traditional structures hinder churches from effective proclamation, the fight against "morphological fundamentalism," the talk of "heretical structures," and much more. Why did these concepts not have any real effect? The statements on structures in themselves are excellent, but the theological foundations on which the demands are based do give rise to concern.

The decisive theological premise of the ecumenical study, that through the death and resurrection of Jesus Christ "every person has become a member of the new humanity,"[38] whether they know it with their minds or not, is the fatal mistake of the whole approach. This concept, which aims at universalism, is exactly the point at which the central achievements of the first two reformations—for example the Lutheran *sola fide* and the Pietistic *praxis pietatis*—are denied.

Christian Möller rightly comments, "The total lack of a boundary between the church and the world which characterizes the ecumenical study as a result of the way it blends Christ as the Lord of the world and as the head of the church, fails to take account of the divisive power of the gospel."[39] In the last resort it leads to "a specific deceit of the world by the church," which, according to Manfred Seitz, consists in "no longer wishing to be the church."[40] Michael Herbst makes a similar comment: "The verbal emphasis on evangelism goes with a denudation of the content of evangelism from its most urgent cause."[41]

---

36 Cf. *Wagner: 1981,* p. 83.
37 Cf. *Margull: 1965.*
38 Ibid. p. 45.
39 *Möller: 1987,* p. 76.
40 *Seitz: 1979,* p. 108.
41 *Herbst: 1987,* p. 194.

Where the theological and spiritual foundation is missing, the standard that should guide structural reform is also shifted. The aim of church development, which the ecumenical structural reformers regard as being far too "ecclesiocentric," plays no role in this concept. The result of this debate has largely been that the discussion about functional, effective structures has been further burdened down. Groups that place particular emphasis on the dimension of personal faith and its appropriation tend to identify the quest for functional structures with the structural reform debate of the Ecumenical Council. In such circles, the whole subject has become a "red flag"—perhaps an understandable result, but a disastrous one.

Structures and Life

There seem to me to be seven reasons that should lead us, as long as we stand theologically and spiritually on the ground of the two preceding reformations, to take the structural question more seriously.

First, structures are never neutral. Any other view betrays traces of a dualistic world view. Structures can be useful for church development; they can also be a definite hindrance. And they have clear effects on the spirituality and theology of a church.[42]

Second, our surveys[43] of over 1,000 churches all over the world have shown that the quality characteristic "functional structures" is one of the eight essential signs of a growing church. In other words, if this point is absent (or too weakly developed), the church is likely not to grow, irrespective of how strongly developed the other seven quality characteristics are.

Third, the same surveys showed that the measurable difference between growing and declining churches is nowhere as great as in the area of "structures."[44] This, then, is the area in which growing and declining churches differ most.

Fourth, in the churches we have studied so far, it has become apparent that, of the eight quality characteristics, the point "functional structures" is one of the most frequent "minimum factors,"[45] in other words the area that is the greatest hindrance to growth and in which tangible action would be most liable to bear "fruit."

---

42 Cf. *Kopfermann: 1991*, p. 172: "There is a reciprocal relationship between the church organism and the structure. A foreign, inadequate structure of the church is not value-neutral; rather, it threatens and endangers the life of the church as an organism, and it can even destroy it. This happens today a thousand times over!"

43 For further details see: *Schwarz: 1996*.

44 Cf. *Schwarz: 1996*, p. 39.

45 For a more extensive treatment of this concept and the ministry approach behind it, see pp. 248-251.

Fifth, it is in the nature of the spiritualistic and institutionalistic paradigms not to take the question of functional structures seriously. Anyone who has recognized the dangers of these two paradigms and wishes to overcome them cannot remain halfhearted in the area of structures. Such halfheartedness could easily become the back door by which—however much we theologically reject spiritualism and institutionalism—the wrong paradigms can creep back into the life of our churches.

Sixth, biological research has shown that what differentiates "dead material" from "living organisms" is not—as a lay person may assume—a difference in substance, but the specific structure by which the individual parts are connected to each other.[46] This in itself is reason enough to put aside the cliché that structures and life are opposites. The two concepts are especially closely related to each other, as surveys of numerous churches have confirmed.

Seventh, the biblical analogy of the body of Christ[47] points us in a similar direction. This illustration makes it clear that each Christian has a specific function in the body, which is determined by his or her spiritual gifts. What is the structure of the church in this illustration? It can best be compared with the central nervous system of a body which makes sure that the coordination between the different limbs and organs works. This is a life-sustaining function for the health and growth of the organism.

It was the achievement of the first reformation that it *rediscovered* the dimension of personal faith and the priesthood of all believers. The achievement of the second reformation was to start *exercising* these central concepts. The task of the third reformation will be to structure the church in such a way that the concerns the first two reformations fought for can become normal in the daily life of the church.

---

46 Cf. the statement made by the bio-cybernetician, Frederic Vester: "Thus, that which makes dead material into living material is also . . . not due to a different type of substance, not in the parts themselves, but here, too, in their arrangement, in their structure, their individual pattern" (*Vester: 1988*, p. 28).

47 Romans 12:5; 1 Corinthians 12:27.

Part 2

The Theological Paradigm Behind Natural Church Development

What effect do the paradigms portrayed in part 1 have on some of the controversial systematic theological issues of today? As soon as we begin to regard these subjects from the perspective of the bipolar paradigm, we find a whole new range of possible solutions, as we will see. The questions under discussion are so varied and complex that it is self-evident that this book cannot, to put it metaphorically, examine them under a microscope—rather, we will need to adopt a "macroscopic" perspective. But this need not be a disadvantage. The macroscopic point of view can help us to see the issues in perspective. In this section, then, I do not aim to provide answers for these contentious issues, but to point out criteria which can help us to find answers which are helpful in our context. At the same time I aim to demonstrate how the spiritu-alistic and institutionalistic paradigms dominate—and handi-cap—literally all aspects of the theological discussion.

Diagram of the
Bipolar Paradigm

The diagram on page 99 is a visual representation of the bipolar paradigm—a concentrated summary of the content of part 2 of this book. It is a combination of the systematic theological quest for the "true church" and the practical theological task of church development. The diagram is based on the hypothesis established in part 1 that the true church must work for a structure which stimulates the development of the church as an organism.

I have classified the dogmatic issues which will be treated in this section into the three basic forms of expression of any Christian church: (a) faith, (b) fellowship, (c) service.[1] However, all three aspects are so closely—even inextricably—bound up with each other that this classification automatically appears a little bit artificial. But it can serve its purpose as an organizational principle in our context.

Each chapter is divided into three main sections. After a short introduction in which I show the relevance of the distinction between the dynamic and the static pole for the question under discussion, I then consider first of all the "Danger to the Right" (the institutionalistic paradigm with its monistic thought pattern), then the "Danger to the Left" (the spiritualistic paradigm with its dualistic thought pattern), and finally, under the heading "The Bipolar Approach," I show what consequences the theological paradigm of natural church development can have for the issue involved. The terms "bipolar paradigm" (which focuses more on the underlying thought structure) and "paradigm of natural church development" (which focuses more on the goals) are used largely as synonyms. In general, the bipolar approach will be illustrated by reference to one of the "eight quality characteristics of growing churches."[2]

I repeat that the terms "institutionalistic" and "spiritualistic" in this typology are nothing more than labels used to designate the two misconceptions of the Christian faith described in detail in part 1. Whenever I refer to a thought paradigm that is determined by a leaning towards objectivism, heteronomism, formalism, rationalism, and magic, I use the term "institutionalistic." The same applies by analogy to the term "spiri-

---

1   Cf. p. 17ff.
2   Cf. p. 21.

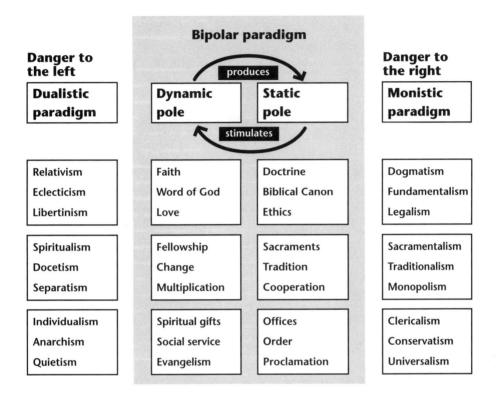

Fig. 12: The theological paradigm behind natural church development (bipolar paradigm).

tualistic." It always represents a thought paradigm characterized by a tendency to subjectivism, autonomism, dualism, irrationality, and mysticism. If the terms "institutionalistic" and "spiritualistic" are separated from this content, they can easily become misleading.

Perhaps it would have been more consistent to speak simply of "paradigm A" and "paradigm B." But this would lead to an extreme degree of linguistic abstraction which would not be very helpful for our subject. Probably most of the other terms I have selected to characterize the different positions are just as questionable. Every term has developed historically and acquired a whole range of meanings. Not all of them are identical with the meaning I associate with the terms. I will therefore attempt to explain clearly which meaning the individual terms have within our paradigm.

My use of secondary literature in this context is in some ways eclectic. The quotations used have been carefully selected, but they do not have the function of presenting the authors' positions in the context of their own thought systems. Instead, I use quotations from literature largely as *illustrations* of the three competing theological paradigms.

Readers who are interested in the overall picture presented, for example, by frequently quoted authors such as Wagner, Brunner, Tillich, or Luther are strongly advised to refer to the primary literature.

My concern in this section is not that the reader should agree with me in all the details of the positions I outline. In spite of my attempts to present an interdenominational theological position, the solutions I suggest will here and there inevitably betray my own (denominationally determined) background. It is a positive thing if there are different emphases within the body of Christ at this point. The suggestions I make for various contentious dogmatic issues are only meant to point out possible ways in which the bipolar paradigm can be related to these topics. I do not wish to convince the reader of the *details* of my theological positions, but I do hope that he or she will accept the bipolar *perspective*.

As we turn to a consideration of each of the subjects mentioned in the diagram, it is important to be aware of the significance of each aspect within the bipolar paradigm. It is in the nature of language that we can only deal with these subjects one after the other, but in reality they belong inextricably together. We cannot understand the details correctly if we don't pay attention to their significance in the overall picture.

In seminars, I try to do justice to this methodological problem by displaying the diagram of the entire paradigm on the wall with an overhead projector at the same time as I explain the concepts one after the other in words. This helps seminar participants to grasp each detail we talk about in the context of the overall picture, which leads to better understanding. The detail and the paradigm can thus, in a way, interpret each other. On the following pages I will frequently refer to the overall paradigm. I therefore recommend that you constantly call to mind the diagram on page 99 (fig. 12).

A.
Christian Faith

The revelation of which the Bible speaks is undoubtedly objective. But this objective element is not the church, nor doctrine, nor tradition—it is Jesus Christ himself. Faith is the event by which what Christ has objectively done becomes a subjective reality for us. It is only then that revelation achieves its aim. "Between the decisive objective content of revelation, Jesus Christ, and doctrine lies that subjective revelation event—or rather, that event which occurs in the subject—which we call faith."[1] Faith is the restoration of our right relationship with God.

The New Testament word for "believe," *pisteuein*, means something different from the connotations of the word in English. We believe what we do not know; we believe what we regard as true.[2] This "believing something to be true" misses the point of the biblical concept of faith. The word *pisteuein* is hardly ever linked with believing that something is true,[3] and the Old Testament equivalent can never be used in this way. In English, however, the concept of "believing that something is true" is the most common usage of the term—a fact which heightens the danger (which is present in other ways, too) of an intellectualistic distortion of the biblical concept of faith.

Pistis in the New Testament does not mean accepting a doctrine, it means trust in God: commitment, relinquishing internal security and external guarantees, complete dependence. We can only be so dependent on someone who is so reliable that we need no guarantees. This is aptly expressed in the Hebrew term for "believe," *aman*, which describes "the way in which the weak person draws strength from another who is strong."[4] The source of this strength is neither the institution *(heteronomism)* nor the person's own devoutness *(autonomism)*, but God himself *(theonomy)*.

Therefore, the biblical concept of faith must be protected from the (monistic) misconception that regards the essence of faith in assenting to a doctrine *(dogmatism)*, accepting biblical contents as "true" *(fundamentalism)*, or following a particular moral code *(legalism)*. However, faith must

---

1   *Brunner: 1960 a*, p. 53.
2   The word "believe" has largely the same intellectualistic undertones as the Latin word *credere*.
3   E.g., Hebrews 11:3, 6.
4   *Zimmerli: 1982*, p. 128.

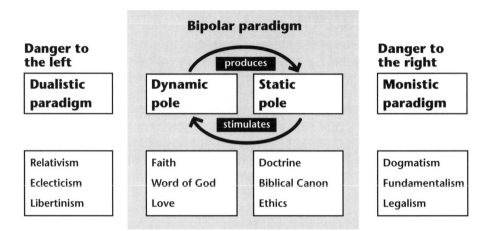

Fig. 13: The biblical concept of faith (pistis) and the dangers to the right and to the left.

also not be understood in a *relativistic, eclectic* or *libertinistic* way, as adherents of the spiritualistic paradigm tend to do.

The influence these misconceptions of faith have on modern theological debate—in very subtle ways—will become plain in the following three chapters.

1
What Is Truth?
The Conflict About
Correct Doctrine

To distinguish the biblical *pistis* concept from an abstract, philosophical concept of truth and knowledge, I like the term "truth as encounter."[1] This phrase, which was coined by Emil Brunner, and which Brunner himself regarded as his most important contribution to theological epistemology, puts into words better than any other phrase the historical, personal and thus existential components of the Christian faith. "Faith in Christ," Brunner emphasizes in his *Dogmatics*, "is not only the answer to the question: What is true? It is also the answer to the question: What is fellowship, and how can we find it?"[2] Here, the knowledge of truth is not a thought process restricted to the intellect—as abstract objectivism would have us believe—but rather an event which encompasses our whole existence.

Diagram 13[3] makes it clear that this personal faith always leads to theological reflection—to "doctrine," "dogmatics" and "articles of faith." The dynamic pole of the church involves personal *pistis* ("truth as encounter"), whereas doctrine is part of the institutional side. The two elements must not be regarded as identical (as the dogmatistic misconception tends to do), but they must also not be separated from each other (which is the mistake of the spiritualistic, relativistic misconception).

The distinction between "doctrine" and "faith" is nothing less than the distinction between *credo* as an objective truth to be believed and *credo* in the sense of the subjective appropriation of faith. It is largely identical with the distinction that has been rather overemphasized in theological history between the *fides quae creditur* (the content of the faith) and the *fides qua creditur* (the act of faith). A *fides qua* which separates itself from

---

1 Cf. *Brunner: 1984*, p. 13: "'Truth as encounter' is a concept of truth unknown to philosophy and scientific study."
2 *Brunner: 1960 c,* p. 159.
3 P. 102.

the *fides quae* is liable to become mere enthusiasm. A *fides quae* which identifies itself with the *fides qua*, and thus eventually replaces it, becomes mere "believing of facts." Faith in the real sense (*fides proprie dicta*) is always the personal faith of trust. Doctrine only fulfills a serving, protective function. It is therefore problematical if the word *faith* is used for the doctrinal element as well.

Theological discussion about this subject largely suffers from the fact that the two elements are either played off against each other, identified with each other, or placed in a rather nebulous "dialectic tension"— whereas the functional relationship between faith and doctrine is only rarely worked out. This functional relationship is, however, part of the theological paradigm behind natural church development: theological doctrine must be useful[4] in helping personal faith to grow. Seen from the perspectives of the institutionalistic and spiritualistic paradigms, it is understandable that this "in-between" position is exposed to a variety of misunderstandings.

Danger to the Right: Dogmatism

If we take a closer look at the institutionalistic misconception, which manifests itself here in the form of dogmatism, we should not fall into the trap of confusing *dogmatics* and *dogmatism*.[5] Whereas dogmatics (understood as theological doctrine that serves the body of Christ) is legitimate and necessary, dogmatism is not. It is characteristic of dogmatism—with its ideological character—that the usefulness of a doctrine for church development is not regarded as a relevant category. Doctrine is seen as an end in itself.

What is the nature of doctrine? Whereas personal faith confesses: "My Lord and my God," theological reflection picks out one element of this confession—for example the word "God"—and asks what this term means. It does not ask the question, "God, what do you want to say to me here and now in my everyday life?" The act of faith is a confession in the existential dimension, using words like "I" and "you." Doctrine uses more "distanced" language, with words like "he" and "they."[6]

This form of theological reflection is not objectionable, as the spiritualistic paradigm supposes. Rather, it is inevitable. Personal faith is keenly interested in an answer to such questions. Problems only arise when the results of theological reflection are equated with the content of faith, rather than understood as an instrument which aims to assist the expression of personal *pistis*.[7]

---

4   This formulation draws on the concept of "usefulness" described on pages 65-74.
5   Cf. my remarks on this distinction on page 44.
6   Cf. *Brunner: 1960 a,* p. 48.
7   A typical example of a dogmatistic approach is the assertion made by the orthodox theologian, Johann Gerhard, that nobody can be saved without a *knowledge* of the

A typical feature of the dogmatistic concept of faith is the use of formalistic reasoning, such as quotations from church fathers, which are cited as proofs, not illustrations. Such methods of debate are typical for Catholicism, but can be found in Protestant churches as well. If we look at the function of quotations from theologians such as Luther, Barth, or Bonhoeffer in many Protestant writings, we find the same underlying thought structure. The mere reference to "accepted" names is enough to transfer their authority to the writer's own theses. Authority here arises, not from the self-evident truth and relevance of the statement in the eyes of the impartial observer, but rather by traditionalistic adherence to formalistic patterns of reasoning.

In the view of this approach, a theological statement is not correct because it aptly states for our time a concern that is consistent with the biblical message (perhaps in opposition to centuries of wrong thinking); it is correct because someone else—who is, probably even in contrast to his or her own intentions, regarded as a sort of infallible witness to the truth—used similar words in a completely different time towards a completely different audience.

This method overlooks the possibility that these "church fathers" may not have thought their position through properly in certain areas (for example, in the area of church development). It also overlooks the fact that this method can be used to "prove" absolutely anything, with no reference to whether the statement proved is right or relevant in a specific situation. The function of theology as a critical corrective is transformed into a method of universal self-justification. That is exactly the *function* that is fulfilled by the dogmatistic proof method—which radically resists being understood in a functional way!

One of the people whose texts are often used to serve this purpose, is Dietrich Bonhoeffer. However, he himself seems to have seen through the demonic nature of this method. "Theology is the discipline in which we have learned to excuse and justify everything. It is a justification by reference to a final authority, the authority of Martin Luther, the doctrinal statements of the church and, in the last resort, the New Testament."[8] A few sentences later, he puts it even more dramatically. "Anyone who has started to justify themselves by appealing to theology is in the hands of Satan. Of course you should be a good theologian. But as such, keep your knowledge at a distance! Otherwise it will endanger your life and you will be caught in the quicksands that will stifle your faith."[9] "Theologism" that hinders faith and finally kills it—there is no better way to characterize the dogmatistic misconception.

---

doctrine of the Trinity. Otto Weber is right to say about this concept: "Statements of this type can be the expression of a hybrid form of dogmatics, which is usually swiftly followed by secularization" (*Weber: 1964*, p. 412).

8   *Bonhoeffer: 1972*, p. 405.
9   Ibid.

The driving force behind dogmatism is once more the security mentality outlined in the description of the institutionalistic paradigm. Wherever this mentality is given a free hand we can observe that—in the long term—it leads to the opposite of what was originally intended. The faith which was meant to be guaranteed by doctrinal statements is simply replaced by them, thus becoming obsolete, and at the end of the process, it may even be classed as "dangerous"—and rightly so. Any form of personal faith, if it is put into action, really is dangerous for a dogmatistic, security-conscious church.

All five characteristics of the institutionalistic paradigm can be studied in dogmatism: objectivism, heteronomism, formalism, rationalism, and magic. We will see later on how dogmatistic thinking, in combination with other symptoms of the institutionalistic misconception (e.g., traditionalism, monopolism, clericalism, and so forth), forms a coherent overall system in which the individual elements reinforce each other synergistically, so that it is impossible to topple this system with arguments on single issues.

Frederic Vester, a biologist who can teach us Christians a great deal in a number of areas, describes the way dogmatism that deliberately builds on taboos has a biological effect. "A taboo is something we must not even think of. It is 'unthinkable,' and therefore it cannot be examined ... If a dogma which could be disproved by the use of common sense is declared as taboo, the following neurobiological effect takes place: the information associated with the taboo is linked with the perception 'fear' ... This means that the forbidden attempt to examine the taboo becomes difficult even on a biological level."[10] Where this sort of dogmatism is effective, there is no need for external punishment. Heteronomism becomes so much part of the inner being of a person that it takes its (neurobiologically demonstrable) course—an effect that is fully intended by adherents of this concept of "faith"!

In extreme forms of dogmatism (especially when combined with a clericalist and monopolist attitude), people may even be explicitly instructed to think that black is white if the church declares it to be white.[11] This absurd approach, which deliberately rejects empirical knowledge, perhaps even by threats of punishment, is nothing more than dogmatism taken to its logical conclusion.

If the subject of "church development" has any place at all in this paradigm (which can by no means be taken for granted in the more extreme forms of dogmatism), it is equated with the defense of correct doctrine. It is not particularly important that personal faith and fellowship are stimulated—and thus hardly any effort is made to speak contemporary language or react sensitively to the needs of a given target group.

---

10   *Vester: 1988,* p. 459.
11   Cf. *Schmidt: 1960,* p. 382.

The "faith" (or what proponents of this paradigm regard as faith) is simply confessed in dogmatic formulas which are loudly proclaimed in public. This, the dogmatist believes, will have its effect. In a sense, the power lies—*ex opere operato*—in the formulas themselves. The structure of magical thinking and feeling can be plainly seen.

Danger to the Left: Relativism

As a reaction to dogmatism, the subjectivist response in the form of relativism is not justified, but at least understandable. The "spiritualist" (in the sense defined in this book) has recognized that dogmas and theological doctrines have often not been a help to faith, but rather a hindrance. Therefore, spiritualism—at least in its more extreme forms—completely gives up reflective thought and seeks spiritual experience only in the inner self, divorced from theological statements and empirical study, and sometimes in a markedly anti-rational attitude.

The mistake of relativism is not that it rejects dogmatism. Dogmatism *is* a hindrance to faith and must be resisted. But the mistake of relativists is just as serious—they separate personal faith from theological reflection. Dogmatics is regarded as irrelevant, with no regard to the question of whether it helps or hinders faith.

It is certainly true that theological doctrine cannot be equated with faith. Faith in the biblical sense is not "believing in something"—a doctrine or dogma—but a personal encounter involving trust, obedience, and love. But this personal encounter is inextricably linked with its "frame," with theological thought and doctrine. "Human insistence on the freedom of the spirit without doctrine is mere enthusiasm."[12]

The demand for a "non-dogmatic" Christianity, which is often voiced today, has some justification if it is directed against the dogmatistic misconception. But if it implies that theological thinking should be replaced by relativism, we cannot leave it unchallenged. Relativism is an illness that is just as dangerous as dogmatism. We should not attempt to use Beelzebub to drive out the devil.

The fatal effects that theological relativism has in practice can be studied in a wide variety of groups that are influenced by the spiritualistic paradigm. Radical spiritualists not only reject all dogmatics; with equal passion they refuse to consider the principles of church development (which unquestionably represent a form of "dogmatics") as well. In both instances they suspect a dogmatism which they want nothing to do with. They want to find out what is right in a particular situation "directly from God," not with the aid of empirically deduced and methodically structured "principles."

---

12 *Brunner: 1984*, p. 140.

The fact that the principles of church development are identified in the same way as dogmatics—by academic study, reflective thought, and abstraction—is, for spiritualists, sufficient reason to reject them. Even where they deem it necessary, for whatever reason, to use some of these principles, they will never achieve an open-minded (let alone passionate) attitude to them. They will always have the uneasy feeling that they have resorted to unimportant—and questionable—practices.

There seem to be exceptions to this rule. There are churches whose "doctrine" is strongly influenced by the spiritualistic misconception—but they have undoubted success in church growth, and they clearly make use of the principles of church development. In my dealings with these churches, I have discovered that there is usually a strange schizophrenia between the practical and the reflective side of church life.

In practice, a lot of those churches work very energetically on the principles of church development—often without realizing it—although their doctrine does not reflect these principles at all. On the contrary, in their teaching, the emphasis is not on the principles which actually brought most people to faith and which have demonstrably caused their growth. The emphasis is rather on the extraordinary—that is, on events which happen only rarely, even in such churches, and which on closer study are found to make only a peripheral contribution to the development of the church. But in spite of this fact, the leaders teach that *these* things, i.e., the extraordinary events, are what really matter. And the principles that God more often uses, and to which these churches largely owe their growth, are in danger of being condemned as "unspiritual."

Of course, this view is a drastic distortion of the truth, and spiritualists sometimes sense the contradiction. But they think that they owe it to their dualistic, other-worldly concept of faith to stick to their position even (especially!) when the facts point in a different direction.

The Bipolar Approach

What, then, is the bipolar approach to doctrine? *The* functional doctrine does not exist, if we understand it in the sense of a static set of theological statements that are valid for all times and in all cultures. The starting point of the bipolar paradigm is that we cannot guarantee truth, neither by an appeal to papal authority, nor by a synod or any other authority. This approach has four important consequences:

First, no Christian doctrine is infallible. The pope and the councils, the synods, and even the Reformers, can be wrong. A church which forsakes this basic insight, for example by claiming its own Reformation statements of faith to be infallible, "would not merely be denying some incidental element of the theology of the 16th century, but rather—in the sense of the Reformation—would be denying its existence as a 'true' church."[13]

Second, Christian doctrine—by contrast with the person of Jesus Christ—is changeable, and must be changed over the years if it is to fulfill its task of serving the proclamation of the gospel in different historical and geographical contexts. No doctrine, not even the famous creeds developed in the history of the church, can "claim a canonical validity for the form of their statements in the sense that they claim to be a-historical, valid independent of time."[14] Theological formulas—even such respectable concepts as the trinity or the doctrine of the two natures—must not be guarded as if they were a magical inheritance. Rather, we should constantly ask whether they demonstrably fulfill their purpose, which is to make the essence of biblical revelation clearer, rather than to obscure it. A statement which is helpful in one historical context can be decidedly counterproductive in another.

Third, every doctrine must be judged by the criterion of whether, in its own context, it has the effect of stimulating the life and growth of the church as an organism. "Functional dogmatics" can thus only mean a doctrinal approach which constantly strives to establish this principle, and which defends it against the spiritualistic and institutionalistic paradigms. What answers this doctrinal approach provides depends largely on the historical context, and thus cannot be definitively laid down for all time.

Fourth, this approach leads to the conclusion that different doctrines can be right at the same time (as they each serve God's purposes in their given context). "The fact that—apart from the boundaries of this pluralism—there is a multitude of theologies and doctrinal positions has its legitimate justification in the fact that the gospel of God's favor, which gives rise to our faith, is a message that is *addressed to people*, and that is directed to people of different identity in wholly different situations and times."[15] Even in the New Testament, there is no uniform doctrine of Jesus Christ or the church, but rather, through divine providence, a variety of types of doctrine, which find their unity in Jesus Christ himself. Unity can never be sought in timelessly binding theological statements—that would be an unhistorical, unbiblical and (for church development) ineffective concept of unity—but only in the *person* of Jesus Christ.

Perhaps actual experience will do more than these rather abstract considerations to illustrate what I am aiming at when I speak of "functional dogmatics." As I mentioned, I am regularly invited to hold seminars in churches with differing traditions in order to help them apply the principles of natural church development in their actual situation. In these seminars I use working material developed by our institute.

---

13   *Weber: 1964*, p. 54.
14   *Thielicke: 1968*, p. 6.
15   *Thielicke: 1978*, p. 308.

Because it is intended for use in groups with different traditions, this material deliberately does not confine itself to the language of any one denomination or devotional style. Yet this material undoubtedly contains doctrine—a doctrine designed to serve the development of the church. Of course I do not claim that the statements and definitions contained in this material are the absolute truth. They are merely an attempt to provide aids to help Christians in church development.

For instance, in our material we describe 30 spiritual gifts, and these gifts are precisely defined. In these definitions—and in our decision to describe no more nor less than 30 gifts—those of us who developed the material conscientiously took into account what we learn from the Bible. However, most gifts are not precisely defined in the Bible, and we find no dogmatic statement about the total number of gifts. The statements we make on this subject have been thought through with great care, and they are painstakingly revised from one edition to the next, but they are not, of course, absolute truths that are valid for all time—just as no theology is valid for all time. Our theological statements must be *useful* for the development of the church in a specific situation—no more and no less.

But almost every time I get involved in discussions on this subject with other Christians, I find out how strongly they are influenced by a static, timeless (and thus unbiblical) concept of truth. Many Christians seriously believe that, somewhere in a heavenly book, God has written down the eternally valid definitions of spiritual gifts, and that he watches to see that we, in our attempts to define them, keep as exactly as possible to the formulations in the heavenly manuals. So there is a precise definition of what is meant by the gifts of hospitality, teaching, and evangelism, and in what ways the gift of helping is different from the gift of service (if there is any difference). There is also, it is assumed, an exact definition of the seven (or three or nine) ways in which Christians should go about finding out what their gifts are, and perhaps even a statement about the percentage of Christians who have each gift. A dreadful concept of God!

With these words, however, I certainly do not intend to justify any sort of relativism. I am completely convinced that God wants us to make *correct* theological statements. But what is "correct" is not formulated in some timeless, heavenly dogmatic work of reference. God is concerned instead that the tools we develop should serve his purposes as revealed to us in the Bible. On the subject under consideration (i.e., the question of spiritual gifts), that means that God wants people to discover their divine calling and to live accordingly. When editing our material, I therefore constantly ask myself whether the last edition helped more than previous editions in the fulfillment of this goal. I am convinced that this approach to theology must also work on other levels (i.e., on issues that are "dogmatic" in the narrower sense). Theology is always a *tool*. Whenever it aspires to be more, it becomes false theology.

Christians who assign theology an exaggerated, magical significance tend to assume (at least, if they are theologians) that somewhere in a heavenly archive God has a precise definition of the doctrine of Himself, dogmatic statements for all areas of theology, and all the details of a correct church structure. At first sight, this sort of position may make us smile. But when we realize how unhistorical—and thus unbiblical—the underlying concept of God is, it doesn't seem funny any more.

Regarding this view of God, Ludwig Feuerbach was right in his criticism of religion. This really is a concept thought up by human beings and projected into the heavenly realm:[16] God is seen as a professor of theology who jealously watches over the correct use of dogmatic definitions! The grotesque nature of this idea should not blind us to the fact that this sort of concept is, in fact, quite widespread—especially among theologians. Because *we* can only think in static, unhistorical categories, we create a *God* who is defined in static, unhistorical categories as well.

---

16 Cf. *Feuerbach: 1981*, p. 224: "The gods are . . . the desires of men transformed into real beings; a god is the human yearning for happiness satisfied in the human imagination."

2
Christian Faith and Fundamentalism: The Conflict About Scripture

When we apply the distinction between the static and the dynamic pole, which is fundamental for the bipolar paradigm, to our understanding of the Bible, it leads us to make a distinction between the "biblical canon" and the "word of God," as can be seen in figure 13.[1] Here, too, we must not regard the two elements as being identical, as the institutionalistic misconception (with its monistic thought pattern) demands, nor may we separate them from each other, as the spiritualistic misconception (with its dualistic thought pattern) tends to conclude.

The mere existence of the written, codified biblical canon is not, in itself, a guarantee that the word of God will "happen," that it will touch and change our life. But it is characteristic of the concept of the word of God revealed in the Bible that this word "happens." It is no accident that the Hebrew term *dabar* has a double meaning: "word" and "event." A person who knows the Bible does not necessarily know the living Lord. That only happens at the moment when the word of God becomes an existential reality in a person's life through the power of the Holy Spirit, so that the perfect tense is translated into the present tense, the written word becomes a "living word."

It was one of the greatest achievements of the Reformation and one of Luther's most important theological contributions to point out this fact. In the struggle of the Reformers against the Papalism of the Roman Catholic Church, it could have been a convenient tactic to argue on the basis of a fundamentalistic approach to the Bible. It is a sign of Luther's genuine concern for truth that he, who appealed so radically to the principle *sola scriptura* and who quoted Scripture as his only "weapon" against his clerical opponents, should not let himself be drawn into a formally authoritarian or literalistic view of Scripture.

The bold comments Luther included in his introductory remarks to biblical books are an impressive witness to the way he made an effort

---

1   P. 102.

to avoid an unhistorical, static understanding of the Bible. For him, different passages of the Bible had different levels of authority. His guiding principle was: "That is also the right touchstone for judging all books, that we see whether they advance Christ or not, for every holy scripture advances Christ (Rom. 3), and Paul wishes to know of nothing but Christ (1 Cor. 2). Everything that does not teach Christ is not apostolic, even if Peter or Paul teach it. Conversely, everything that preaches Christ is apostolic, even if Judas, Annas, Pilate, or Herod should preach it."[2]

For Luther, Christ is *the* word of God. Because the Bible "advances Christ," it is a binding authority, but only insofar as it advances Christ. Luther recognized the danger that the letter of the Bible could take the place of Christ, and for that reason he set up the principle that "Christ is the Lord of Scripture" *(Christus dominus scripturae).*[3] By contrast with an approach to the Bible that consists of a rationalist, heteronomic acceptance of biblical truths, his concern, as in other areas of church life, was with the personal appropriation: "It is not enough that you say, 'Luther or Peter or Paul said this or that,' rather, you must sense in your own conscience, in Christ himself and without wavering, that it is God's word ... As long as you do not have this feeling, you have truly not yet tasted God's word."[4] These words describe—in the language of those days— more or less the same as what we mean today when we distinguish between the "word of God" and the "biblical canon," and when we emphasize that the word of God should "happen" in our lives.

I am not saying here that we should take over the judgments that Luther made about various biblical books on the basis of the criteria he set up. I, for one, could not do so. But the *principle* that Luther established of regarding the authority of the Scriptures from the point of view of whether they "advance Christ" is, in my opinion, a classic way of phrasing what we could call a functional approach to the Bible.[5] Luther was the first theologian to put forward a biblical faith that could come to terms with critical Bible research, and is thus fundamentally different from the formally authoritarian, fundamentalistic view of the Bible which culminates in the dogma of verbal inspiration.

The same (spiritually motivated) freedom in dealing with the Scriptures which Luther formulates theologically[6] can also be seen in his function as a Bible translator. "The unique quality of Luther's translation,

---

2   *Luther: 1964,* p. 141.
3   Weimar Edition 40, I, p. 420.
4   Weimar Edition 10, II, p. 22.
5   Cf. Luther's bold statement that we, as Christians, "can make new decalogues, as Paul made them throughout his epistles" (Weimar Edition 39, I, p. 47).
6   However, we should not deny that Luther, who so clearly formulated the new scriptural principle in so many places, in other places also shows the formally authoritarian or axiomatic view of Scripture. Not everywhere did his functional reformation principle prevail over the traditional approach to Scripture.

which far surpasses all earlier attempts, stems from the deep, independently discovered understanding of the biblical contents and from the translator's power of language, which does not adhere slavishly to literal correctness, and which, in its re-creative translating principle, is more faithful to the biblical original than any word-for-word translation."[7]

Luther, like the other Reformers, did not even leave the generally accepted limits of the biblical canon untouched. For the first time for centuries, the biblical canon was not regarded as a closed, unchangeable whole. By deciding in favor of the Palestinian and against the Hellenist canon, the Reformers excluded the Old Testament "apocryphal" books from the Bible. In the 16th century, that meant breaking with a canonical tradition that had been more or less unquestioned for more than a thousand years—a fact that is hardly realized by modern Protestants. As the formation of the canon was a decision made by the church, the doctrine of the Reformation was that this canon must be re-examined. To absolutize the limits of the canon would be to make an element of tradition absolute.[8]

When we wonder today whether the definition of the canon by the church can be regarded as definitive and final, I believe that the position proposed by Hans-Georg Fritzsche points us in the right direction: "It is practically and historically final, but not in theological principle."[9] In principle, we could imagine circumstances which could cause us to reconsider this question.[10] However, these considerations are more than hypothetical because there is an overwhelming consensus in Christianity that the canonical decisions of the church fathers were amazingly "on target."[11] "There is hardly likely to be any other writing that we could now wish to be added to the canon. There may be some books on the edge of the canon that are debatable. But there can be no doubt of the significance and value of most New Testament writings."[12]

To put it another way, the canonical decision of the church fathers can be regarded as an extremely successful attempt to create institutions that are useful for the life, health, and growth of the church as an organism. The decision was therefore eminently functional, even though it was justified at the time by an appeal to formal, authoritarian arguments. Helmut Thielicke is right when he writes: "The formation of the canon is ... the church's seal under the experience gained with certain texts. The historical quest for authenticity and apostolic origin is, by compari-

---

7   *Wallmann: 1973*, p. 47.
8   Cf. *Weber: 1964*, p. 283.
9   *Fritzsche: 1982*, p. 147.
10   For example, if we should discover new, unknown early Christian documents with contents that turned out to be hitherto unknown elements of the early Christian witness, cf. *Weber: 1964*, p. 281.
11   *Lohse: 1983*, p. 37.
12   Ibid.

son, only a secondary, additional measure, aimed at combining spiritual conviction with historical security. When we use the terms 'conviction' and 'security,' we hint at the hierarchical difference between the two qualities, and we also call into question any motives based on security, insofar as 'security' (beyond the academically justified meaning of the term) is misunderstood as a prerequisite for faith."[13]

Of course, there is some exaggerated *pathos* in the assertion by Karl Barth that the biblical writings, "because of the canonical status they themselves had," ensured that "just these writings could later be recognized and proclaimed as canonical."[14] But Barth is undoubtedly right in his observation that the Bible as a canon "did impress the church, and impresses the church again and again."[15] The separation of the biblical canon reflected the experience of the church with regard to the "kerygmatic efficiency"[16] of these documents, as Hans-Joachim Kraus phrases it. Functionality!

However, it is not without problems to classify the concept "biblical canon" in the bipolar paradigm as part of the institutional side of the church, and thus subject it to the criterion of functionality. If we compare it with the other institutional concepts that are listed in the same column of figure 12[17] (e.g., tradition, offices, order), we can see immediately that these concepts are not equal in value. The difference between the biblical canon and the other eight institutional forms is a fundamental one. None of these eight elements can have a normative function for the church, but the Bible is the decisive normative factor for the church of Jesus Christ in all its forms. It has an identity of its own in relation to the church—a fact that is not expressed in the diagram (because this is not the purpose for which this diagram was designed).[18]

The very word *canon* shows that the early church recognized the existence of something that had absolute validity and authority over the

---

13 *Thielicke: 1978*, p. 154.
14 *Barth: 1948*, p. 524f.
15 *Barth: 1955*, p. 110.
16 *Kraus: 1983*, p. 45.
17 P. 99.
18 This sort of graphical representation is deliberately designed to portray a complicated issue in simplified form by regarding it from one specific angle (and neglecting other angles). In the diagram of the bipolar paradigm, the angle chosen is not the question, "What is the normative standard for the church?" but rather, "What are the organizational and organic elements that are apparent in the life of the church?" The second question is based on the assumption that what is here referred to as the church takes its standards from the Bible. I place special emphasis on this assumption because I have found in my seminars and lectures that, when I have presented the diagram of the bipolar paradigm, some hearers took it as a cause to accuse me of setting aside the normative nature of the biblical canon. They interpreted the diagram from the point of view of a question that it can, by definition, give no answer to, and they projected their interpretation onto its author. It is no surprise that, using this method, some of the results can be rather confusing.

church and all it did. That was where it learned what the church of Jesus Christ is, and how it expresses itself in practice. The church cannot arbitrarily set other writings or authorities in place of the Scriptures. In this context, functionality cannot be taken to mean that Christians can create new Bibles which better express what *they* (and here lies the danger) consider to be helpful for church development. Precisely this tendency would not be functional, as it would inexorably drive the church to random.

The final norm for the church is undoubtedly Jesus Christ; but in order to know who Jesus Christ is, what he has done for us and what he expects of us, we need reliable information about him. To avoid the danger that verbal appeals to Christ should be combined with forms of degeneration (a phenomenon which occurred in the early church and prompted the formation of the canon), it was a wise and necessary decision to subject the church to a normative standard. The usefulness of the biblical canon for the development of faith, fellowship, and service has been so clearly demonstrated throughout history that, for me, the pneumatic functionality of the Bible (in the truest sense of the term) is beyond question.

Danger to the Right: Fundamentalism

For a fundamentalist approach to the Bible, this view of things, like the whole bipolar paradigm, is of course unacceptable. Even though fundamentalism may oppose the magical, institutionalistic misconception in other areas (for example, in the doctrine of the sacraments), the fundamentalist view of the Scriptures shows all the signs of the institutionalistic paradigm. Here, too, the security mentality that has already been encountered several times drives fundamentalism to the (false and dangerous) conviction that a fundamentalist view of the Bible can guarantee the word of God. The thought structures (and practical consequences) of Bible fundamentalism are not different from those of dogmatism or sacramentalism—even though it may oppose these false doctrines in the name of the Bible.

We do not do justice to fundamentalism, however, if we do not understand its underlying concern: it aims to give expression to the secret that the church has experienced in every century, i.e., that when we receive the biblical word, we really do receive the will of God reassuring us and calling us to follow. It is not this concern which I criticize, but rather the questionable methods which, in effect, hinder the fulfillment of this concern.[19]

---

19   Cf. *Weber: 1964*, p. 257: "The dignity of the word of the Bible is not that it was not really a human word but instead, by some miraculous means, a word from God which pushed aside all human words in their humanity and historicity; rather, its dignity is in the fact that God's word in the Bible takes the form of human words that are in no way limited in their humanity."

To safeguard the uniqueness of the Bible as the word of God, fundamentalism takes recourse to the doctrine of verbal inspiration. This theory, which is not Christian in its origin, but stems from Hellenistic Judaism,[20] can be found in similar form in the fundamentalist wings of widely differing religions, e.g., in Hinduism and Islam.[21] According to this inspiration doctrine, Scripture was "dictated by the Spirit," so that the evangelists were only the spirit's *manus* (= hand), *calami* (= quills) and *tabelliones* (= writing slates).[22] The biblical authors—at least, in the more radical forms of the inspiration doctrine—appear as mechanical puppets in the hand of God, a view that we, in our modern computer age, would regard as decidedly "technocratic." The divine inspiration of the Scriptures is seen, in contrast to the historical thought structures we find in the Bible itself, in the theory that the personal and historical elements in the origination of the Bible are eliminated. This is where the true character of fundamentalism is revealed. Fundamentalists do not really believe in the historicity of the divine revelation, but replace it with a timeless system of truth.

It is part of the logic of this mechanistic misconception that bitter battles are fought over the inspiration of every Greek *iota* and every Hebrew vowel mark—a view which is untenable from the outset, as there is no definitive original biblical text, but only a number of differing manuscripts. If the theory of verbal inspiration were true, its advocates would have to admit that the manuscripts on which we base our modern translations are not identical with the original manuscript that was supposedly dictated letter by letter, so that we have no access to the single, authoritative Scriptures, but only to a number of copied and modified manuscripts (some of them with significant differences in the text). Which of these versions is the definitive one (in the sense of historical authenticity) is a question that can only be answered by using historical "textual criticism"—a task that is fundamental to all Bible translations.

A genuine proponent of the verbal inspiration theory would therefore, as a logical consequence of his or her doctrinal position, have to conclude, "We have lost the original, and thus solely inspired Scriptures for ever." However, if we take a *historical* approach to the biblical tradition, we have no cause for such a pessimistic judgment because, with careful historical research and a critical comparison of the various manuscripts, we can come very close to the original text, as biblical research has shown. But we do so, not by eliminating historical methodology, but by using it!

The ideological character of fundamentalists can blind them to such inconsistencies in their reasoning, and even lead them to assert that Luther's German translation (having a historical significance similar to

---

20   Cf. *Weber: 1964*, p. 253.
21   Cf. *Fritzsche: 1982*, p. 154.
22   Cf. *Pöhlmann: 1980*, p. 58.

the English King James version) which was based on the Latin *Vulgate*, (not one of the most reliable manuscripts) is "for church and theology *the* binding, and therefore verbally infallible biblical text for us."[23] This stubbornness, which sometimes leads to the most absurd logical contradictions, is, in a sense, understandable, because for the fundamentalist, the inspiration doctrine is the issue on which the whole of the Christian faith stands or falls. Thus, fundamentalists are in the schizophrenic situation of equating historical criticism with the betrayal of faith, although it is to historical criticism (or at least the discipline of textual criticism) that the fundamentalist owes the historical reliability of the biblical texts, which is all-important for him. An absurd position, but it is understandable from the self-perception of the institutionalistic paradigm with its monistic thought structure!

It is no accident that fundamentalism has a strong tendency to legalism. Whereas the Bible emphasizes that the word of God is *pneuma*, not *gramma*,[24] classical fundamentalism turns everything upside down. Its demand that the infallibility of the Bible be accepted axiomatically is nothing but a law. According to the fundamentalist view, you believe in Jesus because you first believe in the Bible. Faith in the Scriptures, as the orthodox theologian Johann Gerhard phrased it, is not an article of faith, but rather "the axiomatic premise of all articles of faith."[25] There is no significant difference between the Roman Catholic and the fundamentalist concept of faith; they are just different versions of an authoritative, heteronomic doctrinalism.

The deepest flaw in fundamentalism is that it does not really understand (or want to understand) the nature of the incarnation. We could almost conclude from the fundamentalist view that the New Testament teaches that the word became book, not that it became flesh.[26] As Wilfried Joest puts it, fundamentalism gives the impression that after his *incarnation*, the Word of God "was then *in-codified* again."[27]

The danger of fundamentalism is that faith in Christ becomes faith in the infallibility of the Bible. As the two are seen as identical (a consequence of a monistic thought pattern), faith in the Bible can absorb faith in Christ and, in the last analysis, replace it. And that is exactly the point—as was demonstrated by later orthodoxy and the emerging Enlightenment—at which the Bible loses its "living authority" and is finally "pushed aside in favor of the perceptions of reason."[28] "Its true authority comes from the fact that it bears witness to the word *in action*. But if its authority must now be justified by a special quality in the words them-

23   *Echternach: 1937*, p. 9.
24   2 Corinthians 3.
25   *Gerhard: 1863*, p. 9.
26   Cf. *Pöhlmann: 1980*, p. 58.
27   *Joest: 1966*, p. 33.
28   *Weber: 1964*, p. 200.

selves, the word in action which is thus 'secured' is, in fact, overshadowed by the word that bears witness."[29] We should be clear about the fact that it is actually Christ himself who, along with the "word in action," is thus overshadowed.

With regard to church development, fundamentalism (understood as described here, i.e., as a typical variety of monistic thinking) has similar consequences as all the other "-isms" we have used to characterize the institutionalistic paradigm. It is exaggerated, but a thoroughly logical conclusion, when Otto Weber remarks: "If we are to think like that, it is not easy to understand why the church is necessary at all. Reading at home the word of God should surely be enough; perhaps even merely to have a copy of it in the home! The sacred word would be, in itself, the revelation, it would be *theophorous.*"[30]

These remarks, in their exaggerated but logical consistency (that is shared by hardly anyone) point out the real danger of this approach. The personal category—our relationship with Jesus and with brothers and sisters—is not exactly eliminated, but it plays an incidental role by comparison with neutristic, formalistic categories—the right relationship to a theory of the Bible. And any element of the faith that only plays an incidental role can, if necessary, be omitted altogether.

Danger to the Left: Eclecticism

Whereas the fundamentalist approach to the Bible is a consequence of the institutionalistic paradigm, the spiritualistic misconception leads to a view of the Bible which I propose to call *eclectic*. Proponents of this view verbally affirm the validity of the biblical canon, but in practice, they deny its normative function by creating their own eclectic interpretation. There are historical examples of individual forms of spiritualism emancipating themselves entirely from the biblical canon, but such views are rare in the Christian sphere. Generally, spiritualists do not leave their historical religion, but they "heighten" its meaning "without changing a single letter on the surface."[31]

Eclectics choose biblical passages that support their own views and use them to construct their own philosophy. On the outside, they can act like fundamentalists, quoting the "correct" biblical passages for all they do. Internally, however, their appeal to the Bible has a different function than for fundamentalists. For spiritualists, the Bible is a decorative incidental detail, not the standard to which they subject their own actions. However, in *one* aspect there is a parallel between eclectics and

---

29   *Weber: 1964*, p. 200f.
30   Ibid. p. 209.
31   *Richter: 1960*, p. 1238.

fundamentalists: both show a distinctly unhistorical approach to the Bible—which is only reasonable, considering the unhistorical concept of God that these two misconceptions are based on.[32]

Eclecticism treats the Bible as a quarry from which the normative authority of the eclectic's subjective self can break proof texts *(dicta probantia)* as required, and as they fit into his or her own thought system. Usually, eclectics do not even notice that this approach brings them into sharp conflict with biblical concerns. Since spiritualists, as we have seen, regard theological reflection as not very significant, many of them do not realize their own unbiblical tendencies. The proof texts that accompany their actions convince them that they are standing on solid biblical ground, whereas in reality, they have long succumbed to their own subjectivity (or, far worse, to radical anti-Christian influences).

Even where spiritualists officially claim otherwise, personal "visions" and "inner pictures" (which are often, without any testing, interpreted as the voice of God) have a far greater fascination in their circles than the biblical word. This even applies when the contents and the demonstrable effects of these "pictures" turn out to be far weaker than for a thorough Bible study. Spiritualists find it difficult to apply Paul's criterion that everything should serve the building up of the church[33] to these phenomena, because they regard such experiences as "edifying" in themselves (this is, of course, a concept of "edification" that is restricted to the inner person). Spiritualists believe that wherever such phenomena are experienced, the edification of the church happens automatically.

Here, the magic of the word in fundamentalism is replaced by the spiritualistic tendency to do completely without words. Words are seen as an unsuitable vessel to describe spiritual experience. We no longer need the letter, as we rely entirely on the Spirit. Only the Spirit can produce spiritual experience, therefore such "external" and "material" things as the Bible cannot produce faith.[34] This is the beginning of the phenomenon known in theological discussion as mere "enthusiasm."

Here we can understand the passionate opposition of the Reformers to such tendencies—a passion which sometimes made them blind to the distinction between mere enthusiasm and the biblically legitimate and necessary quest for the voice of God in the here and now. It is evident that it is not the concern to hear God's voice today that should be criticized, nor is it the experience of dreams and visions in itself (for these

---

32 This explains the fact that eclecticism and fundamentalism can sometimes be combined in a breathtaking way.

33 Cf. 1 Corinthians 14:26.

34 Cf. Ronald Sider, who summarizes the spiritualistic understanding of the so-called Zwickau prophets as follows: "The Scripture . . . is not powerful enough to teach man: 'Man must be taught by the Spirit alone. For if God wanted man to be taught by Scripture, he would have sent down the Bible to us from heaven.' The inward voice of God has no connection with Christ or the Gospel" *(Sider: 1974,* p. 161f).

things are clearly biblical). But the dividing line to "enthusiasm" (in the questionable sense) is definitely crossed when such experiences are implicitly or explicitly raised above the standard of the Holy Scripture.

The Bipolar Approach

Neither fundamentalism nor eclecticism can do justice to the historical nature of the biblical revelation. Thus it is not surprising that both misconceptions are a hindrance for the quest of church development today. I therefore propose to outline a functional understanding of the Bible as an alternative to both paradigms. The following four principles show in what direction this approach is to be sought.

First, a functional understanding of the Bible should not be identified with destructive Bible criticism. Here, functionality must remain in the limits described in part 1[35] and thus subject to the intentions of the Bible itself. The goal of this functionality is to stimulate faith, fellowship, and service in our times—not to get in their way. A functional understanding of the Bible must be marked by a love for the word of God—a love that is often missing in theologians who indulge in otherwise justified criticism of fundamentalism.[36]

Second, a functional understanding of the Bible is always a historical understanding. The Bible must not be misused as a sort of "collection of oracles" (whether mystical or magical in nature). No quotation from the Bible is, on its own, the word of God—it may be taken out of its context and thus robbed of its original intention. For example, the Bible contains the words: "There is no God."[37] "There can be no greater heresy, no worse nonsense than that which can be proven by a random selection of quotations from the Bible."[38] The custom that is common in many Christian circles of "proving" certain theological statements by generalized reference to Bible verses (which usually contain similar phraseology to those statements) does, it is true, reflect a justifiable concern to be subject to the authority of the word of God, but it has little in common with the historical understanding of the Bible described here.

Third, a historical understanding of the Bible leads us to the question of the "canon in the canon" in the sense of Luther's criterion of "that

---

35 Pp. 67-72.
36 We should, however, take into account that this destructive Bible criticism was, at least to some extent, provoked by a fundamentalistic approach to the Bible. Cf. *Fritzsche: 1982* (p. 155), who writes that the doctrine of inspiration had "fatal historical consequences," in that it led to the very opposite of what it originally intended. "It led people away from the Bible rather than helping them to understand it; it especially provoked the sort of historical Bible criticism that is destructive in its effects."
37 Psalm 14:1; 53:2.
38 *Weber: 1964,* p. 262.

which advances Christ."[39] This is the standard by which we can critically evaluate the various biblical writings. But in our "Bible criticism," we must not impose extraneous criteria (such as our own ideology) on the Bible, but only the criterion of the Bible itself: the redeeming act of God in Jesus Christ. The question of how this act can become a reality in the life of people today is the real "canon in the canon" of the Holy Scriptures. But we must beware of giving a static definition of this "canon in the canon" by disqualifying, or even excluding, biblical writings that seem to be far removed from this central concern. In certain historical contexts and individual situations, different biblical writings can be important and "advance Christ." For example, the Book of Revelation and the Letter of James were obviously not very relevant to the central questions that concerned the Reformers (which is why Luther nearly excluded them from the canon), but at other times—such as today!—they may be highly relevant.

Fourth, a functional understanding of the Bible forbids us to regard the historical forms described in the Bible (such as church structures) as being a divine law. Apart from the fact that there is no uniform New Testament church structure,[40] it cannot be our aim to hold a "procession in the costumes of the church in Corinth,"[41] as Rudolf Bohren once put it. This would be a grossly unhistorical procedure which could only produce anachronistic forms. It would not just be "conservative," but reactionary, and it would flout the real intention of the Bible—to help people to find a right relationship with God. When we accept the Bible as a normative standard for the church, this does not mean that we have to regard this norm as being static and formalistic, as if every statement in the Bible—irrespective of who it is addressed to and what it is about—were a military command to all its readers that required literal, unthinking obedience. This sort of "biblicistic" approach finds no support in the Bible itself.

I am conscious of the fact that many of my readers will not be able to agree with these statements concerning the Bible. As a reaction to *destructive* Bible criticism, a lot of Christians have understandably taken refuge

---

39   Cf. Helmut Gollwitzer, who comments on this formulation of Luther: "Luther does not mean an encyclopedic definition of where Jesus Christ is mentioned, but rather an examination of every biblical text (even in the Old Testament!) to see whether it bears any relationship to the revelation of Christ in action. This examination must not be neglected, even for the driest, most irrelevant pages of the Bible or those texts that seem furthest from Christ" (*Gollwitzer: 1978*, p. 62).

40   Cf. *Schweizer: 1949*, p. 23, where Schweizer summarizes the issue as follows: "Thus it becomes clear to us that, if the Pauline churches are, in a sense, the center, on the other hand there are also the Palestinian early church and the Johannine churches. There is no general pattern that we can apply. The relationships between them are rich, and there is no lack of significant agreement between them . . . And yet, the different concepts of the church in different contexts become clearly apparent."

41   *Bohren: 1975*, p. 146. Cf. also *Kopfermann: 1991*, p. 136: "In questions of church life, the mere imitation of what the early church did is not necessarily helpful."

in an unhistorical, fundamentalist understanding of the Bible, as they—rightly—saw such Bible criticism as a threat to the substance of the Christian faith. Fundamentalism seemed to give them the security they felt they needed in their struggle against the attack on their faith that stemmed from Bible criticism. Thus, in many cases, "personal faith" has become linked with fundamentalism—which in my view is an unfortunate combination. In reality, personal faith in Jesus has little in common with fundamentalism, and is even in danger of being swallowed by it. Whenever the dynamic pole of the church—church as an organism—tries to seek "protection" under the umbrella of the institutionalistic paradigm, a process has started which, in the final analysis, can lead to its own destruction.

It surprises me that fundamentalism is hardly ever seen as a danger in the church growth movement.[42] Undoubtedly we can say that there are totally fundamentalist churches that enjoy strong numerical growth. If we made the ideology of numerical growth the theological criterion, we could then take sides with these churches and say to their critics: "Where is the problem? After all, the church is growing!" But this way of thinking seems to me to reveal a highly questionable pragmatism which cannot be justified theologically. Fundamentalism is inconsistent with the biblical revelation and foreign to the church growth concept. It arises from a security mentality which is related to the technocratic idea, described earlier, that the organic pole of the church can somehow be controlled. Perhaps the tendency to a technocratic paradigm in both lines of thinking is the point at which they can unite with each other.

It is precisely on the issue of the view of the Bible that we can tell whether a church has understood the radical nature of the biblical revelation—or whether it merely advocates a form of (possibly modified) legalism. "No canon can give the church security *(securitas)*. The church can only be certain of the word that is confirmed in its life by the Spirit *(certitudo)*."[43]

---

42 For example, when I asked Donald McGavran, the father of the modern church growth movement, what he thought about fundamentalism, he replied, "I am a fundamentalist!" This statement is not exactly confirmed in his writings, but they do show traces of an unhistorical biblicism which is in contrast to the actual intention of the movement founded by McGavran.

43 *Weber: 1964*, p. 296.

Practical Illustration:
The Quality Characteristic "Passionate Spirituality"

As was mentioned in part 1,[44] empirical surveys in the course of our work have led us to identify eight qualitative characteristics that are demonstrably stronger developed in growing churches than in stagnant or declining ones. On the following pages I propose to treat each of the characteristics at the point that seems most appropriate within the theological paradigm behind natural church development.

It seems reasonable to treat the quality characteristic "passionate spirituality"[45] in the context of the issues of correct doctrine and the correct view of Scripture which have been treated in the last two chapters. In our research, we found that the devotional style of a church is not decisive for its growth (as long as this style is real devotion and not just unbelief papered over with pious vocabulary). But it is decisive that the Christians live their faith with passion. We discovered that the level of commitment in spiritual life is consistently higher in growing churches than in declining ones. Irrespective of the theological position of the church, growing churches are characterized by an atmosphere of expectation. Concepts such as an intensive prayer life, love for the word of God, and encouragement of spiritual maturity are hallmarks of these churches.

The quality characteristic "passionate spirituality" is not the same as the oppressive legalism of the institutionalistic misconception, and it is also far removed from the non-committed randomness of the spiritualistic paradigm. It is the personal experience of love for Jesus and for brothers and sisters (and not just a rational belief) which is the power behind the spiritual dynamic that is found in most growing churches.

In the past, this quality characteristic has sometimes been criticized, particularly by fundamentalists and dogmatists. They point out that "passion" is no proof of the truth. Even the sects, they say, sometimes show a great passion. This observation is undoubtedly true. I have not yet examined any of the sects to find out causes of their growth, but it seems to me that the enthusiasm that is found in them is one of the main causes of their—sometimes remarkable—growth. But this does not mean that the sects are right in their theology. Their doctrine remains false, even if it is advocated with passion and is "successful" in the sense of numerical growth.

On the other hand, though, "correct doctrine" on its own is not a growth factor, as innumerable examples show. Any church, however orthodox its doctrine and its view of the Bible may be, can hardly expect to

44   Cf. p. 21.
45   For a more detailed treatment, see *Schwarz: 1993 b*, pp. 28-31; *Schwarz: 1987*, pp. 128-161; *Beutel: 1995*.

grow if it does not learn to live its faith with passion.[46] This is the reason why churches that are doctrinally orthodox but dominated by the institutionalistic paradigm sometimes rationalize their lack of growth with theological arguments, and thus become (for this reason!) opponents of the church growth movement.

Wherever the "defense of right doctrine" takes the place of practical steps towards church development, we are dealing with the institutionalistic paradigm. It is not surprising that in such an (ideological) atmosphere, we can sometimes observe a tense fanaticism, but hardly ever a released and spiritually relaxed passion.

---

46 Of course, there are also exceptions to this rule: churches that are decidedly "legalistic," repressive and thus anti-passionate in character, but which nevertheless attract people. This shows yet again how inadequate the criterion of numerical growth is. When we analyze churches on the basis of the eight quality characteristics in the course of our work, we deliberately use a *qualitative* criterion. We assume that wherever all eight quality characteristics are developed above a certain level, *quantitative* growth will ensue. We have not (yet) found any exceptions to this assumption (cf. the "65 hypothesis," *Schwarz: 1996,* p. 40f).

3

Between Legalism and "Cheap Grace": The Conflict About Law and Liberty

A ccording to the Bible, the truth of faith is demonstrated when it "expresses itself in love."[1] This love is not something romantic and nebulous, as the secular concept (and, interestingly enough, the spiritualistic concept of love) would have us believe; rather, by nature it has very practical, visible effects. It is the fruit of the Spirit,[2] and thus something that cannot be limited to the private sphere. Love needs to be expressed in public.

As is clear in figure 13,[3] love, if it is not to degenerate into individualistic randomness, needs to be related to an institutional element which is generally known as *ethics*. Following an ethical code is not identical with practicing love (the error of the institutionalistic misconception), but on the other hand, love must not attempt to liberate itself from ethical standards (as that would lead to libertinism).

The ethics that are based on faith are not a mere footnote to dogmatics; they are the other side of "correct doctrine." The church of Jesus Christ has a vested interest in living its faith in an ethically committed way. This commitment must show itself in practice, right down to the order of the church. Church discipline, for example—and in extreme cases the exclusion of pseudo-members so that they do not poison the whole organism—is justified not only in cases of wrong doctrine, but also in cases of wrong practice.

The two dangers to the biblical concept of love—on the one hand institutionalistic legalism, on the other hand spiritualistic libertinism—are closer together than we realize at first sight. It may seem surprising

---

1   Galatians 5:6.
2   Galatians 5:22.
3   P. 102.

that people with decidedly spiritualistic tendencies sometimes show attitudes that seem to be legalistic (although libertinism would be a more logical consequence of their spiritualistic position) and that among people who lean towards the institutionalistic paradigm, libertinistic tendencies can be observed (although institutionalism logically tends more to legalism).

How can we explain this phenomenon? It stems from the fact that both misconceptions, spiritualism and institutionalism, can be traced back to the same unhistorical concept: a "substantial" understanding of God, with a corresponding substantial understanding of humanity and a substantial understanding of sin.[4] A radical personal concept of God and humanity, leading to the category of personal responsibility, is almost impossible for both misconceptions. Against this background, the apparent inconsistencies of the institutionalistic and spiritualistic paradigms can, on closer examination, be easily explained.

Danger to the Right: Legalism

It is not obedience to the biblical commands that we rightly call legalism,[5] but the attempt to make the law into the way of salvation. In the New Testament, the law is confirmed as the will of God, but it loses its role as a mediator between God and human beings. It is not the law which determines our relationship with God, but faith in Jesus Christ. By contrast, legalism describes a heteronomic (and thus formalistic) concept of faith in which—in the last resort—law replaces Jesus Christ.

This legalism has mainly taken two forms in the course of church history, both based on the concept of the church as the mediator of salvation. One form uses force (trying to impose faith by institutional means); the other form does without any form of coercion, but is just as objectivistic in its attempts to claim people for its concept of the "church" (trying to achieve by theological formulas what could not—as proponents of this approach might admit with resignation—be achieved in reality).

The first—coercive—form of legalism was largely restricted to a time when the church had the power to make its ethical standards binding on all by means of state laws. We should not forget that there was a period in which people could be compelled by the police to attend church, and the authorities even checked that attenders did not sleep during sermons.[6] Even though some proponents of the institutionalistic paradigm—

---

4   Cf. pp. 49-64.
5   Cf. Paul Tillich: "Obedience to the law is not, in itself, legalism. Judaism is right to emphasize this point. The law is, above all else, a divine gift. It shows people their essential nature, their true relationship with God, their neighbor, and themselves" (*Tillich: 1984*, p. 90).
6   Cf. *Schmidt: 1960*, p. 359.

understandably in view of their background—tend to regard this period as the prototype of a "Christian era," we must clearly say that, from the perspective of the biblical view of faith and the church, the goal of church development had far less chances in those days than it has now.[7]

Wherever spiritual weapons are confused with statutory and legal force, the "church as an organism" has a hard time. It is pushed into the role of an opposition, a resistance movement—resisting both the state and the institutional church! Faith and love can, by definition, not be forced, and not even God, who could do it, forces us to have fellowship with him. Any institution that attempts to do so is usurping the place of God.

Besides this violent concept, there is also a nonviolent form of the same objectivistic misconception. Proponents of this concept do not try to compel church members to live "holy" lives by legal or ecclesiastical force. Instead, they use theological formulas to declare their members to be "saints," often without their knowledge. Here, the view of the church as a mediator of salvation draws on other expressions of the institutionalistic misconception, such as sacramentalism. The *communio sanctorum* is then interpreted in such a way that the term *sanctorum* is not understood as referring to the saints *(sancti),* but to the sacraments *(sancta).* The personal element is thus replaced—in a way typical of the institutionalistic paradigm—by a neutristic category. In a personal view of the church, the adjective "holy" is applied to the church members, that is, to people, but in a sacramentalist understanding it applies to the holiness of the mediator, the sacraments.[8] It is thus not surprising that in this process, the term *communio* is also redefined. It is no longer understood as the fellowship of the saints (which would be a deeply personal concept), but as the proper *participatio* in the sacraments.

Within this version of the institutionalistic misunderstanding, legalism finds a different expression than the coercive example described above. The life and morals of the church members who, by participation in the *sancta,* are made *sancti,* is no longer so important, as long as they maintain a minimum of religious ritual which is vital for the church, such as infant baptism, formal membership, and occasional participation in the sacraments.

In this framework, sacramentalism fulfills a function that is comparable with indulgences in the Middle Ages (which is not really surprising). Where the slogan of the sale of indulgences, at least in its popular, vulgar form, was "As soon as the coin rings out in the box, the soul leaps to heaven," the vulgar form of the concept of sacramentalism supposes that the soul leaps to heaven when we take the heavenly medicine. Faith is acquired by being baptized into the church. Forgiveness of sins is guar-

---

7   For a more extensive treatment, see pp. 264-271.
8   Cf. *Schmidt: 1960,* p. 125.

anteed by receiving the Eucharist. Thus we do not have to worry about moral standards any longer. People can remain as they are—they merely need to act in the right way towards the church, the "mediator of salvation."

It is quite logical that, against this background, a tendency to a libertinistic morality eventually developed. Why be concerned for personal faith and active love if mere *participatio* in the church is good enough? By contrast with the first variety, legalism is here reduced to a minimum—defined differently by different groups—which is then defended all the more doggedly and fanatically. It takes some effort to identify the deeply legalistic character behind this variety of institutionalism, because it often hides under the cloak of a tolerant, almost libertinistic looking approach.[9]

This "tolerant" version of legalism, at least in its Protestant form, frequently appeals to the biblical doctrine of justification. However, the understanding of justification that is apparent here is not consistent with the New Testament. In practice, it justifies not the sinner, but the sin.[10] This is a doctrine of justification which Dietrich Bonhoeffer in his book *Discipleship* rightly criticizes as "cheap grace." What he writes on this subject seems to me to be such a classical, prophetical characterization of the non-coercive variety of institutionalism, that I will quote an extensive passage.

"Like ravens, we have flocked around the corpse of cheap grace, and from it we received the poison which has made the discipleship of Jesus die among us. The doctrine of pure grace has undergone an incomparable deification; the pure doctrine of grace became God himself, grace itself. Luther's words on every hand, but corrupted from truth into self-deception. 'If our church has the doctrine of justification,' we say, 'then it must surely be a justified church!' That is how we claim to recognize Luther's true inheritance—by making grace as cheap as possible. That is

---

9   One illustration is the system of "church taxes" in the Lutheran and Reformed churches in Germany. Some adherents of the state churches criticize free church financial systems and accuse them of being legalistic, for example on the issue of "tithing." But it is interesting that the tithe, which is by nature a voluntary contribution, is suspected of being legalistic, whereas the church tax (which is a lesser amount, but is collected by the state tax authority) is not. If either system is legalistic in the strict sense of the word, it is rather the church tax system. The church prescribes to two decimal places how much each church member must give. Exceptions are not tolerated. Anyone who wishes to give a single cent a year less must officially leave his church. By comparison with what various churches understand as a "tithe," the church tax is not much. But the question at issue here is not the *amount* of the payment, it is the principle of legalism versus voluntary committment in financial affairs.

10 Cf. Rudolf Weth: "All people have the right to come to know the reconciling and liberating power of Jesus Christ and to accept it for their lives. A church that denies people this basic right, a church of 'cheap grace' (Bonhoeffer) is in reality a merciless church!" (Weth: 1986, p. 153).

our way of being Lutherans—by leaving discipleship to the legalists, the Reformed churches, the religious enthusiasts, and all for the sake of grace; by making the world justified, and declaring Christians who follow Christ to be heretics. A nation had become Christian, had become Lutheran—at the expense of discipleship, and for an all too cheap price. Cheap grace had won the day."

Bonhoeffer continues by describing the consequences of this understanding of faith, which claims to be so merciful to people: "But do we also know that this cheap grace has been extremely unmerciful toward us? Is the price that we must pay today, with the breakdown of the organized churches, not a necessary consequence of the availability of cheap grace? We provided proclamation and the sacraments cheaply, we baptized, confirmed, and absolved a whole nation, unasked and unconditionally, out of human love we gave the sanctuary to the mockers and unbelievers, we gave streams of grace without end, but the call to follow Jesus in discipleship was rarely heard. Where are the insights of the old church, the questions in the baptismal catechism that watched over the boundaries between the church and the world, that watched over costly grace? Where are Luther's warnings against proclaiming a gospel that makes people feel secure in their godless lives? When was 'Christianization' more cruel and devastating than now? What are the 3,000 Saxons killed by Charlemagne against the millions of souls that are dying today? We are experiencing in ourselves the truth of the saying that the sins of the fathers are visited on the children to the third and fourth generation. Cheap grace has been merciless to our Protestant church. Cheap grace has undoubtedly been merciless to most of us in a personal way. It has not opened up the way to Christ, but closed it to us. It has not called us into discipleship, but made us hard in our disobedience."[11]

Perhaps we find it difficult to recognize this sort of doctrine, which cannot be distinguished from libertinism in its effects, as an expression of the legalistic misconception. But it betrays the same belief in the church as the mediator of salvation, the same objectivistic, institutionalistic thought structure that we identified in the more violent, coercive form of the same misconception. In both cases, faith can be achieved without personal responsibility, without love—and, in the last resort, without Christ.

Danger to the Left: Libertinism

In the framework of the institutionalistic paradigm, as we have seen, the ethical concept is determined by a profanity that arises from its formalism; in the spiritualistic paradigm, it is influenced by an other-worldly dualism, which I described in part 1.[12] Depending on whether the world

---

11   *Bonhoeffer: 1981*, p. 24f.
12   Cf. pp. 34-37.

is regarded as *irrelevant* or as *evil* (as we have seen, both views are possible within spiritualistic dualism), the resulting ethical concept can take different forms.

Thus, it is no accident that within the spiritualistic paradigm we find not only plainly libertinistic aspects, but at the same time other tendencies, which can seem almost legalistic. Spiritualists tend to embrace the former view if they regard created life and its structures as being *indifferent*, and therefore not worth paying attention to; they lean towards the latter view if they regard the world as the essence of *evil*, and thus aspire to mortify their remaining worldly lusts by ascetic discipline. Right from the early church, there have been countless examples of both forms.

Some spiritualistic groups concluded from their alienated view of the world that it is unimportant how we live physically in this world—as only the soul is important, not the body. Physical acts, they believed, were morally indifferent. They could indulge in wild orgies that were infamous in Christian and non-Christian circles alike. In the New Testament, for example, the letter of Jude warns against a group that celebrated the *agape*, the love feast, with wild excesses.[13]

Christians who were influenced by this version of spiritualistic dualism claimed that, in face of the meaninglessness of pagan deities, it was completely unimportant whether they ate meat sacrificed to idols,[14] or whether they offered incense in honor of the Emperor. These things were "mere formalities"; such "purely external acts," they claimed, did not affect the "inner devotion of the heart."[15]

From the same dualistic starting point, other groups drew completely opposite conclusions. They demanded the mortification of the flesh, and therefore a life of asceticism. In particular, marriage (or, at least, reproduction) was often forbidden so that the divine soul should "be liberated from the fetters of the senses and bodily instincts and more easily able to aspire to higher things."[16] This form of asceticism should not be confused with the legalism that is found within the institutionalistic paradigm, although its consequences are similar. Whereas adherents of the institutionalistic paradigm overestimate the effect of the law formalistically—as a result of a profane objectivism—the ascetic disciplines of the spiritualist have a different motive. They arise from an otherworldly subjectivism; spiritualists use the world to resist the world, exercising asceticism to mortify their desires, which is more a concession to the fallen world (or the world created by the *demiourgos*) than a genuine, personal conviction.[17] Thus it is that those who passionately oppose the law

---

13   Cf. *Chadwick: 1972*, p. 35.
14   Cf. 1 Corinthians 8.
15   *Chadwick: 1972*, p. 28.
16   Ibid. p. 35.
17   Cf. the helpful remarks made by Paul Tillich, which do not quite reflect my terminology, but which point in a similar direction (*Tillich: 1984*, p. 91).

become legalists themselves—a phenomenon that has marked religious enthusiasts throughout church history. "They speak of the Spirit, but they are slaves to the letter" (von Loewenich).

The ascetic variety of the spiritualistic misconception is shown in the endless lists of self-tortures that Christians have thought up through the centuries. Henry Chadwick's description of the life of Syrian monks in the fourth century gives us some insight into this phenomenon: "One frequent ascetic exercise was to wear a heavy iron chain as a belt. Some lived the life of an animal and fed on grass; they lived in the open, with no shade from the sun and a minimum of clothing, and they justified their way of defying society by claiming to be 'fools for Christ's sake.'"[18] This life in the open air should not be confused with the modern, popular practice of living "in harmony with nature"; it was rather a deliberate exposure to nature as an enemy of humanity. The suffering experienced in such exercises was therefore not a necessary evil; it was the deliberate goal of these exercises to suffer.

We must be fair in our judgment of such practices. Not all groups that indulge in ascetic exercises do so on the basis of the spiritualistic, dualistic world view. Many Christians use ascetic exercises (such as fasting) with the expressed aim of equipping themselves better for service in the world—a meaningful, even functional intention! *This* form of ascetic exercises, which is certainly not rejected by the Bible,[19] can be of positive use even today.

The Bipolar Approach

Perhaps the bipolar approach is more important in the area of ethics than in any other issue. It can help to safeguard Christians from both legalism and randomness—two basic faults with which, in my experience, all churches have to struggle.

It is at this point that it becomes apparent how important it is that we really use a biblical understanding of functionality (i.e., an understanding formed by the Bible), as was described at length in part 1.[20] A prime example of this approach to ethics is found in 1 Corinthians 8, where Paul remarks on the question of whether Christians should join in eating the meat of animals that was consecrated as sacrifices to pagan gods. To put it briefly, Paul's view was as follows: in principle there is no objection to eating this meat, as we have only *one* God and *for us* there is no other god. Therefore, any meat that has been sacrificed to other gods is, for us, still only food, not sacred, loaded material. In principle, then, eating meat sacrificed to pagan deities is *adiaphoron*, indifferent.[21]

---

18   *Chadwick: 1972,* p. 209.
19   E.g. Matthew 6:16; 1 Corinthians 9:27, etc.
20   P. 67ff.
21   Cf. *Thielicke: 1968,* p. 113ff.

But it is characteristic of Paul's approach that he does not stop at this point. When Paul appeals to the Corinthians to abstain from eating this meat, he does not give theological reasons of principle; his reasons are ethical. There may be Christians at the meal who are not yet far enough developed in their understanding that they can see through the meaninglessness of the pagan gods. If these Christians were to join in the meal, it would be a decision to oppose Christ. Therefore Paul appeals to the Corinthians to refrain from eating—out of love.

It is no accident that Paul follows his remarks about meat sacrificed to idols, which he continues in chapter 10, with the verse that we have called the *locus classicus* of biblical functionality[22]:"Everything is permissible—but not everything is beneficial. Everything is permissible—but not everything is constructive."[23] The principle behind this verse shows the dimension in which functional ethics should move.

First, the church of Jesus Christ should always strive for commitment in ethical questions. However, we should not overlook the fact that the boundary between commitment and legalism can be drawn relatively simply on paper and in theological definitions, but in the everyday life of the church things are much more complicated. Whenever a group tries to live out its faith in a committed way and thus gives itself specific rules, this can be regarded by people outside the group as legalism. A church should learn to live with accusations of legalism that result from this constellation.

Second, the adherence to rules and orders that a church sets up for itself should never be understood as an end in itself, only as a means to an end. All rules serve specific goals and must constantly be examined to see whether they really contribute to the fulfillment of these goals. The goals themselves must also be examined to see whether they are really God's goals. This applies especially to exercises that fall under the general heading of asceticism. Where they help Christians to grow in faith, fellowship, and service, they are to be commended; but the moment they either become an end in themselves or serve wrong purposes, they are harmful.

Third, following a specific ethical code must never be made a prerequisite of faith.[24] Pacifism, abstinence from alcohol, opposition to apartheid and other attitudes that might be, in themselves, valuable and meaningful, must never be seen as conditions that people must fulfill before they can become Christians.[25]

---

22 Cf. p. 69.
23 1 Corinthians 10:23.
24 I will return to these thoughts in the context of the question of a "bipolar approach to evangelism" (pp. 209-212).
25 This is the point of the hotly contested distinction between *discipling* and *perfecting*. Cf. C. Peter Wagner: "Church growth people . . . stress a minimum of ethical content in the discipling phase and a maximum in the perfecting stage of Christianization" (*Wagner: 1981*, p. 157).

Fourth, no ethical code must be allowed to lead us to regard God's will as static, as if God required the same of all Christians in all stages of their lives. Growth in faith and love is a lifelong process which includes progress and setbacks. Particularly in the area of ethics, we must avoid the sort of thinking that I described in the context of the institutionalistic misconception, following Paul Hiebert, as a *bounded set* mentality.[26] The criterion for all ethical standards must be whether they help Christians to grow more and more into Christ. We must not fall into any form of perfectionism.

I now propose to explain what effects the bipolar approach can have on church development by reference to a further quality characteristic of growing churches. We call it "loving relationships."[27]

Practical Illustration:
The Quality Characteristic "Loving Relationships"

In our studies we observed that growing churches have a higher "love quotient" than non-growing ones. The "love quotient" is an attempt to represent how strongly (or weakly) the Christian ideal of love is practiced in the life of a church.[28] In the questions we have developed for this purpose we do not ask about people's intentions, but rather about the practical effects of love. How often do the Christians invite each other for meals or for coffee? Is there someone in the church they can pour their hearts out to if they have personal problems? How generously (or sparingly) are compliments given in the church? Do the Christians feel at home in their small groups?

The answers to these and other questions are evaluated, and each church is given a value that represents its quality in this area. The results confirm that growing churches have—on the average—a significantly higher "love quotient" than stagnant or declining ones. They are thus demonstrably characterized by a higher degree of mutual concern and sharing. This applies both to the relationships of Christians with each other and to their relationships with outsiders.

I frequently find that Christians have difficulty with the term "love quotient." I am often told that love cannot be represented by such a "quotient" because it is, by definition, invisible. I am not so concerned about the word itself, but I am deeply concerned about the underlying content. And I feel that this content is rather well expressed by the deliberately provocative term "love quotient," which conveys the message that

---

26   Cf. pp. 40-43.
27   For a more extensive treatment, see *Schwarz/Schalk: 1998,* pp. 116-122; *Schwarz: 1998.*
28   Compare also *Arn/Nyquist/Arn: 1986,* p. 7f. To my knowledge, Arn's love survey (the "love-care quotient") was the first empirical study to relate qualitative aspects of a church to its growth.

love—as understood in the Bible—is not a romantic feeling that comes on us if we are lucky, and then leaves us in an equally mysterious way. The Bible repeatedly emphasizes that love is more than a feeling. It speaks of love as "fruit."[29] In Luke's Gospel we are told: "Each tree is recognized by its own fruit."[30] There can be no doubt that when the Bible speaks of the fruit of the Spirit, it means visible manifestations. For the Bible, just as for the botanist, there is no such thing as invisible fruit. Søren Kierkegaard rightly writes that love itself is hidden, but adds: "However, this hidden life of love can be seen by its fruits, for there is a yearning in love to be known by its fruits."[31]

In our surveys of more than 1,000 churches, we have observed that churches that showed signs of being influenced by either the legalistic or the libertinistic misconception generally had difficulty in practicing love, which was expressed empirically in a low "love quotient." Of course, there are a multitude of other factors that can cause the "love quotient" of a church to be underdeveloped. But in my estimation, the legalistic misconception of the Christian faith is one of the most frequent causes.

Churches that have a low "love quotient" often have problems with evangelism, too. In such groups, evangelism is usually limited to activities that operate with merely verbal methods. It can be demonstrated that churches with a well developed "love quotient" have a much greater attraction for others than groups that operate only with verbal methods.

The secret of this quality characteristic is the fact that love is here regarded as an art that individual Christians, Christian groups, and whole churches can consciously seek to learn. In the course *The Learning Love Process*[32] which was developed by our institute and has been used in many churches, we aim to train, learn, and practice love in the context of small groups, rather than merely talking about it. Our aim is to help groups to develop a strong commitment in ethical questions, but at the same time to avoid any form of legalism.

---

29 Galatians 5:22.
30 Luke 6:44.
31 *Kierkegaard: 1966*, p. 13. Compare also the statement of Emil Brunner: "The fruits of the faith or the fruits of the Spirit are therefore precisely the factor of the faith that is visible, the signs by which we should constantly check if we are really standing in a living faith or if faith has become a matter of the head, a purely intellectual affair, a faith in the dimension of 'believing what is true.' If this is the only type of faith we know, we cannot speak of the fruit of faith, for head-faith has no fruit. Thus, the fruits of faith are no longer a proof of faith, they become a mere content of faith, so that we lose all possibilities of testing whether faith is genuine" (*Brunner: 1984*, p. 167).
32 *Schwarz: 1998; Schwarz/Berief-Schwarz: 1995*.

B.
Christian Fellowship

I n the horizontal plane, faith in Jesus Christ expresses itself in fellow-ship with Christian sisters and brothers. According to the New Testa-ment, new life in Christ without new ways of living together is un-thinkable.[1] Characteristically, the New Testament uses the same words, *koinoneo* and *koinonia*, for fellowship with Christ and fellowship among Christians.[2] They mean both "sharing by giving" and "sharing by receiv-ing," especially in Pauline use. Thus, *koinonia* is a personal fellowship be-tween people who are themselves in personal fellowship with Christ. The two aspects are inextricably connected, so that Dietrich Bonhoeffer could say with some theological justification: "Being 'in Christ' is the same as being 'in the church.'"[3] Against this background we can more readily un-derstand Bonhoeffer's otherwise ambiguous phrase about "Christ exist-ing as the church."[4]

In my view, one of the most important contributions of the church growth movement to missiology has been to point out that this commit-ment to a local fellowship is an integral part of the faith. Wherever we look, we find exponents of church growth arguing that an individualistic "decision for Christ" is not enough, and that conversion always includes becoming a "responsible member of the church." It is no accident that the issue of incorporation into the Christian church plays a major role in church growth literature.[5]

It is clear from figure 14 that the biblical understanding of fellowship faces dangers from two sides. The attempt to guarantee Christian fellow-ship and bring it under control inevitably leads to the institutionalistic paradigm with its monistic thought structure. There, personal fellow-ship can degenerate to a neutristic participation in the sacraments (*sacra-*

---

1   Cf. *Kraus: 1975,* p. 388.
2   Cf. *Hauck: 1950,* p. 807f: "Fellowship with Christ necessarily leads to fellowship with Christians, the fellowship of the members one with another. Here, too, Paul uses the word *koinoneo* in several relationships, and *having a share* in the brothers, in keeping with the literal sense of *koinoneo,* frequently merges into the concept of *giving a share.*"
3   *Bonhoeffer: 1960,* p. 92.
4   Ibid. p. 138.
5   One of the best examples is given by Win and Charles Arn, who translate this concept into the practice of a specific church growth process (*Arn/Arn: 1982,* pp. 142-159).

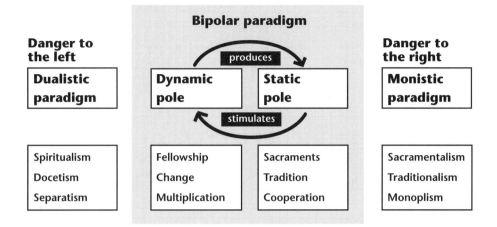

Fig. 14: The biblical understanding of fellowship (koinonia) and the dangers to the right and to the left.

mentalism); the concern to remain in the fellowship of "fathers and mothers in the faith" can switch to *traditionalism;* and if the important goal of the unity of Christians is understood institutionalistically instead of personally and spiritually, a *monopolistic* concept of the church emerges.

This monistic misconception naturally has its dualistic counterpart. The dualistic paradigm is characterized by a tendency towards *spiritualism* (the opposite of sacramentalism), *docetism* (the opposite of traditionalism), and *separatism* (the opposite of monopolism). Here again, the dualistic position cannot only be understood as a reaction against the monistic misconception; it also has its own roots. The final effect of the (individualistic) logic of the spiritualistic paradigm is that the strategic development of the Christian fellowship is regarded as almost completely dispensable.

The next three chapters aim to show the disastrous effect these two misconceptions have on the development of Christian fellowship. But above all, they aim to show how the bipolar paradigm can help to overcome both misconceptions.

1

"The Ritual Makes the Christian": The Conflict About Baptism and Communion

What are known as "sacraments" in large sectors of Protestant churches are especially closely linked to Christian fellowship: baptism as a visible sign of incorporation into the body of Christ,[1] the communion (or Eucharist) as a special expression of the fellowship that Christians have with their Lord and each other.[2] Again it is clear that the institutional elements of baptism and communion cannot in themselves guarantee Christian fellowship (as the magical, sacramentalist misconception holds), nor may faith separate itself from these institutional elements, as is typical of the more radical forms of spiritualism (cf. fig. 14).[3]

The word "sacrament"—at least as a general term for both baptism and communion—does not come from the New Testament. This fact on its own would only be a reason to reject the term on the basis of a strictly biblicistic approach.[4] The real problem is at a different point: the very term "sacrament" seems to imply a sacramentalist (i.e., magical, objectivistic) understanding in the sense of a sort of modified *ex opere operato* structure.

---

1   Cf. *R. Luther: 1976*, p. 205f: "Baptism is presented in the New Testament by definition as the integration into the church. 'Those who accepted his message were baptized, and about three thousand were added to their number (i.e., to the church) that day' (Acts 2:41). The individual people baptized not only received life fellowship with Christ, the head, for themselves. They were at the same time placed in a divine life fellowship with the church, the body and its members."
2   Cf. *Hauck: 1950*, p. 805f: "It is significant that Paul uses *koinonia* for the fellowship that arises in the communion. The sharing in Christ, which is experienced basically and wholly in faith, is implemented and experienced in a heightened form—without a thorough doctrinal definition being given—in the sacrament . . . Paul is not so much concerned with the method, but rather with the fact of the close fellowship."
3   P. 137.
4   Cf. p. 67.

It can distract us from the fact that the only sacrament in the strict sense, i.e., "in the sense of a constitutive linking of *signum* and *res*," is Christ himself.[5] Via this concept, the idea of the *sacrum* in contrast to the *profanum*, which is so well known from the study of religions, can enter Christianity and thus lay the foundations for a *sacralistic* concept of the church. In almost every church that emphasizes the fact that it understands itself in a sacramental way, we can detect—more or less drastic—sacramentalist and thus sacralistic tendencies.

However, I do not consider it necessary to avoid this historical term, as we could similarly criticize terms such as "tradition" (which can degenerate to traditionalism) and "dogmatics" (which can degenerate to dogmatism), although we do not feel it necessary to abolish these terms. Our criticism would even apply to the term "church" itself, as in the course of church history it has become almost inextricably linked with a sacralistic and clericalistic position. Therefore, when I distinguish between the words "sacramental" and "sacramentalist," I am attempting to distinguish a functional concept of sacraments from a magical, objectivist understanding.[6]

The rejection of the magical interpretation of the sacraments in the Roman Catholic Church was the battle front in the struggle of the Reformers which very soon eclipsed the issue of the sale of indulgences. The main Reformation principle in the doctrine of the sacraments, *nullum sacramentum sine fide*, brought the conflict with the Catholic *opus operatum* concept sharply into focus: the inseparable connection between sacrament and faith. In this concept, the sacraments are not effective just because they are performed, but only as we believe the word.[7] "The

---

5   *Thielicke: 1978*, p. 342. This thought was expressed by Luther: "If I want to speak with the language of Scripture, there is only one sacrament *(non nisi unum sacramentum habeam)* and three sacramental signs" (Weimar Edition 6, p. 501). In a disputation, Luther said: "The Holy Scriptures have only one sacrament, that is Christ the Lord himself" (Weimar Edition 6, p. 86). Here, Luther traces the concept of the sacrament back to the element that the New Testament calls a *mysterion*.

6   On the other hand, we could argue with some justification that the term "sacrament" arose in the context of the magical, institutionalistic paradigm and cannot be transported to a different paradigm without changing its meaning. Thus, the mere term "functional understanding of the sacraments" must seem like a paradoxon. With these remarks, I merely wish to indicate certain reservations about the *term* sacrament, although I do not reject it.

7   Cf. Johannes Wallmann: "Whereas God's grace . . . works according to scholastic thought *ex opere operato* . . . without faith necessarily being involved, for Luther, grace comes to a person in the word and must be received by faith, without reception of the sacraments being necessary. This removes the foundations of the sacramentalism of the priestly church of the Middle Ages. His contemporaries were right in regarding Luther's *Babylonian Captivity* (his major work on the sacraments—*author's note*) as being the most radical attack on the foundations of the church. There were not a few who had enthusiastically received his work addressed to the nobility who now, after his *Babylonian Captivity*, turned away from him" *(Wallmann: 1973*, p. 40f).

objectivist categories of the Catholic doctrine of the sacraments were re-placed by personal categories in the Reformation."[8]

However, the personal concept of faith and the functional under-standing of institutions did not eventually prevail. The sacramental doc-trine of the Reformation, like its ecclesiology, reflects a "partially unre-solved tension between the 'inherited' thought patterns, with their ten-dency towards substantial *res* thinking, and the new, personal descrip-tion of the favor of God,"[9] as Helmut Thielicke phrases it. Elsewhere, but in the same context, he rightly says, "Here, Luther needs to be corrected by Luther himself."[10]

The problem seems to be not so much in the inconsistencies in which the Reformers were (understandably) caught up, but in a pseudo-Refor-mation traditionalism which made these inconsistencies into a norma-tive standard. This is why some Protestant churches, for all their rejection of Roman Catholic sacramentalism, practice a modified form of sacra-mentalism themselves. Such churches are torn between being semi-sacralistic and anti-sacralistic, a wild mixture of institutionalistic and functional elements, and their position can only be justified by formula-tions which, to put it mildly, are not exactly convincing in their logic.

Danger to the Right: Sacramentalism

The magical, objectivist nature of sacramentalism becomes all the clearer when its adherents stress that it is not the (subjective) faith that counts, but the (objectively) correct form of the administration of the sacraments.[11] What is accepted as "correct" differs significantly from one denomination to another—ranging from the necessity of a priest who is in the "apostolic succession" through the exact, magical recitation of the words of institu-tion to the "proper" church membership of the recipient. But these ex-

---

8   *Lohse: 1983*, p. 155.
9   *Thielicke: 1978*, p. 328. Cf. also Emil Brunner: "Nowhere else does the theology of the Reformers become so indistinct and self-contradictory as in the doctrine of the sac-raments, and this has an effect even to our own times in the form of a certain sacra-mentalism, for example the concept of the sacraments in the Anglican and Lutheran churches. But above all it was the preservation of the Catholic practice of infant baptism by the Reformers which actually—although it was never admitted—arose out of the desire to preserve the state church, and which made plain the irreconcil-ability of the new understanding of faith with the church situation, bringing both under suspicion of being ambiguous and dishonest" *(Brunner: 1960 c*, p. 120f).
10   *Thielicke: 1978*, p. 367.
11   Perhaps it is necessary to point out that a functional understanding of the sacra-ments must not be confused with a concept that replaces the *ex opere operato* with the principle *ex opere operantis* (i.e., that the personal quality of the *minister* is a guarantee for the quality of the sacrament). Both approaches are signs of wrong thinking, as both give wrong answers to the wrong question (i.e., a question asked out of a insti-tutionalistic concern for guarantees).

amples make it plain where these forms of sacramentalism are the same: in their consistently formalistic nature. The common element is the belief that the sacraments are only effective if they are administered in strictly defined forms.

The nature of this formalism can be illustrated most clearly by reference to its more extreme varieties. Therefore I have chosen an example which may seem too dramatic by comparison with the points of view that are advocated in modern discussion. But this example is not an unfortunate exaggeration of an approach that is basically right—rather, it is sacramentalism taken to its logical conclusion. I am referring to the question of "baptism in the womb."

In a handbook of "pastoral medicine"[12] printed with the permission of the Roman Catholic Church, the authors consider the question of what should be done to save the soul of the infant when there is a risk of a stillbirth. In the opinion of the pastoral medicine authors, a ceremony of *ablutio per aspersionem* should be administered with a special medical instrument "as soon as any part of the infant can be reached."[13] Any danger for the life of the mother and the infant is deemed to be not so important: "The risk of harm to the mother and the possible acceleration of the death of the infant cannot be taken into account in view of the necessary concern for the eternal salvation of the infant."[14] This procedure reflects a consistent application of the magical thought pattern!

But what should be done if the baptismal instrument is not available? In such cases, the authors recommend that the person should "wet the finger thoroughly with the holy water and wash a part of the infant with this wet finger."[15] While the *minister baptismi* feels for the child in the womb (as the baptismal ceremony is regarded as invalid if the umbilical cord is baptized), he should speak the words: "I baptize you in the name of the Father and the Son and the Holy Spirit" (without saying Amen).[16]

Given this formalistic approach, it is important to be prepared for all eventualities in order to react with the correct—that is, previously defined—action. Thus, this manual contains a multitude of regulations for baptism of deformed infants. All sorts of constellations are anticipated: one head and one chest, one head and two chests, two heads and two chests, two faces and one head, one face and two skulls, one head and two hearts, and so forth. For one head and two chests, for example, the authors demand that the head and each chest should be baptized separately: "It is necessary to pour water on *each* chest, as it is impossible to know beyond doubt which chest would be baptized with the head."[17]

---

12 *Capellmann/Bergmann: 1923.*
13 Ibid. p. 257.
14 Ibid. p. 258.
15 Ibid.
16 Ibid. p. 259.
17 Ibid. p. 275.

Even embryos in the first months must be baptized if they show the least signs of life. For the pastoral medicine authors, the only question that arises is whether a fetus expelled in a closed ovum should be baptized after the ovum has been opened, or whether the baptism should (or must) first be performed "conditionally" on the membrane of the closed ovum.[18] This question, the reader learns, is controversial amongst Roman Catholic experts. The details of the controversy cannot be imposed on anyone. But all baptizers who are not specialists are recommended to perform this baptism by immersion, and while doing so, to hold the fetus at an angle and tear the membrane in the water, at the same time speaking the saving baptismal words. The instructions say: "The thumb and index finger of each hand should grasp a fold of the membrane surrounding the ovum and tear it apart so that the content of the ovum flows out, or the baptismal water washes the content of the ovum sufficiently, and then the fetus is lifted out and the remainder of the baptismal formula is said."[19] The general rule for such cases is: "For all objects (!) born of women it is a practical rule that baptism should *always* be administered, at least conditionally."[20]

It is reasonable to assume that the use of the word "object" to describe human life is not a misprint. This neutristic term, and the implied neutristic concept of humanity, is a necessary logical consequence for any who, like the authors, have steeped themselves in the magical, objectivist paradigm, and from one set of instructions to the next discovers more and more of the unfolding (technocratic) possibilities for *soteriology*. The implication that a human being effectively becomes an object in this approach would still be valid if the authors had not used the word themselves; it had already been deprived of all vestige of personal dignity.

Nor can we accuse the pastoral medicine authors quoted of arguing inconsistently on the basis of their own axiomatic presuppositions (namely, the *ex opere operato* efficacy of baptism for salvation). On the contrary: given the institutionalistic, objectivist approach, I see no way in which the authors could have avoided these conclusions. If it is really true that the decisive factor for salvation is not the faith of the person baptized, nor even the parents' faith (nor any other subjective factor), but only the correct performance of a ritual, then we need to search for ways of making sure that as many people as possible have the benefit of this ritual—even if it is against their will, for what importance can the mere subjective will have by comparison with the objective fact of salvation applied through baptism!

---

18   *Capellmann/Bergmann: 1923*, p. 272.
19   Ibid. p. 274.
20   Ibid. p. 265. Compare these remarks with *Deschner: 1972*, pp. 265-267, which I have largely followed. In the context of Deschner's arguments, these examples have a different function than they have here (i.e., *destructive* criticism of the church), although this does not alter the accuracy of his observations.

The materialist notion that grace, or the Holy Spirit, is poured as a kind of "substance" into the person who receives the sacraments, is in no way restricted to Roman Catholic doctrines. For example, the Lutheran theologian Regin Prenter interprets the presence of Christ in the communion as follows: "First of all . . . the real presence in the communion is not a *praesentia personalis* but a *praesentia realis*, the presence of an *object* (!), a *res*, namely, his sacrificed body and blood."[21] By the words of institution, Prenter asserts, the action of a person, Jesus Christ who lived under Pontius Pilate, becomes "a substance, an object that century after century is passed from one person to another to be eaten and drunk."[22] It is hardly possible to phrase the magical, objectivist concept of the sacraments in a more drastic way.

On the theologically unreflected level of the "layperson" (but not only there), sacramentalism shows its effects in the fact that there is a decisive shift in the church's understanding of itself. According to the New Testament, the church *is* the body of Christ; according to sacramentalism, the church *eats* the body of Christ. It can hardly surprise us that this understanding is strikingly similar to the concept of humanity in atheistic materialism, as formulated by Ludwig Feuerbach: "Man *is* what he *eats*." Both systems of thought (secular materialism and its institutionalistic Christian counterpart) are at enmity with the whole concept of the *personal*.

Against the background of the institutionalistic paradigm, the question of infant baptism appears in a new light that has often not been considered in conventional discussion. I must emphasize, however, that not everyone who advocates infant baptism is automatically dominated by the institutionalistic paradigm (there are also decidedly *functional* ways of justifying the practice).[23] However, it is clear that infant baptism is particularly susceptible to magical thinking. Especially pastors who administer infant baptism but are far removed from the institutionalistic paradigm will confirm that many (most?) parents who apply for baptism of their children, particularly in the state churches, have a distinctly magical expectation.

Therefore, I believe that the polemical argument (which I, myself, propagated several years ago)[24] that accuses the state church of using the practice of infant baptism as a way of laying claim on future providers of church taxes and marking children as "church members" from the crib onwards does not really fit. I am not saying that this criticism is

---

21 *Prenter: 1950,* p. 308.
22 Ibid. p. 316.
23 In our institute we have collected numerous examples of how pastors have used the parents' application for baptism of their children as a means to communicate a personal faith, for example by offering courses for parents. I personally believe that these efforts are legitimate, as long as they are *demonstrably* functional and help people to find faith in Jesus Christ (and are not just declared so).
24 Cf. *Schwarz/Schwarz: 1987,* p. 46.

completely misleading, but it does not touch the heart of the matter. Genuine sacramentalists, understandably from their paradigm, are deeply convinced that baptism immediately after birth is the best thing that can happen to an infant. If "original sin"[25] is understood as being an almost genetic, substantial evil that can be cured by swift application of a medicine which acts independent of consciousness, that is, the "medicine" of baptism, then this position has a certain logical coherence.

But Protestants who advocate such theories are in a rather equivocal position. They are caught between two positions, as was Luther in his doctrine of the sacraments. On the one hand, he knew of the personal dimension and the dynamic nature of faith and the church, but on the other hand—for plausible reasons of church politics—he wished to hold on to the practice of infant baptism[26] that was inherited from the Roman Catholic Church. But what, then, became of Luther's formulation that the efficacy of the sacrament depends on the faith of the person receiving it?

As Luther believed that both the principle of *sola fide* and the practice of infant baptism were valid—and he advocated both with equal passion—he had a difficult task justifying his position. He could only do so by making the ridiculous assertion that the infant does, in fact, believe. In a treatise written in 1525 we plainly see how important it was for his line of reasoning that the faith of the infant should be seen as biblical faith in the full sense of the word. He specifically rejected the notion that the baptism of an infant is justified by the promise of a *later faith*. "The excuse does not help . . . that children are baptized on the basis of their future faith. Faith must be there before or even in the baptism, otherwise the child cannot be rid of sins and the devil . . . The minister therefore asks if the child believes, and the answer yes is given on the child's behalf, then he asks whether the child wishes to be baptized, and the answer yes is given on the child's behalf."[27] According to Luther, the immaturity of the child does not hinder faith, only the verbal expression of faith. Therefore, adults must speak on the child's behalf at this point—and only at this point. They do not *believe* on behalf of the child, rather, they *put into words* the silent but existing faith of the child. The line of argument Luther used forced him to describe this faith with the aid of ontological categories, a procedure that he rejected so vehemently at other points.[28]

In post-Reformation theology, this approach was developed even further. Theologians pedantically claimed that the infant had true faith in the sense of *notitia* (knowledge), of *assensus* (assent), and of *fiducia* (trust).

---

25   Cf. p. 60f for a fuller treatment of the problems associated with this term.
26   In the historical context of the Reformation, the adherence to infant baptism was, however, also adherence to a ritual which was commanded by the political authorities and protected by legal sanctions. Woe betide anyone who did not put forward a newborn infant for baptism as soon as possible!
27   Weimar Edition 17, p. 81.
28   For example, with categories of the *habitus* doctrine as a *fides infusa*. Cf. *Thielicke: 1978*, p. 366f.

The justifications used to prop up this axiomatically pre-judged theological postulate became increasingly absurd—although this did not seem to worry academic theologians. If there is any area in which we can study a prime example of an ideology that claims to be academically justified, this is it!

My concern at this point is not to give a thorough treatment of the question of the legitimacy of infant baptism. I only use these examples as (random) illustrations of the way institutionalistic, objectivistic thinking can affect the debate about the sacraments. I am perfectly aware from many discussions that the doctrine of the sacraments is an issue that is extremely emotionally charged for many Christians. Adherents of an objectivistic concept of baptism sometimes appeal to Luther, who, when he was in times of temptation, is said to have told the devil: *baptizatus sum*—"I am baptized." We are told that this was his true comfort and security. Without doubt, it is a right principle that in times of temptation we appeal to something objective. But the fact that Luther sought this objective refuge in baptism betrays the vestige of the same unbiblical objectivism that is also characteristic of other forms of the institutionalistic misconception: when I am unsure of whether I am on the right path as a pastor, I comfort myself with my ordination, and so forth.

In fact, Luther also shows similar objectivist tendencies in other areas. In his struggles with Roman Catholics and religious enthusiasts, for example, he claimed competence to comment from the fact that he had a doctorate—he felt that this gave him "authority" and the "right to speak."[29] Whether his claim was "I am baptized" *(baptizatus sum)* or "I am a doctor" *(doctor sum)*, both arguments are understandable on a human level, but highly questionable on a theological level (as they are purely formalistic).[30] Just as a doctorate doesn't stop a person from talking a lot of nonsense, so also baptism is not able to guarantee personal faith.

Consistent sacramentalism makes church development superfluous. Here, I feel that the criticism of church rituals in the state churches which was voiced by Rudolf Bohren is especially valid. It goes far beyond the question of the administration of the sacraments, but it shows how the same thought structures we have observed in sacramentalism apply to all other areas of church activity.

---

29 *Bainton: 1983*, p. 388.
30 Cf. also the comment made by Helmut Thielicke (*Thielicke: 1978*, p. 362), which points in a similar direction: "Although I am impressed when Luther, when tempted, flees to the permanent 'extra' of God's assurance of grace, and sees it represented specifically in baptism *(baptizatus sum)*, this path out of temptation remains foreign to me. I cannot follow its reasoning, particularly for the sake of an understanding of the sacraments that is based on the priority of the word. Temptation mainly means that our trust in the word vanishes, and that our certainty about the author of the word passes away. But if the 'document' is in doubt, any thoughts of its 'seal' are no help. The seal of an author who does not exist or who (for me) has vanished would be meaningless, and would itself become an element of the temptation."

Bohren writes: "We assure people constantly and at all decisive points of their lives that they are Christians and church members, and thus we give them dispensation from the proclamation, fellowship, and service of the church. Thus, church rituals become the enemy of proclamation, they become an impossible possibility, a sin. It is futile to bemoan the ineffectiveness of preaching, the impersonality and anonymity of churches, and the lack of service in the church, but at the same time to demonstrate by church rituals that proclamation is not really necessary, that faith is superfluous, that fellowship is a hobby and service a hobbyhorse. The practice of such rituals makes preaching, fellowship, and service optional extras, merely useful as spiritual training for the meek, but of no real use for the rough life of this world, and evidently not necessary for eternal life, if there is such a thing. Those who call on the services of the church are doing right—they grow up as Christians, marry as Christians, and go to a Christian grave. The ritual makes the Christian. Those who subject themselves to the rituals are Christians, *ex opere operato*. The mechanics of these rituals create Christians who live without Christ. The rituals build and maintain a fictional church."[31]

Danger to the Left: Spiritualism

The mistake of sacramentalists is to make the sacraments almost into gods—a "cursed idolatry,"[32] as the Heidelberg Catechism phrases it. The separation of the reality and the sign is the mistake of the "sacrament hunters," as Luther called the religious enthusiasts in their impulsive anti-sacramental actions. Insofar as the criticism "from the left" is directed against sacramentalism, it is understandable and right. But where it goes on to make a separation between sign and reality—corresponding to the separation between organization and organism, static and dynamic pole—it errs into the spiritualistic paradigm.

The sacraments, as *verba visibilia*, undoubtedly are more sensory and experiential than the spoken word. In them, "a characteristic feature of the gospel is expressed in bodily form."[33] Where spiritualism is directed against this bodily, sensory character of the sacraments and regards them, at best, as optional extras, we must firmly contradict it—especially from the perspective of church development.

We can fairly reliably predict that adherents of this sort of view will have problems with the whole concept of church development. Just as spiritualists tend to believe that Christ was not really incarnate and not really historical, they tend to reject the bodily, sensory character of the sacraments and thus, implicitly, the empirical, historical dimension of the

31   *Bohren: 1960, p. 19f.*
32   *Niesel: 1938, p. 169.*
33   *Möller: 1990, p. 138.*

church. Here we see the effects of the individualistic implications of the spiritualistic paradigm. The protest of spiritualists against baptism as a visible sign of acceptance into the church can also be explained by the fact that they tend to have problems with the concept of integration into the church, which requires personal commitment.

Arguments put forward from the point of view of the spiritualistic paradigm are often difficult to grasp and thus to criticize, because they do not distinguish between a *sacramental* and a *sacramentalist* approach. Spiritualists say much that is right when they criticize the sacramentalist misconception, but when they oppose the sacraments themselves (and not just a specific concept or practice of the sacraments), they put themselves in the wrong. The anti-materialist concept of faith, which, when taken to its logical conclusion, opposes any form of commitment or visible expression, cannot claim support from the Bible. The whole line of reasoning of spiritualists—although it often sounds so pious—actually has more in common with pagan religious concepts than with the visible, historical, church-building work of the Holy Spirit as described in the Bible.[34]

Traditional debate about these issues, especially the struggles between Luther and the (so-called or real) religious "enthusiasts" of the Reformation period, was hampered by the fact that both sides were unable to distinguish between the legitimate bipolar approach and the ideological misconceptions to the right and to the left. Thus, Luther's insistence on what he called the "real presence" (*Realpräsenz*) must be seen against the background of his struggle against spiritualistic tendencies that devalue everything external and attempt to reduce the presence of Christ exclusively to the inner person. But Luther's ability to distinguish between real and alleged spiritualists was, as we have seen, not very well developed. Thus, he insisted that his dispute with Zwingli was "part of his struggle against the religious enthusiasts."[35] Where Luther's reasoning sometimes seemed to be dominated by arguments that are typical of the institutionalistic paradigm, this was not only due to the influence of his inheritance (e.g., the Roman Catholic concept of the sacraments). To some extent, his writings reflect an overreaction to the spiritualistic misconception.

This corresponds with an observation that can be made in other areas as well. Wherever theologians who have started to work with the bipolar paradigm find that destructive spiritualist tendencies interfere with their work, they tend to seek refuge in the institutionalistic paradigm, which offers them—because of its convenient absolute formulations—a certain security. This mechanism is understandable psychologically, but it has devastating theological and spiritual consequences.

---

34   Cf. p. 70ff.
35   *Wallmann: 1973*, p. 74.

The Bipolar Approach

The debate about the sacraments in church history is a prime example of the way discussions remained caught up in the pattern of "spiritualism versus institutionalism," and the way the bipolar paradigm had hardly any influence. As in other areas, the bipolar paradigm asks here, too, *what form of administration of the sacraments is most likely to stimulate the development of faith, fellowship, and service in a specific context?* It should be clear from the considerations so far that this functional criterion is not to be confused with a pragmatism[36] that dispenses with biblical principles. How, then, can a functional understanding of the sacraments be achieved?

First, the deliberations up to this point lead to the conclusion that different opinions on the sacraments are not necessarily divisive for the unity of the church. (The opposite opinion would be a typical symptom of institutionalism, which has a tendency to monopolistic thinking.) It can even be decidedly beneficial that there are different practices in this area that can appeal to different people. This approach does not, however, mean that all opinions are equally right. Whether they are "right" or not depends largely on how well they serve to achieve the desired results in their particular context.

Second, it is also clear where a functional understanding of the sacraments draws the line. Any form of theological doctrine that aims to convince people that a sacrament is a guarantee of faith is rejected. It makes no difference, for example, whether a magical concept of the sacraments is related to infant baptism or adult baptism. Even a "faith baptism" can be combined with the magical belief that faith is guaranteed by the ritual of baptism.

Third, baptism and communion should always be administered in a way that emphasizes the dimension of fellowship. Any form of individualism implied by the spiritualistic misconception (or other sources) must not be supported by the way the sacraments are administered in the church. The natural place for baptism as a celebration of integration into the church is therefore a full church service.

Fourth, both baptism and communion should be real celebrations. The way people celebrate can differ—ranging from formal, liturgical forms to much more "spontaneous" styles that include unplanned elements. Neither is more spiritual than the other. But where a formal, liturgical approach is used, the church must take care not to be infected by the sacralistic misconception.

While different doctrines of the sacraments are possible on the basis of the bipolar paradigm, these differences lie exclusively in the theological interpretation. It must be clear that the presence and working of

---

36   For a more extensive treatment of this term, see p. 72; cf. also *Schwarz: 1996*, p. 100ff.

Christ—whatever concepts we use to describe them—are not dependent on our *interpretation* of his presence and working. Hans-Joachim Kraus is right to comment that it is a "monstrous theological proposition . . . to try to quantify and define the type and degree of presence occurring in the freedom of the glorified Lord. Who would dare to treat another person like this? But Jesus Christ is treated as a phenomenon, as something we can control, carry around with us, hand out to others. His presence is defined and programmed."[37]

It would have saved us much trouble if the advocates of the various concepts had assumed that the doctrines of the sacraments have no influence on the *reality* of the presence of Christ, but are just a series of human attempts to begin to explain something that is impossible to capture in mere doctrinal formulations. Here, too, we must ask ourselves how *useful* the formulations we have found are for the life of the church.

Practical Illustration:
The Quality Characteristic "Inspiring Worship Service"

At this point I propose to illustrate the practical relevance of the bipolar approach by reference to the quality characteristic that we, in our institute, describe as "inspiring worship service."[38] The adjective expresses the secret of this principle. Irrespective of the form a worship service takes—that is, whether it is more "liturgical" or more spontaneous—in growing churches, attendance at a worship service is seen as an "inspiring experience."

The approach behind this quality characteristic is opposed to any magical understanding of worship services, any concept that implies that the fulfilling of a ritual of some kind (whether Roman Catholic or Lutheran or Pentecostal) can conjure up the presence of the Holy Spirit. Rather, the form of service is judged by the criterion of how useful it is in developing the dynamic pole of the church as a personal and spiritual fellowship. "Inspiring worship services" are characterized by the presence of many enthusiastic Christians who worship God together. They speak of the everyday questions and needs of the congregation, and they project a positive atmosphere both verbally and non-verbally.

The word "inspiring" is here taken in the literal sense of the Latin word *inspiratio*, a form of inspiration that comes from God's Spirit. But where the Holy Spirit is really at work (and not just assumed to be at work), this has a practical effect on the form of the services and, of course, on the atmosphere that can be sensed. Those who attend such meetings agree that they "enjoy" participating in the services.

---

37   *Kraus: 1975*, p. 389.
38   For a more detailed treatment, see *Schwarz/Schalk: 1998*, pp. 86-95; *Douglass: 1998*.

It is thus plain what this quality characteristic is opposed to—the concept of church attendance as a duty (some churches explicitly use the term "Sunday duty"). This concept is extremely widespread—people attend church, not because it is a happy, inspiring experience, but because they wish to do the pastor or God a favor. Sometimes they combine this with the notion that God will bless them for their "faithfulness," that is, for tolerating patiently a relatively unpleasant experience.

It is true, as experience shows, that such an approach may achieve a short-term stabilization (or even increase) of the attendance at worship services. But this method overturns just about all the basic principles of theology (and natural church development), so the medium-term and long-term consequences are negative. The energy expended to appeal to people's guilty consciences and motivate them to attend church must be constantly increased—and the readiness of the people to come of their own accord decreases in inverse proportion to this energy investment. Eventually, the church attenders may develop a grudge against the worship service—and sometimes even against God himself.

But people usually do not admit these feelings, so that those who do their "duty" of church attendance are often the ones who react most violently to any change in the services. For them, absolving a specific form that they are accustomed to (without ever asking whether or not they like it) is identical with faithfulness. People who have adjusted their emotional life to accept that willingly suffering something boring is, in fact, spiritually virtuous, must feel their whole identity questioned if they are told that there is an alternative.

2

Between Supra-Historical and Anti-Historical Tendencies: The Conflict About Tradition and Change

The hallmarks of historicity—transformation and continuity—are characteristics of the church as well. In order to express this fact, I place the terms *change* and *tradition* next to each other in figure 14,[1] where change belongs to the dynamic pole (church as an organism), and 'tradition to the static pole (church as an organization). The church as an organism will always produce traditions and (hopefully) learn from them. The criterion for this learning process, however, is how useful these traditions are for church development.

It seems to me that the Reformers aimed to express this relationship between tradition and change in the formula *ecclesia reformata semper reformanda:*[2] "the church of the Reformation must constantly reform itself." However, like so many slogans of the Reformation, the principle of the *ecclesia reformata semper reformanda* has only halfheartedly been put into practice by most Protestant churches. The Lutheran and Reformed branches of Protestantism very soon arrived at a state of Protestant traditionalism which made a consistent application of this principle almost impossible.

In this area we can study the disastrous consequences of the unhistorical concept of God described in part 1,[3] which influenced Christian theology in the process of Hellenization. It almost inevitably leads to an unhistorical concept of the church, which can express itself either in a *supra-historical* tendency (characteristic of the traditionalism of the institutionalistic misconception) or in an *anti-historical* tendency (as can be found within the spiritualistic paradigm which tends towards ecclesiological docetism).

---

1   P. 137.
2   The Reformers in no way rejected tradition; rather, they subjected it *(subicienda)* to the authority of Scripture.
3   P. 53f.

Danger to the Right: Traditionalism

Traditionalists believe that, by passing on traditions of experiences made in the past, the church as an organism can be secured. But they find that the physical law that unused energy crystallizes even applies to the realities of church life. When traditions are not subjected to the criterion of continual actualization and the need to demonstrate their functionality in each new situation, they become fossilized.

The institutionalistic misconception understands traditions technocratically. They are transported from one generation to the next, and traditionalists believe that formalistic adherence to every detail assures faithfulness to the cause. The interesting point is that many traditions were usually, in their original form, highly functional. This functionality has only been lost because the traditions have been handed down without changes into a different time or context. But traditionalists are convinced that functionality is, almost like a substance, automatically included in the ancient forms or formulas they use—an expression of their magical thought structure.

Otto Seeck describes this mechanism in his *Development of Christianity* as follows: "What became established for practical reasons first became a church custom, then a holy law, and soon nobody remembered that it had ever been differently. It is therefore possible to have the pious Christian conviction that Christ and his apostles founded the church just as we now see it before us, for no changes were carried out deliberately, they happened just by force of circumstances. Thus it is that forms of church administration could become a truth of faith that is valid, like the doctrine of Christ, for all eternity."[4]

Perhaps the mechanism that lies behind traditionalism can best be clarified by a few practical illustrations rather than by abstract words, although the following examples may seem a little trite:

- It is said of Arturo Toscanini that he had such bad eyes that he could not read the notation on his conductor's rostrum. He therefore had to learn the whole score by heart so that he could conduct without using a written score. His successors kept to the same style of conducting in the conviction that a great conductor *must* work without written notation.[5]

- Originally, priests of the Roman Catholic Church wore their normal everyday clothes even when they officiated in a church service. What was later made mandatory as "church robes" for all priests was, in fact, none other than the normal secular fashion of antiquity. In the church, this fashion was retained for traditionalistic reasons, even after it had been changed everywhere else.[6]

---

4   *Seeck: 1921*, p. 376f.
5   Cf. *Younghusband: 1991*, p. 199.
6   Cf. *Chadwick: 1972*, p. 189.

- Martin Luther's Bible translation was such a success largely because he "looked the people in the mouth" and managed to put biblical texts in the everyday language of his time. However, in many traditionalistic churches we find that this language of the 16th century, which nobody speaks any longer, is not only still used, but is sometimes even regarded as particularly "spiritual."

We could give many more illustrations. These examples enable us to determine exactly the point at which *traditional* behavior crosses the line and becomes *traditionalistic*. The mere fact that Toscanini's successors felt they had to conduct without a score is not in itself traditionalism, nor is the fact that clothes that were originally secular are still used in the church when they are no longer used by anyone else, nor the fact that some Christians can only express spiritual experience in antiquated language. All these phenomena are anachronisms, to be sure, but we can smile at them.

But the smile will disappear as soon as these patterns change into a full-blooded traditionalism. This is the point when the anachronistic behavior that has become established is implicitly or explicitly made into a standard for all, so that every good conductor from now on *must* work without a score, every priest *must* wear the fashion of Roman antiquity, certain antiquated linguistic forms *must* be used if the speaker wants his or her words to be accepted as spiritual. The degree of traditionalism becomes the criterion by which the truth is judged, the anachronism becomes canonical. This is the point at which the content that the traditionalist wishes to preserve is, in reality, betrayed. That is the decisive theological criticism we have to raise towards this way of thinking.

Perhaps the magical character of traditionalism can be seen more drastically than anywhere else in the area of linguistic usage. Some churches deliberately use a language in their ritual that has long fallen into disuse. For example, the liturgy of the Coptic church of Egypt uses the old Egyptian language, and it is interesting that the same structure is found in almost all religions (in the Brahmanic rituals of India, for example, the extinct Sanskrit language is used, and so forth). But even churches that celebrate their services in the mother tongue of the participants tend to make conscious use of archaic language in Christian rituals. As was pointed out above, that in itself is not traditionalistic—for a traditionally minded target group (or for people interested in linguistic history) it may even be decidedly functional. The institutionalistic paradigm is, however, in action if the traditional sound of the words is held to be important for the efficacy of the ritual—and where the archaic form is preserved even with people who find it estranging rather than helpful.

The fact that traditional language can quickly assume a divisive instead of a mediating function can be seen in the language of many liturgies and prayer books. The style being used there seems fairly strange when compared with the way children speak to their fathers, but for many Christians it is such "sanctified" language that they use the same antiquated words in their own prayer life.

Antiquated linguistic forms are then identified with the message itself, so that Martin Walser, one of the great German poets of this century, could describe God as a "magical and quaint authority figure" whose "contorted use of language" we only accept because "God is a thing of the past."[7] With regard to such a language and the underlying traditionalistic thinking, Otto Weber's criticism is right: "Where people think or (more often feel) like this, a doctrinal decision has, in fact, already been taken. The mystery of the word of God has been transformed into the tangible mystery of incomprehensible language."[8]

Perhaps these examples may still seem relatively harmless. Why not let people pray in antiquated language if they wish? It won't stop God from hearing their prayers! The disastrous consequences of traditionalism become apparent, however, as soon as it is extended to cover the structures of church life. Thus the very demands that are made in the name of Christian tradition can actually hinder the development of the church today.

This even applies, we must note, if these structures are based fundamentalistically on the Bible, as was implied in the chapter on our understanding of Scripture.[9] That approach misuses the New Testament in a legalistic way, thus often achieving the exact opposite of what the New Testament authors intended.[10] Walter Kreck rightly comments: "An ecclesiology can only be properly biblical if, instead of making a particular New Testament form into a normative standard, it comes back to the message of the New Testament in each new situation to ask afresh what is meant. This includes the possibility of disassociating ourselves from certain behaviors of the New Testament church in the same way that it had to relinquish stubborn adherence to Old Testament and Jewish laws and forms so that it would not become just a fossilized Jewish sect."[11]

Traditionalists point out, often with great emotion, that revelation is "historical." They are firmly convinced that history is on their side, justifying their point of view. But they don't notice that traditionalism is just

---

7   *Walser: 1964*, p. 347.
8   *Weber: 1964*, p. 36.
9   Cf. p. 122.
10   Cf. the classical sentence by Eduard Schweizer: "*The* New Testament church structure is non-existent. Even in New Testament times, church forms were extremely varied" (*Schweizer: 1959*, p. 7). Michael Herbst rightly comments on this statement of Schweizer: "If, then, the New Testament contains a number of very different statements about the form of the Christian church, if we must even reckon with development and change within the New Testament books (e.g., in Paul, or in Acts after the Council of Jerusalem in Acts 15), then we finally become aware of the historical dimension of the way God speaks and realize that it is not a question of mere legalistic copying of New Testament statements about the church and church development" (*Herbst: 1987*, p. 75).
11   *Kreck: 1981*, p. 16f.

as unhistorical as the docetist tendencies of their spiritualistic opponents. Whereas the spiritualist regards the present tense as an absolute, the traditionalist absolutizes the present perfect (or even the past perfect). But a historical understanding of the works of God requires both, the present and the past. And it also involves the third temporal dimension, the future, as the church growth movement rightly emphasizes.

We can only claim to think historically if we combine all three dimensions. Traditionalism, however, is the attempt to "steamroller" the present and the future with the structures of the past. I find it rather difficult to understand why such an approach is so often described as "historical thinking" in theological discussion.

Danger to the Left: Docetism

In our description of the spiritualistic paradigm, we saw that spiritualists do not necessarily advocate a docetist Christology, such as was typical of the theology of Marcion or other thought systems influenced by Gnosticism in the early days of the church. But even where spiritualists are orthodox in their Christology and assent to the incarnation, rejecting the theory that Christ only appeared to have a physical body (*appearance = dokesis*), their docetist tendencies come to the surface in the area of ecclesiology. Just as for a docetist Christology the humanity of Christ is secondary, irrelevant and, in the final analysis, unreal, for a docetist ecclesiology the same applies to the church, the body of Christ.

Spiritualists demand a direct relationship to God that is unhampered by anything historical. They regard every connection with things past (or external) as aspects that are incomplete, or even dangerous, and therefore something that must be overcome. Thus it is not surprising that they find it difficult to relate to Christian traditions in a constructive, functional way. Behind all traditions they see—understandably, given their thought paradigms—the pathological condition of traditionalism, an externalizing of the faith.

The best illustration of this docetist, anti-traditional tendency is probably the phenomenon of "image breaking" (*iconoclasm*), which occurred in different phases of Christianity, especially in the Byzantine controversy over images in the 8th century and again, characteristically, in the age of the Reformation. The image breaking *iconoclasts* saw the veneration of images as idolatry, as a worship of material things which took the place of God.

The iconoclasts were undoubtedly right in rejecting images that had, in the mind of those who venerated them, taken the function of idols—this substantial superstition was widespread, and is still widespread today. But they went much too far when they suspected idolatry in *every* image, and even in every material, external form. It was a logical conclusion that many of them banned not only images, but also music and other art forms from worship services. "Banish organs, trumpets, and flutes to the theater," demanded the same Karlstadt who was the initiator of the breaking of altars and the images of saints in 16th century Wittenberg.[12]

The iconoclasts, in their struggle for the "purity" of the gospel, showed an unparalleled destructiveness. They not only broke and burned the images of Mary and the angels, they also destroyed artistically designed church windows, defiled the graves of Christians who were regarded as "saints," and plundered monasteries. Luther finally found it necessary to oppose these people who claimed to follow him, and to exhort them to moderation.

Iconoclasm can be regarded as a symbol of the way docetists treat traditions. They use hammers and hatchets to destroy all that is traditional—in the name of the so-called "purity" of the gospel, but from a standpoint that, on closer examination, shows distinct signs of a spiritualistically colored anti-material understanding of the Spirit. It is true that the iconoclasts were justified in many cases, in that they destroyed things that really hindered faith, fellowship, and service. But their choice of means and their lack of discernment in what they destroyed are the points at which they are to be criticized.

Their destructive fanaticism, which often went out of control, could easily destroy things that are essential as aids to faith. The concept of faith that is left at the end of their spiritualistic struggle against false guarantees is stripped of all bodily form, and it is no use for church development. The influence of Puritanism, which goes in the same direction and has molded large sections of Protestantism, is one of the most common obstacles to church development. Everything that can help people to find faith (forms of evangelism that reach people where they are, a good atmosphere, need-oriented ministry, and so forth), and everything that can make life in the church more beautiful (architecture, music, colors, and so forth) is suspected by Puritanical Christians of corrupting the faith.

Influences of this kind are apparent in different areas of Protestantism today—for example even where the vivid, graphical language of the Bible is rejected in favor of abstract philosophical terminology. This abstraction is carried out in the name of the same "purer spirituality" that motivated the iconoclasts, with their hammers and hatchets. Karl Barth is right in his comment on Rudolf Bultmann's program of "demythologization," when he says that Bultmann's New Testament, when freed from (alleged or real) myths, exuded a "strong odor of docetism."[13] This attraction to theological abstraction is no less than an intellectual form of iconoclasm—understandable in its motivation, but self-destructive in its effects.

---

12   Cf. *Bainton: 1983,* p. 210.
13   *Barth: 1952,* p. 34.

The Bipolar Approach

The best way of avoiding the twin dangers of traditionalism and ec-clesiological docetism is to regard traditions from a functional point of view, as with all other institutional elements. Traditions in themselves are neither positive (as the traditionalist thinks) nor negative (as the docetist believes)—they are neutral. Here, again, the real question is what we do with them.

This approach makes any form of traditionalistic tyranny impossible. Many churches identify the historical development so strongly with the truth itself that any new people who come along have no choice—they must become traditionalists before they can become Christians. If they dislike certain traditional forms, these churches don't regard this as what it is—a different aesthetic taste—but rather see it as a "revolt" against the "faith handed down from the fathers." New people are expected to spend time getting accustomed to these strange structures and formulas until they can see them as positive. What was once an aid to faith has now become a hindrance, and there is an expectation that all newcomers should go back mentally and emotionally into the past until they find these traditions helpful—a procedure that actually can work, though with difficulty. This mental re-programming into a traditionalistic frame of mind is then, to make things even worse, confused with "maturity" and "growth in the faith."

A functional approach to traditions is not concerned with decorating the graves of the prophets, church fathers, and Reformers; rather, it is concerned to serve those who live today. In this quest, however, the expe-riences of the prophets, church fathers, and Reformers can be a great help. If we adapt a famous sentence coined by Friedrich Nietzsche, we could say: "We will only serve tradition insofar as it serves the develop-ment of the church." This functional approach is not directed against tra-ditions; rather, it attempts to put into practice their real intention, and in this way—to use a common but ambiguous term—to "honor" them.[14]

First, a functional understanding of tradition assumes that we can learn an enormous amount from the experience of our spiritual mothers and fathers. We don't need to invent the wheel over again in every gen-eration. Church history gives us a wide range of helpful stimuli that are useful for church development, and we accept them gratefully.

Second, this willingness to learn from history includes a willingness to learn from our ancestors how *not* to do things. Just as we don't need to re-invent the wheel, we also don't need to repeat the mistakes that our predecessors—sometimes quite persistently—made in the past. I do not

---

14 This term is ambiguous because it could imply a meaning of "honor" which is only rightly given to God.

"honor" Luther by repeating his mistakes in my generation, nor will I feel "honored" if my children take over all of my faults.

Third, it is important for every church that it develops specific habits, and thus "new traditions." It is in the nature of habits and rituals that we don't need to think through each step separately when we are using them. The whole procedure is more or less automatic, which can greatly simplify our lives, including the life of the church. New habits are established by repetitions—and here the benefits and dangers lie close together. We can demonstrate in many churches that frequent repetition (e.g. in liturgical formulas) does not so much deepen faith as immunize against it. When we have heard the same formulation often enough, we become so accustomed to it that we don't take it seriously any more.

Fourth, a functional understanding of traditions cannot ignore the fact that there are traditions that must be broken. Whenever traditions have the effect of hindering rather than stimulating faith, we can speak of traditionalism. But if we do not wish to fall into the error of the iconoclasts, we must consider two things. First, what one person sees as hindering can be helpful for another person. We must beware of making our own feelings the judge of all things. Second, even traditions that are misused in a clearly magical way can be redirected in a functional way. It is possible to reinterpret traditions and to make them helpful for the gospel, rather than reaching for the hammer and smashing them.

Fifth, this understanding of the relationship between tradition and change includes the aim of encouraging the church to dare to experiment more. There are experiences, both positive and negative, that cannot be passed on by tradition—we must go through them ourselves. The widespread resistance to experiments in Christianity (which does not only stem from traditionalism) is one of the greatest obstacles to finding new ways. Whereas in business it is quite normal that for every successful attempt there are ten failures (which is the only way to achieve the one successful attempt!),[15] in many Christian circles there is an assumption that mistakes must be avoided at all costs. No wonder Christian churches produce so little that is creative and innovative.

To repeat the main point briefly: institutions can and should be passed on. The church as an organism, however, cannot be passed on in

---

15   Cf. for example the comments on this subject by the management experts Tom Peters and Robert Waterman. In their classic bestseller *In Search of Excellence* the authors tell of a company that manufactures refrigerators and endeavors to encourage its researchers to be "willing to learn and take risks." "To this end, it was defined precisely what may be regarded as a 'total failure,' and on each such occasion, a salute was fired. The concept of the total failure is based on the simple insight that every piece of research and development involves risks, that the only chance of success lies in making enough attempts, and that it should therefore be the paramount goal of the management to encourage as many attempts as possible, and that a failure that you can learn something from is a cause to celebrate" (*Peters/Waterman: 1984*, p. 95f).

the same way. It must become a reality in each new generation, the *factum esse* must again and again become a *fieri*. This constant actualization is a work of the Holy Spirit. If we make an effort to preserve structures and create new ones that fulfill this purpose (God's purpose!), then we are part of a process that we have elsewhere called "pneumatic functionality."[16]

Practical Illustration:
The Quality Characteristic "Functional Structures"

The question of tradition and change has a close affinity to the quality characteristic that we describe with the term "functional structures."[17] This quality characteristic signifies that it is not important how many or how few structures a church has, or whether its structures are old or new, but the criterion is how useful they are in a specific situation. I have frequently emphasized that this criterion must not be regarded as merely pragmatic, but rather that it is the only possible way to justify structures *theologically*.[18]

This quality characteristic should not be thought of as more important than the other seven—all eight must be present if a church is to grow in quality and quantity—but it does play a key role in natural church development. This is due to the fact that the decisive biotic principle of "interdependence"[19] is expressed particularly in the structures of a church.

It is interesting that this element is the most controversial of the eight quality characteristics. I assign that to the probability that advocates of both the spiritualistic and the institutionalistic paradigms find it much more difficult to open themselves to the implications of this element than to the other seven. Whereas the mere word "structures" sounds like an unspiritual foreign term to spiritualists, traditionalists just cannot fit the concept of "functionality" into their thought paradigm.

What, then, are functional structures? It is in the nature of the historical approach proposed here that we cannot give an answer to that question that has a timeless validity. Just as there is not *the* New Testament church structure, there is not *the* functional structure for churches today. What is right in one church may be wrong in another. Which structures are most appropriate in which situation depends on the philosophy of ministry, the mentality of the people, the devotional style, the rules of the denomination, and countless other factors.

In our institute we have collected numerous examples of church structures that are very different from each other, but that fulfill their

---

16 Cf. p. 71.
17 For a more extensive treatment, see *Schwarz/Schalk: 1998*, pp. 74-85; *Schwarz: 1987*, pp. 162-190.
18 Cf. also the comments on the relevance of the structural question on p. 94f.
19 For a more extensive treatment, see pp. 224ff and 244.

purpose in their situation, and are therefore appropriate and functional. However, if we compare these structures, they do have some—evidently significant—elements in common.

First of all, all structural efforts are directed towards clearly formulated church guidelines ("philosophy of ministry"). Second, all "successful" structures concentrate on the specific focus as defined in the philosophy of ministry, which includes the willingness to eliminate all that is not useful. Third, the structures of growing churches are almost entirely multiplication structures, that is, they are not geared to additive growth (which at some point comes up against natural limits), but rather on the ongoing multiplication of the work. To make this multiplication possible, appropriate substructures are created, which have a certain degree of autonomy and are therefore self-sustaining.

3
Spiritual Unity or Monopolism? The Conflict About Church Planting and Cooperation

The question of the unity of Christians is probably the issue where identifying the church as an "organization" with the church as an "organism" has the most disastrous consequences. Those who identify these two concepts with each other—logically—think of unity in organizational, institutional terms. Unity is therefore assumed to exist wherever Christians are members of *one* church institution. The fewer different church institutions there are, the greater is the unity among Christians. From the perspective of this thought paradigm it is inevitable that any form of church planting (at least if it results in churches outside the denomination of the observer) is regarded as separatism.

This thinking simply reflects the institutionalistic, monopolistic paradigm of the Middle Ages. However, it is in no way restricted to that age; it still comes to the surface today, as I have experienced in innumerable discussions on the subject.[1] It can be demonstrated that most misunderstandings in this area could be overcome if we would learn to distinguish between the church as an organization and the church as an organism, and then place the two in a functional relationship to each other. Then we

---

1   It was during an interview with the German church historian, Joachim Rogge, the Lutheran bishop in Görlitz, that I realized how strongly the concern for unity in Jesus' high priestly prayer has, in theological debate, been mixed with the Constantinian/ Theodosian concept of unity. When I asked him what he thought of the planting of new churches outside the state church, he replied: "I would consider it extremely disturbing." When I asked why, his answer was simple: "Because the whole New Testament is against it . . . In John 17:21, Jesus prayed that all his followers would be one." In the course of the interview the bishop relativized this position (as a Protestant he had no other choice), but for anyone reading the interview it is noticeable how often he switched between the personal, spiritual concept of unity and a purely institutional, organizational understanding (cf. *Gemeindewachstum* 1/90, p. 14).

would no longer seek "unity in Christ" in uniform structures and formulations, but rather in the living fellowship between Christians.

Where the church "happens" as a personal, spiritual reality, the sort
of unity that Jesus prayed for happens as well (John 17). This unity is
interdenominational in its character, so it is in no way endangered by the
fact that there are different church institutions—as long as these institutions do not fight against each other. In the course of my own interdenominational ministry, which takes me into a wide variety of church
situations, I see how wonderfully God can give unity in Christ even with
members of churches that I didn't know existed until a few years ago.
I find I can pray with them, plan with them, think things through with
them, work with them, read the Bible with them, and worship with them.
The unity in faith, fellowship, and service that I have with these brothers
and sisters would be no greater if they were members of my denomination (or I joined theirs).

It is certain that the issue of church planting and Christian unity is
one of the areas in which mutual understanding is just not possible without a paradigm shift. People who live within the institutionalistic paradigm *must* think in monopolistic terms. They have no choice about it. No
argument—neither biblical, nor strategic, nor doctrinal—will convince
them. They have to leave their accustomed thought pattern before they
can even consider the idea that new churches (at least outside their own
church family) can arise and multiply. As long as this shift does not take
place, all well-meaning teachings on this subject are in danger of being
in vain.

In figure 14,[2] I indicated the effect the bipolar paradigm can have on
the question of church planting and unity. I chose the two concepts of
multiplication and *cooperation*—both of them necessary elements of what
we call the "true church." The first term relates mainly to the church as
an "organism," whereas the second term relates more to the institutional
side of the church.[3] Here, again, the two concepts must not be regarded
as being in a "dialectic tension" (that would be a pathological symptom,
indicating that therapy is needed), but should be related functionally to
each other. Whereas the church as an organism must always keep to
structures of cooperation, these structures must be useful in helping the
church to multiply. That is the real point of cooperation. When a church
attempts to free itself from all cooperation with others, it opens the door
to *separatism* (danger to the left). But on the other hand, if cooperation
becomes an end in itself, there is the danger of ecumenicist thinking,
which can even develop to *monopolism* (danger to the right).

---

2   P. 137.
3   Cf. Ako Haarbeck, who suggests in his critical review of our *Theology of Church
     Development* that it should be considered whether the relationship between the church
     institution and *ekklesia* could not "be thought through afresh under the aspect of
     complementarity and conciliarity" (*Haarbeck: 1986*, p. 30).

I find it questionable that the necessity of planting new churches is frequently justified by reference to the sorry state of existing churches.[4] Although the existing churches are certainly not above criticism, this argument is problematical because it links the question of multiplication, which arises from the organic nature of the church,[5] with a completely different question: how effective (or New Testament based or theologically legitimate or innovative) the specific structures of the existing churches are. Both questions are certainly justified, but they should not be linked together. If we do combine them, church planting must inevitably appear to be a protest movement against existing churches. This is one explanation why the subject causes so much anxiety among Christians.

Church planting is not the need of the hour because there is too little evangelism in the existing churches. The subject would still be the need of the hour if all—really all!—the existing churches were working flat out on evangelism. Even if, for example, every church in Germany could double the number of people it reached with its church services within the next ten years (an obviously overoptimistic expectation), there would still be about 90 percent of the population unevangelized. In other words, the existing churches on their own are simply not capable of fulfilling the task that lies before us. Thus, we should not support church planting out of opposition to the existing churches, but with the aim of supplementing the work they already do.

Great controversy was caused in Germany by a number mentioned by Donald McGavran in an interview with me in 1987, which I published in a magazine.[6] McGavran said that, in his estimation, West Germany needed at least 20,000 new churches. The publication of this number caused people in many circles literally to throw up their hands in horror. This controversy and the aggressions it released can only be explained by assuming that these people—caught in the institutionalistic paradigm, with its monopolistic concept of unity—regarded these words of the patriarch of church growth as being a 20,000-fold attack on the existing churches.[7]

---

4   This impression can be deduced, for example, from Wolfram Kopfermann's famous book about the "end of the state church" *(Kopfermann: 1991).* I in no way question the validity of his criticism of the state church. The book has undoubtedly helped to stimulate discussion on the necessity of new churches, and thus to remove the taboo on the subject. But it also had the effect of making the link between the issue of church planting and the debate about the state church even stronger than it already was in many European countries anyway. The (unintentional) impression could therefore arise that church planting is primarily an issue for people who regard their existing church as not being biblical or spiritual enough—an impression that does not do justice to the real challenge of the subject.

5   Cf. my comments on the biotic principle of multiplication on p. 244f.

6   Cf. *Gemeindewachstum* 1/88, p. 10.

7   For a more extensive treatment, see my article about church planting as the strategy of the church in the nineties *(Schwarz: 1989,* pp. 112-127).

One of the aims of this chapter is to help make debate on this issue less emotional. Above all, I would like to show that—depending upon which theological paradigm we base our thinking—certain consequences for our approach to this subject are inevitable. My hope is that the bipolar paradigm I describe will not be regarded as "hostile towards existing churches" (as, for instance, "state church ideologists" sometimes allege), nor as "ecumenicist" (as some "church planting ideologists" see my position) but rather as the groundwork for a discussion that can help us to tackle the tricky question of "church planting and Christian unity" in a more solid framework.

Danger to the Right: Monopolism

The monopolistic concept is expressed most consistently in the Roman Catholic Church. Thus we read in an official paper: "This church, constituted and structured as a society in this world, is realized in the Catholic Church, which is led by Peter's successor and by the bishops in fellowship with him. This does not exclude the fact that a variety of elements of sanctification and truth can be found outside it which, as gifts belonging to the church of Christ, support the Catholic unity."[8] The focal element in this understanding of unity is the bishop. Leaving the bishop means leaving the church, and "no one can have God as a father who does not have the church as a mother," as Cyprian wrote in his tract on the *Unity of the Church*.[9]

This is a concept of unity which, although it does not stem from the New Testament, is at least intrinsically consistent and logical. The one true church is the Roman Catholic Church, and outside it—note the tolerance!—there may be "elements of sanctification and truth," but on no account a true "church." People who separate themselves from the Roman Catholic Church in an institutional, legal sense are therefore separated from the body of Christ.[10]

No Protestant would be able to argue in such a simple—or even simplistic—way. The principle of the Reformation, as I have attempted to show elsewhere,[11] expressed itself in the fact that the institutionalistic, monopolistic paradigm was broken by a functional approach. We can, however, show how strongly the Roman Catholic, juridical ideal of unity continues to operate within Protestant churches—beginning with the

---

8   *Hampe: 1967*, p. 277.
9   *Cyprian*, De ecclesiae unitate, 6.
10   It must, however, be added that this alleged "ideal" of a single, undivided church (in the institutional sense) was hardly ever a reality. "Even in the early church, there were divisions. Movements such as the Donatists would today be called a denomination. And, of course, we must not forget the division between the Greek church and the Latin church which took place many centuries before Luther" *(Lohse: 1983,* p. 158).
11   Cf. pp. 82-86.

Reformers themselves.[12] This mixture of institutionalistic, monopolistic arguments and functional, spiritual elements means that Protestants are inevitably caught up in a web of contradictions.

A typical example of the way Protestants deal with these contradictions is the *Church History* by Kurt Dietrich Schmidt, one of the most widespread textbooks for students of theology in Germany. After explaining the "special love" with which Protestant theologians will continually turn to the Reformation, he goes on: "But the history of the Reformation also contains a serious problem even for Protestant Christians. On the one hand, they can only regard the rediscovery of the gospel as a gift from God, which they wholeheartedly assent to . . . But why the unity of the western church was lost through the Reformation remains a problem even for Protestant theologians. It is true that we can show from history that this unity was only preserved till then by the use of force against heretics. True, it only came into being through state intervention from Constantine onwards; before Constantine, there was a plethora of schisms and heresies . . . And yet the unity of the earthly, visible church is a high value, and its loss is very painful. A really satisfactory theological explanation for the separation must therefore be sought. In spite of all efforts, it has not yet been found . . . Since the Reformation, theology has struggled to come to terms with this fact doctrinally. It has not yet really succeeded."[13]

If we examine the terminology used here ("unity only by the use of force," "came into being through state intervention," and so forth) it becomes clear what sort of (extremely dangerous)[14] concept of unity underlies this argument—the same Constantinian/Theodosian concept we find in the Roman Catholic Church. Given this axiom, it is obvious that a committed Lutheran concerned to justify the variety of churches in the post-Reformation age must get tied up in contradictions. It is to Schmidt's

---

12   The inconsistencies of the Reformers are shown, for example, in the fact that they regarded the attempts at church planting by the "Anabaptists" as being "sectarian"—thus borrowing the term used within the Roman Catholic Church to describe Protestants in the state churches. According to Roman Catholic thinking, every Christian fellowship founded outside the Catholic Church was regarded as a "sect"—which is entirely consistent with the Catholic understanding of the church. The Reformers interpreted the New Testament teaching about the "unity of the church" as meaning that there should be only one church in each geographical location. The fact that this undermined their own right to exist was hidden by their claim that their church was not a new one, but rather the true catholic church "reformed according to the word of God," and that the papal Roman church was really a "sect." Characteristically, though, they refused to allow the Anabaptists the right to make the same claim for themselves. These inconsistencies reflect the fact that can also be observed in other areas that in principle the Reformers vaguely recognized the relevance of what we have called the "bipolar paradigm," but that in other areas they largely remained within the framework of the institutionalistic paradigm.

13   *Schmidt: 1960*, pp. 274, 393.

14   This term is not exaggerated, as is underlined by Walter Kreck in his comment on the practical consequences of this ideal of unity: "From this perspective, the dreadful fact of the persecution of those who believe differently, and specifically the

credit that he at least admits to the contradiction, rather than trying to gloss over it by pseudo-logical formulas about the "paradox dialectics of a unity and not-yet-unity." However, these contradictions are resolved when we begin to think through our theology in terms of the bipolar paradigm with its functional implications—the direction of thought that takes the Reformation to its logical conclusions.

Schmidt himself demonstrates in a different part of his book where the medieval ideal of unity has its historical roots: in "neo-Platonic philosophy."[15] That is not surprising when we remember that neo-Platonic thought patterns have also led to an impersonal way of thinking in other areas (such as the concepts of God, humanity, and the church).[16] Juridical, institutional monopolism is just the logical conclusion of this profoundly unbiblical (even anti-biblical) thought structure.

But apart from these philosophical roots, there were simple political interests that caused unity to be understood in institutional terms. Emperor Constantine's interest was in having a unified church rather than a church split into several groups.[17] This was his motive for getting so involved in internal dogmatic conflicts even though he was no theologian, and for ensuring that ambiguous but diplomatic compromise statements were drawn up which aimed to preserve the doctrinal unity of the church by formalistic means.

"The emperor had a vested interest in a large, strong church because the church was intended to help the state."[18] Thus we cannot say that Constantine's concept of unity was not functional. But it was not functional in the sense of the pneumatic functionality I propose in this book, which aims to stimulate the development of the church as an organism. It was functional in a completely different sense: it helped to stabilize the power of the emperor. As a side effect, this policy also gave the church more power, so it is not surprising that *this* sort of functionality (which was pragmatic in the worst sense of the word) finally won the day.

The effects of Constantine's approach can be seen in European Protestantism today in the way the original monopolistic, all-embracing concept of unity—out of historical necessity—has largely retreated to the provincial level of parochial, territorial thinking in some of the mainline

---

persecution of Christians by Christians, the heretic trials and burnings at the stake and even the extinction of whole denominations can, it is true, never be excused, but their motives can at least more readily be understood. They were not just products of sadism and brutality; the best representatives of the church, in all their blindness and unspeakable cruelty, were crusading for the glory of God, for the unity and purity of the church as they understood it, even for the salvation of the souls of those persecuted, about which they often showed their concern right up to their last breath on the gallows" (Kreck: 1981, p. 254).

15   *Schmidt: 1960*, p. 251.
16   Cf. pp. 50-61.
17   Cf. *Schmidt: 1960*, p. 91.
18   Ibid. p. 92.

churches. At least within the boundaries of church parishes, proponents of this approach feel justified in thinking and acting monopolistically. This does not mean that the parochial *structure* in itself is automatically a hindrance to church development. There are many examples that show how it is possible to work effectively for church development within a parochial system. It is not the strategy of dividing the country into territories that hinders church growth, but territorial *thinking*—that is, a thought structure that makes monopolistic claims on a certain territory.

This sort of thinking is still widespread today, as is demonstrated by the monopolistic language that is often used. For example, many people in Germany, especially within the state church, speak quite unashamedly of *the* church when referring exclusively to their own organization. A change of membership from the Lutheran state church to a Lutheran free church, for instance, is labelled as "leaving the church"; the attempt to set up new churches outside the structures of the state church is regarded as church planting "outside the church," and so forth.[19] The similarity with the way people in East Germany (and other Communist countries) spoke of *the* party is not only linguistic, there is also a similarity in the underlying thought structure, which is based on a monopolistic concept of unity. Representatives of "the party" could tolerate, although perhaps grudgingly, the so-called "bloc parties" (which were under the communists' control), but they could never tolerate independent, free groups. Any attempt in this direction drew the anger of the governing communists until, eventually, the free groups won the day and drove the political monopolists out of power.

This comparison does not mean that I identify the communist system with the state church, as has been alleged in a different context. That would be absurd. I merely want to emphasize *one* point of comparison, namely the monopolistic attitude that can be found in both groups. This monopolism is—thank God—not shared by all representatives of the state churches. There are many adherents of the state churches who humbly, and without any monopolistic claims, join in the alliance of local Christians, knowing full well that, alongside the Baptists, Methodists, independents, Pentecostals, and many others, they are just one segment of the local body of Christ.

Danger to the Left: Separatism

It is clear from what has been said above that, from the point of view of the monopolistic paradigm, every form of church planting that results in churches outside the observer's own denomination must be regarded as

---

19 The matter is even more drastic when spokespersons for the state churches call free churches "sects." Under the Theodosian compulsory church system, which also applied to the churches of the Reformation, every attempt to plant free churches was regarded as a "sect."

separatism. This is the understanding of separatism that is often used in theological discussion. Like the institutionalistic paradigm itself, it is so omnipresent that it is even used by theologians who are otherwise not representatives of the institutionalistic paradigm.

Wolfram Kopfermann is right to comment: "Some critics of so-called schism base their comments on a highly questionable ideal of the church. For them, anyone is causing schism who attempts to build churches outside the organizational and juridical structures of the existing churches. Such critics justify variety, but insist that it must exist within the large churches. This position is theologically, historically, sociologically, and ecumenically untenable. In the Federal Republic of Germany alone, there are dozens of completely different denominations and many more independent churches. From an ecumenical point of view, the German state church model is the exception rather than the rule."[20] We must beware of equating the terms "separatism" and "church planting."

However, to pretend that there is no such thing as separatism is only possible from the perspective of an unhistorical, Platonic concept of the church (with the motto: "Somehow we are all connected in a mysterious way in the invisible church"). People who argue on the basis of the "invisible church" can opt out of the challenge of giving our unity in Christ a visible form. But the concept of the "invisible church" is biblically untenable, and it is incompatible with the bipolar paradigm of natural church development.[21] The church of Jesus Christ, especially in its spiritual and personal dimension, is something highly visible. Therefore, its unity must also take a visible form.

It is true that "unity in Christ" cannot be produced by institutional measures, nor can it be destroyed by institutional differences. But it *can* be destroyed—and this happens wherever the individual parts of the body of Christ abdicate their spiritual (and therefore visible) unity. Within the bipolar paradigm, we call the attempt to achieve a unity of churches with different denominational backgrounds that is expressed at a structural level, *cooperation.*[22] Cooperation does not mean organizational uniformity, but rather a symbiotic relationship between different

---

20 *Kopfermann: 1991,* p. 47.
21 For a more extensive treatment, cf. *Schwarz/Schwarz: 1987,* p. 50.
22 The participants in the "Pasadena Consultation" expressed very aptly how the relationship between the individual local churches and the overall body of Christ should work in practice. The delegates agreed "that in many situations a homogeneous unit church can be a legitimate and authentic church. Yet we are also agreed that it can never be complete in itself. Indeed, if it remains in isolation, it cannot reflect the universality and diversity of the Body of Christ. Nor can it grow into maturity. Therefore, every Homogeneous Unit church must take active steps to broaden its fellowship in order to demonstrate visible unity and the variety of Christ's Church. This will mean forging with other and different churches creative relationships which express the reality of Christian love, brotherhood, and interdependence" (Quoted from *Gibbs: 1981,* p. 101).

church organizations in pursuit of a common goal.[23] A church that withdraws from any form of cooperation with other churches must, indeed, be called separatist. It is isolating itself from the body of Christ. We should not be afraid to call it what it is: a sect.

It should be clear, however, that the danger of this sort of sectarianism is not restricted to independent groups. The established churches are also at risk of separating themselves from the body of Christ; for example when they refuse to work together with other (for instance, newly planted) churches in a local setting. We must beware of making words like "sect" dependent on the *size* of an institution. The term signifies an ideological *set of behaviors* that sees its own organization as an absolute—and this sort of attitude can be found in groups of all sizes.

Here we can see that, at least in one area, monopolists and separatists are not as far apart as it seems. Both have a profoundly ideological thought structure. Perhaps it is really only the small size of their groups that stops some separatists from adopting a monopolistic attitude.

The Bipolar Approach

The bipolar approach to the question of church planting and cooperation is based on the assumption that a variety of churches is basically positive. Here, the paradigm of natural church development is close to the famous proposition of Ernst Käsemann that the New Testament canon does not justify the "unity of the church" so much as the "multiplicity of denominations."[24] This does not mean that all of the 22,000 or so denominations in the world are automatically beneficial. We can be sure that they include many false teachings and false practices, and that there are many that we would wish had never been set up.

But it seems quite in keeping with the will of God that he showed us a number of different church models within the New Testament canon. When we encounter theologically questionable church forms—and who can doubt that there *are* questionable forms today—we need to remember that even a questionable variety is better than the medieval ideal of a monopolistic church.

What practical effects can the bipolar approach have on the question of church planting and cooperation? Five aspects seem to me to be important:

First, the bipolar approach should not be confused with a sentimental idea of unity that attempts to water down existing differences in a spiritualistic way. Most of the organizational and doctrinal differences between churches are not really divisive (in that they do not hinder unity); but there *are* some differences that certainly are divisive. This applies wherever one

---

23 For a more extensive treatment of the principle of symbiosis, which is fundamental for natural church development, see p. 245f; *Schwarz/Schalk: 1998*, pp. 167-175.

24 *Käsemann: 1960*, p. 221.

church contests the claim of another one to be a "true church" just because it has different forms. In the dialog between such churches, the bipolar approach could be especially beneficial if it is applied to the issue of truth.

Second, ecumenism should never pursue the goal of uniting churches organizationally, and certainly not the goal of creating a worldwide super-church. Such attempts are counterproductive for church development. Studies of fusions between denominations show that they almost always result in a lower effectiveness in evangelism. "Cell division, not cell fusion, produces healthy bodies."[25]

Third, the idea behind the term "cooperation" must be put into practice on a local, regional, national, and international level. Churches with differing traditions must find ways to work together to fulfill the great commission. One of the most promising approaches, which attempts to make use of the different natures of the churches involved, is the DAWN strategy.[26] We can already see that local and national groups made up of members of different churches can often achieve a greater spiritual unity than similar groups drawn from within a single denomination.

Fourth, in our interdenominational projects and discussions, we should beware of what C. Peter Wagner calls "hyper-cooperativism."[27] People with this view regard the cooperation of the different churches as being more important than the project that has to be carried out. Many studies have shown that this approach is counterproductive, especially in the area of evangelism.[28] Cooperation should never become an end in itself—it must always put itself at the service of the development and multiplication of churches.

Fifth, each church should not only ask how it can grow better than it has done up to now; perhaps more importantly, it should consider at the

---

25 *Wagner: 1985 b*, p. 73. There, following a thesis stated by Lyle Schaller, Wagner writes: "Church mergers, in particular, are often a clear sign of approaching decline, if not death. Church splits, hopefully intentional, are often signs of vitality and growth." The principles proposed by Wagner for the church apply in a similar way in business. Thus, for example, Tom Peters writes: "Most studies come to the conclusions that mergers don't pay." He quotes an article from the *Economist* which says on the same subject: "The biggest mistakes were made by industrial strategists who insisted that bigger is better." The motto is very often: "If you join us, we can be inefficient together for longer" *(Peters: 1988*, p. 18f).

26 DAWN = Discipling a Whole Nation; cf. *Montgomery: 1990; Simson: 1995*.

27 For a more extensive treatment of this concept, cf. *Wagner: 1985 b*, pp. 64-76.

28 For example, C. Peter Wagner writes about such attempts: "For at least a couple of decades, evangelicals, who have always been interested in effective evangelism and church growth, have been told that one way to evangelize more effectively is to cooperate interdenominationally on a local or regional level . . . There has been little or no evidence that this premise is valid. In fact, research that has been done to date seems to indicate that just the opposite is true—the more churches cooperate interdenominationally in evangelistic projects, the less effectively they evangelize" *(Wagner: 1985 b*, p. 65).

same time how it can multiply. Nowhere in the western world are there enough churches.[29] "The most effective method of evangelism is to plant new churches."[30]

The criterion for the question of whether we have really understood what is meant by "Christian unity" is whether we can rejoice over new churches from our hearts, and whether we can practice with their members unity in Christ. Usually it is just the other way around. In the name of Christian unity, new churches are actively resisted, sometimes with highly aggressive methods.

When I speak of "rejoicing," I do not mean the sort of condescending benevolence that we sometimes hear from adherents of the established churches when they speak about new groups, as if they were saying: "Unfortunately we can't stop new churches from arising. But if it does happen, we don't want them to be dismissed as sects."[31] Such condescending reactions only reveal how deep-seated the old thought paradigm is. The former monopolists concede to the new groups—which arose against their will, but are now on the scene—a certain right to exist. People who speak like that have not understood much about the nature of Christian unity.

Practical Illustration:
The Quality Characteristic "Holistic Small Groups"

I wondered whether a quality characteristic called "planned church multiplication" should follow at this point. The problem is that this quality characteristic does not exist. The eight quality characteristics do not describe what I, or anyone else, wishes or has dreamed up. Rather, they came about through the empirical study of churches on all six continents. In these studies it could be proven that church planting has a positive correlation to both quality and growth; but it is not, in the light of research, an indispensable essential for any healthy church, as the eight quality characteristics are.

However, the central principle behind the concept of church planting, multiplication, can be illustrated by reference to one of the quality characteristics we identified. We call it "holistic small groups."[32] Within the

---

29 Cf. the comments by C. Peter Wagner on whether any region can have "too many" churches (*Wagner: 1990*, p. 40).
30 *Wagner: 1990*, p. 12.
31 Cf. a similarly worded press statement by the organizers of the "Nuremberg Church Congress," the "German Church Growth Association." They expressly stated that "in spite of the reports that suggest otherwise, it is not our intention to plant new churches, although this cannot be avoided. If it happens, these new churches should not be automatically regarded as sects" (*Gemeindewachstum* 1/92, p. 27).
32 For a more extensive treatment, cf. *Schwarz/Schalk: 1998*, pp. 96-104; *Schwarz: 1987*, pp. 191-221.

microcosm of a small group, the same process occurs that should be characteristic of the whole church—the small group life increases by multiplication.

One of the decisive aspects we found in our study of small groups in growing churches is their "holistic" character. This means that they provide a situation in which individual Christians can find personal relationships and the opportunity to share spiritually. These small groups are places where "fellowship" has a strong affinity to "friendship." The larger a church becomes, the more decisive is the function of small groups in the life of the church organism.

These groups can fulfill a variety of different tasks. They are a suitable setting for learning to use spiritual gifts, a place where Christians can offer counseling to each other, the members can find ministries which suit their gifts, and some groups have a definite evangelistic aim. Small groups are an ideal place for experimenting. Before something is introduced to the whole church, it should be proved in the context of a small group. Last but not least, such groups can be a recruiting ground for the future leadership of the church. The decisive point for church growth is that small groups should be designed for multiplication. Permanent multiplication only happens where it is deliberately encouraged. Every group should therefore have a plan to show how it can contribute to the reproduction of new groups.

The specifically "biotic"[33] nature of this quality characteristic includes the principle that small groups must be allowed to die. Many groups suffer because they attempt to put off this time indefinitely rather than drawing the sober conclusion that it is quite normal for groups to come to an end after a certain period. If we speak of reproduction, we must also speak of dying. It is the end of a natural development. The dissolution of a group can be a happy occasion if the group has, for example, given life to two "children," six "grandchildren," and fifteen "great-grandchildren." This is God's plan how life multiplies.

---

33   Cf. p. 223ff.

C.
Christian Service

As being a Christian involves being a member in the body of Christ, there is no such thing as a passive Christian. This term is, theologically speaking, an *oxymoron*, that is, a phrase (like hot snowball or dry tears) that consists of two elements which, by definition, do not fit together.[1] In the "body of Christ," as Ernst Käsemann writes in his classic essay about office and church in the New Testament, "there is no passive membership."[2] The *ministerium verbi divini* is "assigned and commanded to every Christian who does not wish to cease being a Christian."[3]

In the New Testament, the ministry of the Christian church is mainly described with the term *diakonia*. This term denotes acts of service that arise "from the right attitude of love."[4] "The decisive element for the meaning of this term is that the young Christian church regarded every activity that is important for building up the church as *diakonia* . . . With every such activity, Christians do not only serve their brothers—they serve Christ himself."[5]

It is a logical consequence of this understanding of service that the New Testament does not use an official, hierarchical term such as *time* or *arche* to describe it. The secular term *diakonia* "never implies any association with a particular status or position."[6] Rather, it denotes service of slaves at the table. The model of Christian service is therefore not the political ruler, the scribe, or the priest—but rather the slave serving others at the table.

Figure 15 (next page) shows the dangers facing the biblical concept of *diakonia* to the right and to the left. The monistic misconception distorts gift-oriented service into *clericalism*; instead of social involvement

---

1 Therefore it is untenable to speak of "dead members," as, for example, the so-called "Spandau theses" do (in: *Baden: 1961*, p. 59). This term betrays a despairing thought pattern that tries to equate what, for logical reasons, cannot be equated. As the New Testament shows, there will be weak and sick members of the body of Christ, but a dead member is inconceivable—or if it existed, it ought to be quickly amputated to avoid poisoning the whole body!
2 *Käsemann: 1960*, p. 117.
3 Ibid. p. 123.
4 *Beyer: 1954*, p. 87.
5 Ibid.
6 *Schweizer: 1959*, p. 157.

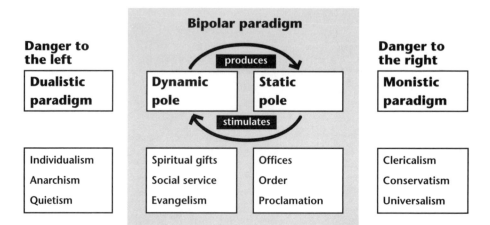

Fig. 15: The biblical understanding of service (diakonia) and the dangers to the right and to the left.

which implies critical reflection of political structures, it demands structural *conservatism;* and the evangelistic efforts of Christians can be replaced by a *universalistic* theology. In all three areas we see yet again that what was originally intended to preserve the service of the Christian church in fact replaces it, and in the last resort makes it impossible, at least unnecessary.

However, the tendencies that can be found within the dualistic paradigm are also far removed from the biblical concept of *diakonia.* Neither the *individualistic* concept of spiritual gifts, nor the approach that rejects order on principle and tends towards an *anarchist* political position (of a violent or nonviolent kind), nor the tendency to adopt a *quietist* attitude to planned proclamation of the gospel are consistent with the concept of service we find in the New Testament.

Here it is clearer than in other areas that the true church must not only show itself in right doctrine *(orthodoxy),* but also in right practice *(orthopraxis).*[7] But this *orthopraxis* cannot be safeguarded by theological formulas, ecclesiastical structures, or any other institutional measures. The decisive point is to develop theological reflections and structures that stimulate the development of *diakonia.*

---

7   Cf. *H. Lochmann: 1972,* p. 64f.

1

"The Priesthood of All Believers": The Conflict About Gifts and Office

We can see from figure 15[1] the distinctive character of the concept of spiritual gifts that is advocated by the church growth movement. Spiritual gifts must always be matched with practical tasks ("offices"), and these offices must be useful in stimulating "charismatic service" (understood in this sense) to develop. When Jürgen Moltmann writes, "The whole church is spiritually and charismatically gifted, not just its ministers,"[2] he not only has the church growth movement behind him—he is backed by the Bible, too![3] The concern of natural church development is, quite simply, to release this biblical concept from the abstraction of a theological postulate.

The basis of this understanding of gifts is the concept of the church as the "body of Christ." Every Christian has certain gifts (*charismata*), but no Christian has them all. When the Holy Spirit gives all Christians at least one gift, he gives them a position and function to fulfill in the body of Christ. The well-worded phrase of Ernst Käsemann that a *charisma* is the

---

1   P. 174.
2   *Moltmann: 1975*, p. 23.
3   We must, however, remember that there are different emphases on this question even within the New Testament, including tendencies that are on the edge of an almost institutionalistic approach (e.g., in the pastoral Epistles; cf. *Conzelmann: 1973*, p. 397). However, even here, the borderline to the institutionalistic paradigm is never crossed, as the functionality of structures for building up the church is always taken for granted. Thus, Eduard Schweizer writes: "We do see that the first church was more concerned with firm structures than the Pauline church; but this structure in no way assigns specific functions, such as binding and loosing, only to the holders of certain offices. This is consistent with the fact that in Acts it is assumed that everyone can baptize—and surely also break the bread. But even in the most institutional parts of the New Testament, in the pastoral Epistles, it is still assumed that every man can teach, and it is not an office or an office holder but the church that is the 'pillar and foundation of the truth'" (*Schweizer: 1949*, p. 18).

"actualization and individualization of grace"[4] in the life of the individual Christian makes the point of this approach clear: we do not choose the area in which we wish to be actively involved, rather, we accept what God gives us in his grace.[5] When we discover our gifts, we have at the same time identified where our calling lies.[6]

Spiritual gifts are not meant to glorify the person who has them— they are meant to serve for the building up of the church and thus for the glory of God. Therefore they must be matched with specific tasks.[7] The concept of "offices" used in the diagram of the bipolar paradigm is not without problems,[8] as it could imply a formalistic, clericalistic misconception (in a similar way to the problems that surround the term "sacrament").[9] But there are many examples which show that it is possible to talk of "offices," but to understand them as strictly functional. If offices are regarded in such a way that they are consciously harnessed to support church development, this reflects a theologically legitimate understanding, regardless of the terminology used.

The concept of spiritual gifts presented here is one of the keys to understanding the practical implications of church growth. C. Peter Wagner's book *Your Spiritual Gifts Can Help Your Church Grow*[10] played a pioneering role in this area. The idea behind the book is simply to draw the conclusions out of the Reformation doctrine of the "priesthood of all

---

4   *Käsemann: 1960*, p. 117. This is implied by the very word *charis-ma*. The ending *-ma* in Greek "usually means the result of an action." A *charis-ma* is thus "the result of the *charis* in action" (*Conzelmann: 1973*, p. 393).

5   Cf. *Conzelmann: 1973*, p. 384, who emphasizes that the linguistic starting point of Paul's *charis* concept is the meaning "bringing joy by giving, an act of favor that is given, not earned." Thus, the "freedom of the giving is the constitutive element."

6   Cf. *Käsemann: 1960*, p. 120: "Everyone should remain in that in which they are called, i.e., . . . in their *charisma*. Grace makes us free for new obedience in the possibilities given specifically to each one of us. It does not give us the freedom to buccaneer whatever we take a fancy to . . . We can follow Barth's exposition of this passage in Romans and say that my *charisma* is, for me, the only ethical possibility . . . I cannot choose my calling or reject it for another. Even from this point of view alone, the ideal of the pastor and theologian who is always and everywhere competent is not tenable."

7   Cf. *Schweizer: 1949*, p. 7: "Precisely to enable this service of all, the structure of the church is necessary. Precisely because not everyone is given every gift, the life of the church must be so structured that others always have the opportunity to put their gifts into practice. This does not mean that certain areas are reserved only for those who hold office, but it does mean that all must be willing to hold back with their service so that others can also serve the building of the church."

8   Cf. Helmut Thielicke: "It can be doubted whether the term 'office' fulfills these functions, as it is unbiblical, and it also has the association of ruling, hierarchy, and officialdom. Closer to the New Testament at any rate is the term *diakonia*, which applies to discipleship and is also linked with the promise that those called to it will have the support of the Spirit, so that *diakonia* and *charismata* can correspond to each other" (*Thielicke: 1978*, p. 302).

9   Cf. p. 138f.

10   *Wagner: 1979*.

believers" for the local church. It seems to me that the bridge-building doctrine of spiritual gifts that is advocated by the church growth movement is one of the areas in which its unadmitted theological roots (Reformation and Pietism) are most fruitful.[11]

Danger to the Right: Clericalism

According to the clericalistic misconception, the presence of a spiritual gift cannot be seen as a precondition for taking over an office in the church. The whole issue is turned upside down. When clerics take up an office, the charismatic "gifting" is conferred by the act of ordination. The underlying magical paradigm is highlighted even more clearly where objectivistic, formalistic considerations determine the act of ordination (apostolic succession, academic degrees, and so forth). From Cyprian on, the Holy Spirit has been "bound" to offices.[12]

It is interesting that the tactics used by clericalism in all ages are so similar in different religions that it is hard to tell them apart. In ancient India, for example, the caste of the Brahmans secured their privileged priestly position by telling the people that only the Brahmans had "knowledge about the right way to deal with the divine powers, and they kept this knowledge carefully and surrounded it with mystery; they skillfully propagated the opinion that even the smallest deviation from the correct ritual can spoil its success and bring great harm instead of blessing. Furthermore, the priestly knowledge about the old forms and formulations acquired a certain dark incomprehensibility and a mysterious sacredness that grew with the increasing distance in time and space from the origins of that knowledge. The Brahmans thus became indispensable mediators in all the important events of private and public life. In war and peace, coronations, birth, marriage, and death the secret of blessing or curse lay in the correct performance of a sacrifice that only they could do properly. They also had a monopoly over all higher education, which was entirely in their hands."[13]

Anyone who wants to study the functioning of what we can only call the "deceit of priests" has a choice—they can choose whether to study it

---

11 Particularly in the areas in which the concept of spiritual gifts goes further than what was implemented by Reformation and Pietism (both movements remained too strongly dominated by clericalism), it is actually fulfilling profound *concerns* of both Reformation and Pietism.

12 Even though there are, as was already mentioned, different levels in the New Testament, including those represented in the pastoral Epistles, it can be said for all: "The concept that an office holder, by virtue of the fact of holding office, and independent of spiritual qualifications and experience, merely on the strength of the act of ordination, has any specific authority, is not found even at the fringes of the New Testament age" *(Brunner: 1984,* p. 189).

13 *Störing: 1950,* p. 42.

in the Brahman system or in the Christian church. The mechanisms are almost identical even in their details.

It was mentioned earlier[14] that clericalism particularly legitimates itself by reference to the related phenomenon of sacramentalism. If the Eucharist is interpreted sacramentalistically and thus becomes the real center of the church, the person who administers this sacrament, the priest, acquires a dominant position. *He* constitutes the church again and again by the sacrament. The priest becomes a holy person. With this concept, the Old Testament sacrifice cult, which, according to the Letter to the Hebrews, was ended once and for all, is reintroduced into the church. Once again, there is a spatial holy place *(sanctum)*, the altar, and thus a division between those who administer the holy elements, and the *profanum*.[15] The new element in the New Testament, the overcoming of the contrast between profane and holy, is negated. The priest, the altar, and the chancel are holy, the everyday world of "lay" people is profane. In this way, ordained priests become indispensable as mediators between God and the church—or rather, they make themselves indispensable, for this doctrine was thought up entirely by priests.

It is true, however, than none of the many Protestant churches would argue for the above understanding of church office. It largely reflects the Roman Catholic concept which was sharply attacked by the Reformation. Nevertheless, distinct traces of clericalism can be found in Protestant churches, especially in the form of the following five concepts.

- *Concept 1: The pastor as an all-rounder.* This logical consequence of the clericalist misconception can be illustrated particularly drastically by the picture of the pastor as an "egg-laying, wool-giving, milk-producing pig" created by Eduard Steinwand. The pastor is a speaker, counsellor, academic, public relations specialist, organizer, social worker, evangelist, master of ceremonies, teacher—"and competent at everything else, except perhaps at walking on water."[16] This ideal, which in reality condemns a pastor to be mediocre in all these areas, cements the pastor-centered consumer mentality in many churches. "Pressed into the role of an all-round charismatic, he is often, in effect, a sort of substitute for the church."[17] Thus, the gifts are "entombed within the pastor's office. The pastor is largely the king, priest, prophet, and teacher. All serve one, and one serves all. In this way, the church remains immature and the pastor overburdened."[18]

- *Concept 2: Lay members as the pastor's "helpers."* Where people want to justify the cooperation of "lay workers" in spite of the clericalistic,

---

14   Cf. p. 138f.
15   The *profanum* is what is "in front of the temple." It is the direct corollary of the *sacrum*.
16   *Wagner: 1979*, p. 142.
17   *Krause: 1989*, p. 42.
18   *Bohren: 1969*, p. 155.

pastor-oriented paradigm (which is, strictly speaking, not really necessary in clericalism), it is interesting that they normally do it by using purely pragmatic arguments—and here I use the word pragmatic, which can be interpreted in several ways, in its most negative sense.[19] The argument then runs like this: "Unfortunately, the pastors cannot fulfill all the tasks that they should perform. Therefore we need active lay people to support them. It would be better if the pastors could do everything themselves, but as that is not possible, there is no way to avoid having lay people as the pastor's helpers." The psychology behind these words is woefully common in Christianity—even where churches make theological statements of the "priesthood of all believers." But the relation between the two concepts— "lay people helping their pastor" and "priesthood of all believers"— is an "either-or."

- *Concept 3: The leader as a spiritual "guru."* In this concept it is expected of the members that they "subject themselves" in ways that are similar to the non-Christian idea of the "guru." People do not subject themselves to their leaders because of the leaders' competence in certain areas, but simply because they are their leaders. They try to get a guiding (and absolutely valid) pronouncement from their spiritual guru even in areas in which his or her competence is demonstrably weak. This servitude to Christian (and secular) authorities seems to me to be a particularly persistent vestige of clericalism, which can even be diagnosed in groups which reject theologically, for example, the sacramentalist authority legitimization of the cleric. Here, "obedience to the authority is equated with morality."[20] The leader as a general![21]

- *Concept 4: Active involvement as a spiritual form of "Taylorism."*[22] This concept is probably the most drastic expression of the impersonal view of humanity which, as we have repeatedly seen, almost always lies behind the institutionalistic paradigm. The starting point in this thought pattern is not—as it is characteristic of the concept of "gift-oriented ministry"—the spiritual gifts of the individual Christians, which are then, in a second step, related to specific ministries. The opposite procedure is followed: a list of tasks is fixed in advance, then "volunteers"

---

19 For this concept, cf. p. 72.
20 J. M. Lochmann: *1972*, p. 136.
21 This image is not only problematic from a theological point of view; outside the Christian sphere, for example in business, its ineffectiveness has long been unmasked. The company consultant, Gerd Gerken, writes for example: "People no longer want father figures (paternalistic principles of pioneers), because, although they often impress them, they give hardly any opportunity for others to develop." New leaders, according to Gerken, "love criticism. They love contradiction" (*Gerken: 1990*, p. 175f).
22 Named for F. W. Taylor (1856-1915), who attempted to rationalize working processes by developing a strictly methodical procedure to increase the working achievement.

are sought to do them. In this technocratic concept, those who actively get involved are no more than parts in a statically defined cog system. The tasks that need doing are the fixed points, and the Christians must adapt to them. This model can be described as a spiritually clouded form of "Taylorism."

- *Concept 5: Service in the church as a sacrifice.*[23] This concept is the culmination of the misconceptions outlined so far. In this approach it is almost impossible (and sometimes regarded as a danger to be avoided) that anyone might actually enjoy their ministry in the church. Pastors and "lay" people are permanently in the wrong place (i.e., not in the place that the Holy Spirit showed them when he gave them the corresponding gifts). Therefore, they experience the frustration of having a task that is inconsistent with their gifts. But this frustration is not interpreted as a direct consequence of their self-willed disobedience, or at least ignorance; rather, it is seen as a sign that a Christian is in the right place, because in this concept, real service for Christ is always a "sacrifice." My intention here is not to criticize the biblical concept of "service as sacrifice"; rather, I wish to criticize a sacrifice mentality that arises from an approach that is not gift-oriented. People who suffer from doing tasks that they are not gifted for mainly have themselves to blame. They should not expect this ineffectiveness (and even spiritual arrogance, as we often see on closer examination, cf. the image of the "egg-laying, wool-giving, milk-producing pig") to be spiritualized with a pseudo-spiritual claim to be "suffering for Christ's sake." We must carefully differentiate between self-imposed suffering arising from unsound theology and genuine suffering for Christ's sake as described in the Bible.

However the clericalist misconception expresses itself in practice, it certainly shows a tendency to lead church members—not surprisingly—to make the "hair-raising statement"[24] that, in a certain sense, "the church is the pastor and the pastor is the church."[25] This identification is the real point of clericalism. The church is dethroned in favor of the pastor, and thus it is finally in danger of being superfluous.[26] The very career group

---

23 In his book about spiritual gifts, C. Peter Wagner calls the underlying attitude "consecration theology" (*Wagner: 1979*, p. 34).
24 *Herbst: 1986*, p. 92.
25 *Hild: 1974*, p. 276.
26 Adolf Schlatter makes it clear to what extent even the Reformation—in contrast to its own doctrine of the "priesthood of all believers"—based its concept of the church on the pastor: "With the justification of the pastorate, the impulse to action ended. It seemed that enough had been done for the proclamation of the word and the provision of the sacraments." The logical consequence of this thinking was plain: "The pastorate is indispensable because the word must be proclaimed; the church is dispensable, because it is possible to believe and love without it" (*Schlatter: 1956*, p. 81f).

that has spent centuries justifying this concept with more or less sophisticated arguments should not complain about its consequences. The "loneliness of the clerics," which is now often encountered and bemoaned, with all its negative effects for their self-esteem, is just the other side of the same theory clerics have used to safeguard their legitimation and self-esteem over the centuries.

Danger to the Left: Individualism

If the different forms of clericalism are the one extreme, at the other end of the scale we find the individualism that is typical of the spiritualistic paradigm. We cannot accuse spiritualism of automatically leading to passivity, although in some cases it does so. In many cases spiritualists can develop tremendous and impressive activities—but this almost always occurs in individualistic ways that consciously bypass the church and its structures. This individualism is an indication of the underlying concept of the *privatism* of faith and service (from the Latin *privatio* = robbery). The church is literally robbed of the service for which God has gifted these people.

Individualistic spiritualism overlooks the fact: "I cannot have the Holy Spirit without having those to whom the Holy Spirit also communicates—and in a different way."[27] Therefore, Gerhard Lohfink is right when he writes: "Discipleship in the New Testament sense is, naturally, not an individualistic occurrence far from the church which each person can fashion as they desire, but rather it is the commitment of one's whole life to the cause of Jesus, which can only be understood and taken hold of in the church, on a local level."[28] As spiritualists have problems on principle with church structures, if not with fellowship itself, their individualistic, privatist concept of service is not surprising.

This basic feature of spiritualism has far-reaching consequences for their approach to spiritual gifts. The inherent tendency in spiritualism to refuse a sober, practical link between gifts and tasks sometimes tries to justify itself by a further argument that is typical of this thought pattern: spiritual gifts are identified exclusively with the extraordinary, spectacular, and supernatural, so that practical "planning" for church development is impossible from the outset.

It is undoubtedly true that spiritual gifts sometimes express themselves in a spectacular way—just as they can also occur in unspectacular ways. The one is no more spiritual than the other. Biblically, a gift qualifies as being spiritual not by the "factuality of the supernatural, but by the modality of proper use."[29] As Ernst Käsemann writes, Paul makes

---

27   *Bohren: 1975*, p. 78.
28   *Lohfink: 1988*, p. 154.
29   *Käsemann: 1960*, p. 112.

"the usefulness the criterion of heavenly energies and revelations, where he counts as 'useful' those things that build up the church."[30]

The criterion of the "supernatural" is theologically unsatisfactory. What we understand by this term depends on our world view, our concept of science, and the current state of research. What a society regards as "natural" or "supernatural" is thus subject to change. It would therefore be disastrous to attach a particular spiritual aura to things that people in our day and age regard as "supernatural."[31] According to the witness of the New Testament, "Everything that serves to build up the church is *charisma*, not just ecstatic occurrences, but also the profane, everyday act of service."[32]

The resistance of spiritualists to practical planning for church development turns out to have particularly dire consequences in the area of spiritual gifts. Thus it is possible—by using pious-sounding words—to prevent the gifts being used for the purpose for which the Holy Spirit has given them, namely to build the church. Rudolf Bohren rightly comments, "Without planning . . . the gifts remain unused. Building up the church without planning is not possible, and it must be noted that even planning is based on a spiritual gift. One of the main hindrances for such planning is the indefinite idea that belief in the Holy Spirit is incompatible with planning."[33]

Here we can clearly see what destructive effects the anti-institutional attitude of the spiritualistic paradigm can have. By an apparently spiritual appeal to our human inability to plan church development, the fundamental fault of this paradigm—its tendency to autonomism, and thus to presumption—can be clouded over. Eduard Schweizer makes it plain in his book about the Holy Spirit that a "purely dynamic understanding

---

30 Ibid. The identification of spiritual gifts with the extraordinary is not based on Paul. In modern non-Christian usage, the term *charisma* is mainly determined by the content given to it by the sociologist Max Weber. It is possible that Weber's concept has influenced theological thought about *charisma* in our culture more strongly than Pauline theology.

31 It seems to me a typical expression of the spiritualistic paradigm with its tendency to other-worldliness to rate spiritual gifts such as "leadership" or "evangelism" as natural, but "healing" or "prophecy" as supernatural, as happens in some parts of the charismatic movement. If we have to use the terms (which is problematic enough), then we must say that each of these gifts has a natural dimension (i.e., which can be explained rationally) as well as a supernatural dimension (i.e., one that cannot, or not yet, be explained). In all of these gifts, we are completely dependent on the anointing of the Holy Spirit, and there is no difference in their spiritual quality.

32 *Conzelmann: 1973*, p. 395. Cf. also *Käsemann: 1960*, p. 117: "Just as nothing is a *charisma* in itself, so also nothing is profane in itself. This concept of a thing 'in itself,' i.e., a neutralized zone, an indifference, does not exist in the eschatological age. The kingdoms of Christ and Satan are facing each other and manifesting themselves on earth through people who are obedient or disobedient. Everything is a gift if we do not defile it. Everything has a charismatic potential and is holy to the extent that the saints of God use it."

33 *Bohren: 1975*, p. 149.

of the Spirit" must be rejected in the name of the Holy Spirit, as it is an understanding "in which the 'spiritual' person regards himself/herself as being so important that structures and institutions are impossible."[34]

Thus it is not surprising that spiritual gifts can be perverted, and often have been perverted in the history of the church. The same autonomism that causes gifts to be isolated from practical tasks, in the last resort leads the gifts away from the giver, from God himself. "The gift, when isolated from the giver, loses the character of being a claim made by the Lord and leads to self-portrayal of the uncommitted, making churches into a hotbed of religious talents, and producing disorder which is the reality of the old world, and thus opposed to the peace of Christ."[35]

Whenever a gift is not used to build the church and *by that means* for the glory of God, it is in danger of being perverted. The "gift bearer" who apparently takes a short cut, and instead of using the gifts to build up the church uses them *directly* to the glory of God is usually only seeking his or her own honor. This emancipation of the gift from church development, and thus from God himself, can be illustrated by spiritual gifts such as "prophecy," "healing," and "speaking in tongues," as painful experience shows. However, critics of these gifts overlook the fact that the underlying mechanism is in no way restricted to this category of gifts. There are just as many examples of the disastrous effects caused if gifts such as "teaching," "evangelism," or "counseling" are used, not to build up the church, but for the glory of the "gift bearer."

I know of a number of examples of Christians to whom God has given the gift of leadership who misuse it to project their own personality, to play power games, to intrigue against others, to assert their own interests at other people's expense, to suppress the gifts of fellow Christians, and so forth. These cases are examples of perverted spiritual gifts, too—and interestingly enough, they often occur in churches that are concerned to protect their people from (real or alleged) "charismatic" perversions.

Misuse of spiritual gifts can be found in all sorts of groups, amongst so-called "charismatics" as well as among so-called "anti-charismatics."[36] This misuse cannot be avoided—as some "anti-charismatics" suppose—by allowing no room in the church for certain gifts that are thought to be particularly "dangerous." On the contrary: if we refuse the place in the church to use certain gifts, we contribute to the isolation of the gift from the task, and thus to a possible perversion of the gift. We should then not be surprised if these gifts "go underground"—and sometimes have

---

34 *Schweizer: 1978,* p. 175. Cf. also *Schweizer: 1949,* p. 14: "Life in the Spirit and legal authority in the New Testament sense are no contradiction."

35 *Käsemann: 1960,* p. 119.

36 The term "so-called" is indispensable here, as the labeling of such groups as "charismatic" or "anti-charismatic," whether from within or from without, has nothing to do with the Pauline concept of giftedness, which is that every Christian, having a share of the *charis,* can also be regarded as a "charismatic."

disastrous effects. The only way to prevent the misuse of spiritual gifts is by giving opportunities for their proper use, which means that we need to show practical ways in which a particular gift—whether it be hospitality or giving or healing or whatever—can be put into practice for church development.[37] In other words, the misuse of gifts can only be prevented by a functional understanding of offices.

The Bipolar Approach

The doctrine of spiritual gifts is perhaps the area where we can see most clearly the practical effects of the *pneumatic* functionality proposed in this book. We do not build the church to fit our own concept—which adherents of the institutionalistic paradigm tend to do when they define the ministries of the church in advance rather than working with the actual gifts of the members. On the other hand, we draw a clear distinction to the concept of the Spirit in the dualistic paradigm (which tends towards randomness, if not to chaos).

The concept of gifts behind natural church development is based on a specifically *theonomous* approach: we begin with the gifts that God has given us, and we let him show us how he wants our church to be. We do not need to fulfill all ministries that people (such as our denominational leaders, our members, and so forth) expect of us. Rather, we assume that God has equipped us as a church for precisely the service he expects of us.

C. Peter Wagner describes in the German edition of his book on gifts how inadequately our theological tradition has prepared us for the sober use of spiritual gifts. None of the church fathers—including Augustine, Luther, Calvin, and Wesley—"developed the concept of spiritual gifts as the starting point for Christian service."[38] Yet the gift-oriented approach is a logical expression of the biblical doctrine of the "priesthood of all believers." No one—at least within Protestantism—will contradict the statement that the priesthood of all believers is fundamental for building up the church. But who would think of drawing the practical conclusion of giving each member practical help to discover his or her spiritual gift(s) and to develop an appropriate ministry? Thus theological theory and church practice are in tension with each other, a tension that we could—literally—call "paradox dialectics."

How, then, can we overcome this paradox, which is not just illogical but also unspiritual, and unhealthy? In the ministry of our institute, we have found the following four guidelines helpful.

---

37 Cf., for example, *Käsemann: 1960*, p. 112: "Paul by no means . . . rejected the ability of miracles and ecstasy. With the term *pneumatika* in 1 Corinthians 12ff. he can commend these abilities. But he does it, as these chapters show, by putting them at the service of Christ and his church, in other words by allowing them to be spiritual gifts."

38 *Wagner: 1987*, p. 159.

First, it should be one of the most urgent tasks of church leadership to help all Christians to discover their spiritual gifts. To judge by our surveys, we can assume that 80 percent of committed Christians do not know their spiritual gifts.[39] This shocking state of affairs does not arise because these Christians do not have gifts (as they sometimes think), but because no one has ever helped them to discover and use their gifts. In our experience, the discovery of spiritual gifts is one of the aspects of church development which is least complicated to put into practice, quite apart from the fact that those involved usually enjoy the process. Wherever we start church development by using the gifts that already exist, we are starting with the treasure that God has given our church. That is what makes it such a happy, liberating process.

Second, each of the gifts discovered should be matched with specific tasks. In my experience this is the point where many churches that have helped Christians to discover their gifts fail. They then wonder why the concept of spiritual gifts, which they had expected so much of, fizzles out. Christians do not have to do everything—but they must do the things that God has gifted them, and thus called them, to do. "Gifts of grace that we do not perceive are, for us, nonexistent. But as the non-perceived spiritual gifts are given and present, the non-perception of gifts implies guilt."[40]

Third, this approach means that "leadership" should be seen as one gift among many. A charismatic understanding of ministry—in the New Testament sense—does not make the *charisma* of leadership superfluous; it stimulates it. The stronger this gift is in those who have the responsibility of leading the church, the less they need to insist on their formal, juridical authority. In other words, we recognize leaders by the fact that they lead others, not by the fact that they have a leadership position, and perhaps even complain that nobody follows them.

Fourth, anyone who discovers that the task they are currently doing does not correspond with their spiritual gifts should leave this ministry as soon as possible (whether it is service as a street evangelist, a small group leader, a pastor, or a bishop). After taking this step, they will normally experience two things. First, they themselves will be happier (at least if they then live in keeping with their real calling), and second, this decision has a positive effect on the people they have tried to serve. When a position occupied by the (spiritually) wrong person becomes

---

39 This number, which was arrived at in 1987 by a survey we carried out with 1,200 members in churches in Germany, Austria, and Switzerland, must, however, be relativized: in my experience, some of the 80 percent who do not *know* their gifts nevertheless *live* according to their gifts—and that, after all, is what is important. The survey results, however, point to a real lack in our churches.

40 *Bohren: 1975*, p. 146. Cf. also Michael Herbst: "If a Christian refuses to join in building up the church, the church is missing something and the individual does not find his or her calling (1 Cor. 12-14)" (*Herbst: 1987*, p. 101).

vacant, a climate arises in the church that will encourage those Christians who have the appropriate gift to take over the vacant position.

Rudolf Bohren writes that the church becomes "beautiful" in the "concerted action" of its gifts.[41] The important point is that such statements should not be regarded as poetry, but as theological statements that have practical consequences. Two of the eight quality characteristics of growing churches have a special affinity with the concept of gifts and office presented here: "gift-oriented ministry" and "empowering leadership."[42] Therefore, I would like to use these quality characteristics to illustrate how the concerted action of the church's gifts can be put into practice and help to develop churches that are healthy—and thus "beautiful."

Practical Illustration 1:
The Quality Characteristic "Gift-Oriented Ministry"

The starting point of this quality characteristic is the recognition that it is not enough to preach the concept of gift-oriented ministry, or to teach in a way that confuses the teaching process with purely verbal lecturing. Whenever I am invited to hold a seminar in a church, I endeavor not just to lecture on the subject but, as far as is possible in one weekend, to apply in practice the principles of which I speak. The seminar participants need to experience what effects the gift-oriented approach can have on their personal situation and their church.

In these seminars—and not only there—I experience the liberating effect that the concept of spiritual gifts can have. Individual Christians and whole churches are freed from the widespread "all-rounder" syndrome. The biblical concept of spiritual gifts seems to me to be a healthy alternative to a masochistic self-denial syndrome (which is not to be confused with spiritual self-denial), and also to an egotistic insistence on "self-fulfillment." For none of the other eight quality characteristics are the effects that this approach simultaneously has on both personal lives and the life of the church as great as here.[43] I am not surprised that the working material that we have developed on this subject[44] has the greatest echo of all our materials for church development.

We should not pretend, however, that this approach to spiritual gifts is completely without its problems. Even though it rightly can claim to be based on the New Testament, it can sometimes only be implemented

---

41   Bohren: 1975, p. 145.
42   For a more extensive treatment see *Schwarz/Schalk: 1998,* p. 55-62.
43   It is true that the quality characteristics "passionate spirituality" and "loving relationships" also have immediate consequences for both areas; however, the results of change in these areas take effect much more slowly than for "gift-oriented ministry."
44   *Schwarz: 1997; Schwarz/Berief-Schwarz: 1998.*

after overcoming resistance (Paul experienced the same). And we should not hide the fact that this approach can be misused. I know of Christians who fall back on the principle of gift-oriented ministry (and even quote our working materials!) whenever they *don't want* to do a particular task. Where earlier they would been honest and said that they are not in the right mood to do it, now their excuse is, "I haven't got the gift."

It should be clear that these cases are really a misuse of a concept which is basically right. Working on the gift-oriented approach certainly does not mean being led by our urges of the moment, but asking in great seriousness, "What do *you* want me to do, God?" Our experience with this approach is that the spiritual benefit that individual Christians and whole churches gain is so overwhelming that the occasional misuse is insignificant by comparison.

Practical Illustration 2:
The Quality Characteristic "Empowering Leadership"

Contrary to widespread opinion, natural church development does not regard it as desirable that pastors should be freed from "management tasks" to devote themselves to their "real" ministry (which is usually taken to mean preaching and counseling). This demand is almost routine in the ranks of many Christians, but it certainly does not express what I mean by the concept of empowering leadership.[45]

Our surveys revealed something else: pastors of growing churches are noticeable for the fact that they spend a lot of time fulfilling their *leadership responsibility*, an area that has a fairly clear affinity to the unpopular "management tasks."[46] Leadership, however, does not express itself, as is sometimes supposed, in a dictatorial style, but in the fact that the gift is placed in the service of the body of Christ. Leaders of growing churches are helping the church members to find their calling. They concentrate their energy on empowering other Christians for ministry. They do not use "lay" workers as "helpers" in attaining their own goals and fulfilling their own visions. Rather, they invert the pyramid of authority so that the leaders assist Christians to release the spiritual potential that is already in them. These leaders equip, support, motivate, and mentor individuals, enabling them to become all that God wants them to be. This concept of leadership means that the pastor's function will be "less like that of a shepherd of sheep, and more like that of the trainer of a team."[47]

---

45 For a more extensive treatment see *George/Logan: 1987.*
46 However, management should not be *equated* with leadership. In our teaching on gifts, following C. Peter Wagner, we distinguish between the gift of "leadership" and the gift of "organization." Whereas the gift of organization is not necessary for the pastor, the gift of leadership is important for him or her.
47 *Krusche: 1970,* p. 302.

Leaders who realize their own power by empowering others experience how a lot of problems are almost solved "all by themselves." Rather than handling the bulk of church responsibilities on their own, they invest the majority of their time in discipleship, delegation, and multiplication. Thus, the energy they expend can be multiplied indefinitely. This is how spiritual "self-organization" occurs. God's energy, not human effort and pressure, is released to set the church in motion.

The problem is that most pastors are trained to be preachers and counselors, but that nothing in their training prepares them for the tasks of an empowering leader.[48] This in itself causes many of them, depending on their mentality, to seek refuge in the institutionalistic or spiritualistic paradigm, because within both thought patterns, their theological existence is assured without the need of being an empowering leader.

The secret of empowering leadership is that the personal, spiritual level and the institutional, organizational level are related to each other. Empowering leaders are both goal and relationship oriented. The bipolarity which we have described as fundamental for the paradigm of natural church development, must be incarnated in the personality of the leaders. In part 3 of this book we will examine the practical implications of this approach more closely.[49]

---

48   Cf. Manfred Josuttis, who writes about the state church: "In our church it is expected that a person can become a decent minister if he or she was an average high school and average university student and passed two exams with average results" (Josuttis: 1982, p. 215). For a church that merely requires "administrators" for the word and the sacraments and that assumes that these things in themselves have an automatic effectiveness, these qualifications are probably good enough!

49   Cf. pp. 214-218.

2

The Dream of the Christian State: The Conflict About Christians in Politics

Christian ministry cannot restrict itself to the private sphere; it inevitably has a public effect. This creates the theological problem of how the church should do justice in public life, and thus also in politics, to the Christian commandment to love. Controversy today rages not so much about whether the church should face up to this task—it is *how* it should do it that is controversial.

There are Christian groups that believe they can escape this question by claiming to be completely unpolitical. However, this claim is pure fiction. The attempt to keep out of politics is in itself a political decision—a decision for the *status quo*.[1] Helmut Gollwitzer rightly says, "Nonparticipation, disinterest out of principle, is out of the question. Where this is proclaimed as Christian, God is given notice to end his preserving work, and an area as important as the forming of society is removed from the saving action of God. To accompany political events attentively, in prayer, in active thought and advice, forming judgments and taking sides is an inviolable part of the calling to be a disciple in this world."[2]

For me, the question of the political dimension of Christian churches has always been an important issue, and the moment I became active in church development, I realized even more what is at stake. The naïveté with which many Christian groups—in the United States just as much as in Europe—flee to an alleged political neutrality and fail to notice *whom* they are thus serving, is frightening. Whenever I have been able to

---

1   C. Peter Wagner comments: "The choice not to get involved in the political process is a vote for the status quo, and should be recognized as such. Some may choose not to endorse any of the political options that the system offers, but to move outside the system and either start a counterculture or join the revolution. That is clearly a political decision" (*Wagner: 1981*, p. 185).

2   *Gollwitzer: 1978*, p. 191.

publish anything about the church growth issue, I have therefore tried to point out the social and political significance of faith, fellowship, and service—knowing full well that in some circles I would be making enemies. I am, on the other hand, glad that even critics who are rather skeptical of the evangelistic implications of natural church development could never accuse us of opting out of the political issues and escaping into a purely subjectivistic piety.[3]

We must agree with Karl Barth when he writes that it is the task of Christians "to seek the best for the city, to honor the divine decree and appointment of the state by voting and striving, to the best of their knowledge, not for the false state, but for the good state, a state that will not dishonor the fact that it has a power 'from above,' as Pilate did, but will honor it."[4] This commission is so fundamentally Christian that I consider it dangerous to degrade it to a question of personal taste—even if some substitute the word "calling" instead of "taste" to give a greater theological respectability to their personal preference. Therefore, when I thought through the bipolar paradigm, I found myself compelled to ask the question: What, on the basis of this paradigm, are the political consequences of natural church development? (This, of course, should not be confused with the personal voting choices or the party membership of people who are active in church development!)

In figure 15,[5] I attempted to show the bipolar position in this area. The church as an "organism" will, by nature, always display *social service*. This must be related to the organizational element of existing *orders*. If Christians refuse on principle to relate to orders, there is a danger of *anarchism*. On the other hand, if they identify social involvement with adherence to the existing orders, they have succumbed to the danger of (structural) *conservatism*, which has such a paralyzing effect on many churches.

The problem is all the more complex because we are dealing here not only with church structures, but also with state structures.[6] By nature, these structures function with legal compulsion: a police force that must arrest criminals, a legal system which metes out punishment, a military force that protects a country by force of arms—all these things are indis-

---

3   Thus, Reiner Strunk (*Strunk: 1986*, p. 120) comments on my book *Theology of Church Development:* "The accusation of eliminating or even condemning the political relevance of the Christian faith in favor of an inner piety cannot be leveled against *this* evangelistic concept." Cf. *Schwarz/Schwarz: 1981; Schwarz/Schwarz: 1983; Schwarz: 1995.*

4   *Barth: 1947*, p. 133.

5   P. 201.

6   Strictly speaking, this overstretches the significance of the diagram of the bipolar paradigm—in which the organizational aspect is always related to *church* organizations. However, as the thought patterns in the relationship of the bipolar approach to state structures are analogous to church structures, I feel that this inconsistency is justifiable.

pensable parts of any state order. If it were not possible to enforce legal rights (which is not possible without the threat, and the use, of force), the rule of law would not be possible.[7] What attitude does the Christian church have to this legal compulsion?

In the history of the church there have been two tendencies which are related to whether the particular Christian is more influenced by the spiritualistic or the institutionalistic paradigm. Whereas spiritualists live in the illusion of ruling the world by *spiritual means*, representatives of the institutionalistic paradigm tend to establish the kingdom of God by *secular means*. This statement is, of course, greatly oversimplified, as there are a great number of modified intermediate positions as well as the two extremes. The extremes do, however, describe the direction in which the two paradigms move with regard to the social and political responsibility of the church.

Danger to the Right: Conservatism

When I speak here of conservatism as an expression of the institutionalistic paradigm, this term needs explanation. There is undoubtedly much in church and society that is worthy of conserving. Particularly Christians will, in an age of disintegrating values, fight for values that are worth preserving, and thus be conservative. But besides this legitimate, even necessary conservatism there is another version which is called by the same name, but which has little in common with this attitude: the preservation of structures, forms, and orders for *their own sake*.

Here I find the distinction proposed by Erhard Eppler between *value* conservatives and *structural* conservatives most helpful. "Structural conservatism," he writes, "comes into conflict with a conservatism that is concerned not so much about structures as about values, that insists on the inalienable value of the individual, whatever he or she achieves, that regards freedom as an opportunity and a call to solidarity, that searches for justice in the knowledge that it can never be achieved completely, that risks peace even at the price of sacrifice."[8]

Whereas the value conservative strives to establish things worthy of preservation even *against* the resistance of existing structures, the structural conservative is concerned with a different quest: the "conservation of power, of privileges, of authority."[9] This structural conservatism is, according to Eppler, "an ideology in the strict sense of Karl Marx's

---

7   It seems to me a wise decision of the Reformers that, in their conflict with both religious enthusiasts and Roman Catholic ecclesiocrats, they based the state not on Christology, but on the law. This means that where legal compulsion is applied, it is not Christ who rules, but it is still an expression of God's created order.

8   *Eppler: 1979*, p. 35.

9   Ibid.

definition: a superstructure for the protection and justification of power."[10]
The slogans of structural conservatism are, typically, "authority, state, and
law."[11] While the value conservative considers "*what* authority, *what* state,
what law result from the esteemed values, the technocrat clings to structures just because they are structures."[12] Technocracy and structural conservative thinking are, for Eppler, interchangeable concepts. We are faced
with the question "whether we wish to preserve structures at the expense
of values or values at the expense of structures. Those who try the former
will, in the long run, not resist the pull of the reactionary. Those who wish
for the latter will find themselves among the progressives."[13]

What Eppler calls structural conservatism is the same as what, in the
sphere of the church, is called "morphological fundamentalism." Structural conservatism stems from the same security mentality and displays
the same heteronomic tendencies that I described in the characterization
of the institutionalistic paradigm. When representatives of this paradigm
turn to politics, they will always tend towards structural conservatism,
as this is the approach which corresponds to their thought pattern, their
emotional life, their whole mentality.

I am not surprised by the similarity in the thought pattern between
Erhard Eppler, the politician, and the bipolar paradigm of natural church
development. It is my impression that in both cases this thought pattern
has been inspired by the same source, the study of the Reformation. Thus,
Eppler writes: "When the Reformers discovered the message anew, they
found that it could not be put into practice in the structures of this church.
The 'return to the Bible' led to the Reformation."[14] Reforming the structures with the goal of preserving the content—that is the nature of value
conservatism or the reformation principle (the two are almost synonyms
at this point). When I use the shorter form *conservatism* from now on, I am
always referring to structural conservatism, whereas the thought pattern
described by Eppler as value conservatism largely corresponds to the
concerns of the bipolar paradigm.

The mistake of conservatism lies in the illusion typical of the institutionalistic paradigm, the belief that by defending structures it is possible

---

10   *Eppler: 1979*, p. 35.
11   Ibid. p. 44.
12   Ibid.
13   Ibid. p. 45.
14   Ibid. p. 38. With regard to the church sphere, Eppler describes the relationship be-
      tween value conservatism and structural conservatism as follows: "If resignations
      from church membership reach a level that would endanger the existence of the
      state church in the medium term, structural conservatives will look nervously to the
      right and left at every step in order to avoid giving cause for more resignations,
      whereas value conservatives will find it understandable that people who have long
      had no real link with the church do not wish to pay taxes any longer. They will ask
      how the message given to the church can be presented credibly so that it has an
      effect on our society, even if that involves the danger that the church will have to
      look for new organizational forms" (Ibid.).

to guarantee what these structures were designed to protect. When problems arise, conservatives are quick to call for a strong state. They tend to wish that adultery were legally punishable, that prayer in school were compulsory, that blasphemy were forbidden, that abortion were severely punished. The mistake of conservatives does not always lie in their demands for laws and corresponding punishments (which sometimes can be useful); their mistake lies in the illusion that when such laws and punishments are passed, they have achieved their aim. "Right" laws (as ends in themselves) are more important than the effect they actually have—a typical thought pattern of heteronomism.

It is in the logic of Christian conservatives that they long for a Christian state. This state would then make all that is of value for Christians compulsory for the whole of society. However, we have had enough experience of such Christian states to be able to assess fairly realistically whether they really lead to the results the conservatives would wish. In the course of church history, this has mainly been put into practice in two forms: first in the attempt to instrumentalize the state for church purposes (the prototype being *papalism)*, and second in the attempt to instrumentalize the church for state purposes (here, *caesaropapism* can serve as a prototype). In the first form, the state is part of the church, and in the second form, the church is part of the state.[15] But both forms are only possible on the basis of a similar "Christian" concept of the state.

The concern of *papalism* is to form the world as a *civitas dei*. This is done by incorporating it into the kingdom of God, which, in the Middle Ages, meant that it should be governed by the *vicarius Christi*, the Pope. The symbol of this distribution of roles was that the emperor promised to hold the stirrups for the Pope, as Pippin literally did in Ponthion.[16]

Caesaropapism proceeds in the reverse order. The Christian emperor nominates the bishops and has dominion over the wealth of the church (as, for example, Charlemagne had). This is explicitly justified as being to the benefit of the church,[17] but in practice it means that the church loses all opportunity to be critical of the state. It only retains the possibility of blessing the state and all it does—as is so characteristic of the *byzantinism* of the eastern orthodox churches. *Caesaropapist* tendencies can also be displayed in a less radical form when pastors are called on to be state officials. For example, under the German Emperor Frederic II (1740–1786) they were obliged to plant mulberry plants, bring in the potato harvest, and proclaim police regulations from the pulpit.[18]

From the point of view of politics it may be very significant whether a particular age tended to *papalism* or whether the *caesaropapist* tendency won the upper hand. From the point of view of church development,

---

15 Cf. *Pöhlmann: 1980*, p. 295.
16 Cf. *Schmidt: 1960*, p. 192.
17 Cf. Ibid. p. 195.
18 Cf. *Wallmann: 1973*, p. 177.

however, the relevance of this question merely is who has to hold whose stirrups (i.e., it is negligible). The common elements in both forms are far more important than the differences in power politics. Both reveal the institutionalistic thought structure that is geared to security and believe that state laws can enforce the kingdom of God.

Fortunately, we now live in an age in which neither the Emperor nor the Pope has to hold the stirrups for the other. But the dream of a Christian state is still very much alive in many believers—which shows how widespread the underlying institutionalistic thought structure is. We can surely anticipate that if Christians influenced by this misconception had the power, they would not hesitate even today to institute their Christian state with all the means of compulsion that we know only too well from history. May secularization preserve us from this dream coming true! In my estimation, such authoritarian Christian states are among the political constellations in which the issue of the right of the Christian to resist the state is particularly relevant.[19]

Danger to the Left: Anarchism

The term I have selected to characterize the "danger to the left," *anarchism*,[20] describes a line of thinking which assumes that "power is in itself evil."[21] Anarchists do not reject state structures because they think that particular rulers are unsuitable, but because they reject any sort of power structure. In our context we are not so much concerned with the secular form of political anarchism, which began to be formulated in the 18th century,[22] but rather with a line of thinking that arose on the basis of Christianity and that comes to similar results, and which I therefore describe with the same term.

Whereas in conservatism, the heteronomic need for security dominates the political stance, in anarchism, the autonomous desire for freedom prevails. Christian anarchism can be found in two forms: either in the form of a pacifist escapism, with a rejection of all forms of force on

---

19   The ethical issue of the right of resistance is too complex to be treated here; in fact, it seems to me problematical to try to solve it without reference to specific situations. My remark is merely meant to indicate that the right of resistance cannot only be necessary in atheistic states, but also in so-called Christian states, which may become a threat especially to the dynamic pole of the church by dint of the means of compulsion they use for every area of life.

20   Cf. this definition of anarchism: "Anarchism can be defined as a social, philosophical doctrine which postulates a lack of rulership on principle, and justifies it exclusively by a criticism of authority. This criticism is directed mainly, if not exclusively, against the state, whatever form it takes (including the democratic state)" (*Heintz: 1957*, p. 353).

21   *Heintz: 1957*, p. 355.

22   Cf. Ibid. p. 353.

principle, or, as history has shown, the very same approach can turn to revolutionary violence. As the force of the state is rejected in both cases, the pacifist and revolutionary forms can be combined under the heading of anarchism. Which of these two ways is embraced depends, among other factors, on whether the spiritualists regard state structures (along with all other sorts of institutions) as *irrelevant* or as something that is *evil* and must be actively resisted.[23]

How closely these two forms of anarchism are related to each other can be seen clearly in the Anabaptist movement in the Reformation period. In its origins, this movement—in contrast to Luther—rejected any form of violence and demanded that Christians should not take on any official position in the state; but for a period, some of the Anabaptists adopted what seemed to be a completely opposite position. After they had suffered severe persecution for ten years, numerous Anabaptists had a "revelation" in 1534 that they should no longer be like sheep for the slaughterer, but more like the angel with the sickle that cuts the harvest.[24] Adherents of the former Lutheran lay preacher, Melchior Hofmann, flocked from the Netherlands to Münster in Germany, where they set up the "New Jerusalem" to await the second coming of Jesus. The newcomers soon exceeded the local populace and finally succeeded in electing an Anabaptist town council.

Jan Matthys, who organized the Anabaptist realm of Münster as its "prophet," decided to kill all the "ungodly." After his death he was succeeded by Jan Bockelsen, who had himself declared king of Zion and, as one of his first policy decisions, introduced communalism and—interestingly—polygamy. He governed Münster "with a mixture of religious hysteria, unabated moral excess, and hard cruelty."[25] After a fourteen month siege, the town was finally conquered by the Bishop of Münster— and the revenge was just as cruel as the reign of terror had been. The corpses of the executed Anabaptist leaders were packed into cages, and hung on the spire of the Lamberti church—which can still be viewed today.

This episode brought the rest of the Anabaptist movement to its senses. Through the initiative of Menno Simons, it returned to the old form of a defenseless movement that rejected all forms of violence—a tendency that still influences the Mennonite church today, but which is also characteristic of other Anabaptist groups such as the "Hutterian Brethren."[26] They are not against the state, but they trust "that God will call people who will lead the world and create calm and security for the masses. They know themselves called to follow God's word without compromise, to perform untainted baptism and to celebrate the Lord's

---

23   Cf. pp. 34-37.
24   Cf. *Bainton: 1983*, p. 400.
25   *Wallmann: 1973*, p. 89.
26   Cf. *Eggers: 1985*.

Supper as a fellowship meal in brotherly love, to separate themselves from evil influences, and to lead a church life that is ordered by elected lay preachers."[27]

I personally have a strong tendency to the pacifist form of anarchism. Even though I do not share the implications of anarchism that are so typical of the spiritualistic misconception—for example, its negative view of institutions—I still feel that Christian groups that adopt a decidedly pacifist position have an extraordinarily important function in society. I mention my own sympathy for the pacifist position only because I wish to add that this can, of course, *not* be the position of natural church development. My concern in this book is not to justify dogmatically what is important to me personally (which is, inevitably, strongly influenced by my own biography and my encounters with certain people). Far too many theological works are written from this motivation, and their function as a self-justification strategy for the theological existence of their authors is only too transparent.

The pacifist version of anarchism cannot be a model for church development, if only because of the fact that merely a small proportion of Christians will choose this path. An attempt to make it compulsory for all Christians would be a new form of legalism. Furthermore, whatever positive things we can say about pacifism, we must also critically remark that it has not been able to contribute to a constructive, functional use of legal compulsion. The greatest danger of pacifist anarchism is that it tends to disparage all uses of force, thus making it almost impossible to organize force in a way that best serves the people in society.

I am grateful that, apart from the minority who are pacifists, there are also many who get involved as Christians in politics, justice, the penal system, the military, and other areas of public life. We can only hope that they do not take sides with structural conservatives, but instead try to bring Christian *values* to these areas, even if this frequently brings them into conflict with existing structures.

The Bipolar Approach

The bipolar approach has as its starting point the fact that the Bible gives us many *principles* that have high political relevance. On the other hand, the Bible does not portray a political *program*[28] which tells us in detail what to do in every single situation (such as abortion laws, operating permission for atomic power stations, pension insurance, economic subsidies, arms control, and so forth). Anyone who interprets the Bible in this way has not understood its nature. On the other hand, those who

---

27   *Wallmann: 1973*, p. 62.
28   For the distinction between *principles* and *programs*, cf. p. 238f.

regard biblical *principles* as irrelevant for these issues rob themselves of an important source of help in the evaluation and solution of social and political problems of our time.

Our question cannot be *whether* biblical principles apply to the social involvement of Christians, but only *how* these principles should be applied to each situation. Here, I find it normal that there are differences of opinion within the body of Christ. The different opinions are not only due to a different interpretation of the *Bible*, but more importantly to the fact that the specific *situation* can be assessed in different ways.

When trying to relate biblical principles to social questions, a number of aspects seem worth noting:

First, the question at issue here is not whether a church *wishes* to be socially involved or not. To abdicate this responsibility, for example by rationalizing that evangelism is more important, would betray a deeply unbiblical way of thinking. The widespread teaching that converted people automatically change society must be rejected as wishful thinking.[29] As long as Christians do not learn in practice how they, as changed people, can change society, there is a danger that all will stay exactly as it is—as countless examples show.

Second, the aim of social involvement with a Christian motivation will be to bring God's love to the world, and thus to make the world more loving and more "Christian." But any attempt to establish a "Christian state" must be rejected as an expression of the institutionalistic paradigm. Within the state, Christians should struggle for freedom of conscience—not only for themselves, but also for those who believe differently or are unbelievers. To demand freedom for ourselves which we do not grant to others is theologically and spiritually highly questionable.[30]

Third, a church must be able to allow differences of political opinions to exist amongst its members, and to accept Christians being involved in different political parties and social groups. In a church there will be, for example, soldiers and conscientious objectors, union members and business owners, house owners and squatters. Uniformity on these issues would give us reasons to suspect that the church is ideologically

---

29 That is also the position adopted by C. Peter Wagner: "Every Christian and every church must contribute in some way to the effective fulfillment of the cultural mandate. It is not enough to think and theologize about it. It takes doing. It is not enough even to pray about it. It takes energy and involvement. Changed persons do not automatically move out to change society. They need to be taught, they need to be encouraged, they need to see exemplary models that they will desire to imitate" (*Wagner: 1981*, p. 13).

30 Cf. the characteristic words of Heinrich Albertz, who comments self-critically on the Christian resistance in the Third Reich: "That was the great and terrible mistake, or even the guilt of the church and Christians in the year 1933, and even before, that they only started to cry out—and even then only a minority of them—when the freedom of Christians and the church was at stake, whereas they had watched completely unmoved when the social democrats, the communists, and the Jews were sent to prisons and concentration camps" (*Albertz: 1980*, p. 7).

oriented. Especially in such complex questions as when, in what areas, and in what way civil disobedience may be justified, the church must not provide a single solution that is legalistically imposed on all. These decisions should be made by individuals in good conscience under the non-directive encouragement of the church.

Fourth, the distinction between "social service" and "social action" which C. Peter Wagner introduced to the discussion of church growth seems to me to be extremely fruitful.[31] Although the two areas cannot be entirely separated from each other, they do indicate different tendencies. Wagner's thesis, which is well justified, is that the area of social service (focused primarily on helping individuals) is best taken care of by the local church, whereas social action (including the political dimension) is usually more effectively undertaken via the structures of a para-church organization.[32] In this argument, Wagner is not trying to exclude political issues from the body of Christ. He just thinks that the para-church structures are more effective for fulfilling the political mandate, a position which, on closer examination, makes a lot of sense.

The content of this chapter is not illustrated by reference to one of the quality characteristics of growing churches. The reason is this: What we have referred to as social action is not counted as a quality characteristic of a local church, because of the arguments given above (which are backed by our empirical research). What we have called social service, however, is part of the quality characteristic "need-oriented evangelism," which will be considered in the context of the next chapter.

---

31   Cf. *Wagner: 1981*, p. 35f.
32   The underlying supposition is that organizations that extend beyond the local church can choose their staff for their suitability for the work (which, in this case, would include their political attitude and competence), whereas this approach would be beset with problems at the local church level. I must admit that formerly I thought differently about this issue, but that I was then convinced by Wagner's arguments. In my estimation, his book "Church Growth and the Whole Gospel" *(Wagner: 1981)* is one of the best that has been written on the subject of Christians in politics in recent years.

3

"Make Them Come In": The Conflict About Evangelism and Conversion

No missiologist in the twentieth century has fought so tenaciously to ensure that the *proclamation* of the gospel is not confused with *evangelism* as Donald McGavran, the father of the modern church growth movement.[1] The proclamation of the gospel, he says, is never an end in itself, but always a means to an end. Thus, C. Peter Wagner also writes: "Proclamation itself, while it is as necessary as presence to evangelize effectively, does not in itself constitute evangelism. Evangelism has only been accomplished when disciples are made."[2]

This functional relationship between proclamation and evangelism underlies the diagram of the bipolar paradigm in figure 15.[3] To separate the two elements from each other, which the spiritualistic misconception tends to do, would be just as harmful as the far more widespread attempt to identify the two with each other, which is the tendency of the institutionalistic paradigm. The question of how the proclamation is perceived by the listener and what effect it has in him or her is a necessary part of responsible reflection upon evangelism.

Danger to the Right: Universalism

The term "universalism" which I have selected to characterize the consequence the institutionalistic paradigm has for the understanding of

---

1   Cf. *McGavran: 1980*, p. 36: "To *God*, as He has thus revealed Himself, proclamation is not the main thing. The main thing is the salvation of persons. This is so obvious, it is almost embarrassing to state. Is it conceivable that God our Savior is more interested in the form than in actual saved men and women? Is He more pleased by 'grateful witness to the fact of Christ'—or by lost sons and daughters welcomed to the Father's house? The proclamation of the Gospel is a means. It must not be confused with the end, which is that men—multitudes of them—be reconciled with God in Christ."

2   *Wagner: 1981*, p. 56.

3   P. 174.

evangelism, needs some explanation. The gospel is undoubtedly universal in its nature, in that it is directed to all people and ethnic groups. The participants in the Council of Jerusalem who had been influenced by Paul expressed this, as reported in Acts 15. They resisted the attempt to narrow down the gospel to one ethnic group, and thus they paved the way for missions to the gentiles. *This* sort of universalism describes precisely the path that every Christian should be committed to.

Normally, however, the term universalism is used to describe a different understanding that is influenced by the institutionalistic paradigm. It is the attempt to make "all the world" into disciples by institutional means (or, with similar effect, by theological reflection). This is the understanding of universalism I will use on the following pages. I propose to illustrate the effects it can have in three different versions of universalism. The first version is the *compulsory church* misconception, which dominated Europe for many centuries from the Constantinian/ Theodosian reform onwards; the second is a concept of proclamation that can best be called *sermon magic*; the third version consists of universalistic *theological formulations* which declare people to be Christians without them having to become believers. However great the differences between these versions, they all have a common starting point. The commendable desire to make as many people as possible into disciples is deflected, as is typical for the institutionalistic misconception, into the attempt to claim as many people as possible for the church by institutional means.

The most drastic form of this tendency is, of course, the *compulsory church* misconception. From Constantine onwards, the church not only claimed that there was no salvation outside itself *(extra ecclesiam nulla salus)*; in the context of the Roman Empire there was literally no possibility to *exist* outside the church. This state of affairs lasted in Europe almost to the French Revolution, thus applying also to the churches of the Reformation which identified themselves with the Constantinian state church and the Theodosian compulsory church.

Although the attempt to use the force of arms for the propagation or defense of the Christian faith (or to cause the state to use such force) must be rejected as a perversion of the Christian faith, we do not do theological justice to this phenomenon if we do not take into account the justified concerns behind this approach. It is reasonable to assume that the Christians of those days (or at least many of them) were genuinely concerned to bring as many people as possible into the body of Christ. It is not this *aim* that should be criticized, but the *means*, which were, as a logical consequence of the institutionalistic paradigm, inadequate to achieve this aim.

The "theological" justification for the use of force was, of all things, a word of Jesus himself. "Make them come in," Jesus made the master of the great feast say when he sent his servants to the "roads and country lanes."[4] In the Latin translation *cogite intrare*, the words that were meant to express the loving coaxing of God had a devastating history. They were first used by Augustine to justify the use of state force against the Donatists, and in the sequence for almost all forms of compulsory measures. From the Inquisition of the Middle Ages to the "missionary methods" that were based on the power of the sword, the phrase *cogite intrare* was repeatedly quoted as justification.[5]

These practices of using force were not "mistakes" by the church that can be explained by the times they occurred in; rather they are completely logical consequences of the institutionalistic paradigm. The fact that modern advocates of this paradigm would not take up weapons or give approval to the use of force for the defense of the gospel is not a sign that they have adopted a pacifist position. Its historically demonstrable cause lies in the way that the *world*—thanks to the Englightenment and the French Revolution—took this prerogative from the church against the church's bitter resistance. The fact that Christianity did not renounce the use of force through "better insight," but that it was "rather the determined opposition of secular people and the worldly powers" that hindered it, "is one of the most shameful parts of church history, and has damaged the church's credibility more than all the propaganda of the godless."[6]

At this point we could seek the easy way out and claim that the concept of compulsory church universalism is historically long past and does not merit serious consideration. However, a glance at contemporary works of church history shows how pervasive compulsory church *thinking* is even today. Hardly any modern church historian would express approval of the use of force and compulsion on behalf of the church. However, those who try to maintain a neutral, distanced position in their works are betrayed by their biased language (which they themselves might not notice). A single paragraph from the *Compendium of Church History*[7] by Karl Heussi, even today one of the standard works for students of theology in German-speaking Europe, will illustrate what I mean by this assertion.

In his chapter about the "spread of Christianity in the north and east of Europe,"[8] Heussi uses the word "missions" in a way that is totally synonymous with expressions like "the advance of Christianity," "pushing back the border to heathendom," "fight against the heathen," "military advance," "force to adopt Christianity," "rule of the church," and other phrases.[9] He blithely speaks of the "conversion" of whole countries,

---

4   Luke 14:23.
5   Cf. *Schmidt: 1960,* p. 119.
6   *Kreck: 1981,* p. 142.
7   *Heussi: 1979.*
8   Ibid. pp. 204-207.
9   Ibid. p. 204ff.

which mainly occurred under threat and application of force and thus had nothing in common with the biblical meaning of conversion. Forced baptisms, which took place often enough, are possible. But how a "forced conversion" is supposed to work remains a mystery. However, Heussi does not even hint at the fact that his descriptions have nothing to do with conversion in the New Testament sense and that this form of "missions" is a radical betrayal of the gospel. The term "conversion" is not even placed in quotation marks to indicate a certain distance from the events of those days.

Quotation marks are—*nota bene!*—used for the word "conversion" in a different context—when talking about the evangelical movement of "Pietism,"[10] which managed without swords and torture chambers and aimed for the voluntary decision of the individual. The link between "conversion" and phrases like "struggle of repentance," "breakthrough of grace," and such is, according to Heussi, a sign of the "one-sidedness" of Pietism.[11] The Pietists are accused of "separatist errors" and "sectarian tendencies"[12]—value judgements that we seek in vain in his description of the use of force to compel people to join the church.

The theology student and future pastor learns here, without it being expressed openly, that an emphasis on the "struggle of repentance" makes one suspicious and causes accusations of separatism and sectarianism—but the use of swords and torture chambers does not. There is not a single word that expressly justifies the compulsory church concept, but the finer points (or missing finer points) in the language make it amply clear which way the wind blows. This contemporary view of things should show us the extent to which the categories of the Theodosian compulsory church, and thus the institutionalistic paradigm, even today dominate the feeling, thinking, and theologizing of many Christians.

The second variety of universalist thinking, a *magical understanding of the sermon*, is worlds removed from the compulsory church concept. Proponents of this view can even claim that compulsory measures of all sorts are completely unsuited for church development. For example, Christian Möller emphasizes how little all "force or urging" achieves for church growth, as the use of such measures only produces "hypocrites."[13] According to Möller, this was also Luther's opinion, from whom he quotes: "Summa summarum: I will preach it, I will say it, I will write it. But I will not urge anyone with force, for faith wishes to be accepted willingly and not by compulsion."[14] Anyone who reads these words and compares them with the concept of the compulsory church as described above can only say: "How true!"

---

10   *Heussi: 1979*, p. 397.
11   Ibid.
12   Ibid. p. 398.
13   *Möller: 1990*, p. 67.
14   *Luther: 1983*, p. 280.

However, on closer inspection we notice what strange alternatives are presented here. We are all agreed that force and violence are completely unsuitable means for church development. But what alternative is proposed to this compulsion? Möller's answer, which he correctly quotes from Luther, is "I will preach it, I will say it, I will write it." But however much we like this "I will preach it" by comparison with the *cogite intrare*, we must ask if this is the right alternative for church development.

It seems to me to be one of the major weaknesses of Protestant theology that almost everything it has to say about church growth is related to preaching, and that this is largely identified with the pulpit lecture delivered by the pastor. The turning point in theology that began with Karl Barth and led to theology as a whole being understood as "proclamation theology" had as its cause the "specific minister's problem of preaching."[15] The discovery of the task of proclamation was a positive development, but we must face the question whether it goes far enough. Behind this concept of proclamation, in the final analysis, lurks the idea that church growth results automatically, *ex opere operato*, from the pastor's pulpit lecture. Advocates of this opinion even stress that it is not crucial whether the proclamation finds a hearing, whether it has any effect or leaves its hearers untouched. The effect of the sermon lies, almost like a material substance, in the words themselves (a line of reasoning that is parallel to sacramentalism).

This theory and practice of preaching must face up to Paul Tillich's accusation of arrogance: "Church terminology, and to a large extent biblical terminology, is far removed from our historical situation. If it is still used with that priestly arrogance that repeats the biblical words and leaves it up to the hearers whether to be touched or not, it surely ceases to be 'God's word,' and is rightly not heard. And the minister who feels a martyr of divine ineffectiveness has become guilty by a lack of contextualization."[16]

However, these words of Tillich, which I fully agree with, still do not touch the heart of the matter with regard to the magical understanding of preaching, because even the more appropriate "terminology" demanded by Tillich remains in the realm of the verbal. We should not underestimate the importance of verbal proclamation, but in terms of church development it is only *one* of many measures that can be adopted. Here are just a few other aspects: if we do not set out to build up cell groups, create multiplication structures, motivate need-oriented ministry, analyze our church situation, help Christians in the discovery of their gifts, create specific plans for church development, train church members for evangelistic service (and the list could go on and on)—then even

---

15   *Zahrnt: 1966*, p. 15. Cf. also Karl Barth: "The task of theology is one with the task of preaching" *(Barth: 1957*, p. 10).
16   *Tillich: 1961*, p. 105.

the most orthodox and biblical sermons will not help. To be sure, they might bring some people to faith here and there (usually in a purely individualistic sense), but on their own they certainly do not build up the church. The belief that all the above elements will automatically come about if we only speak about them in a sermon (or simply preach about biblical texts)—that belief betrays the same *hocus pocus fidibus* expectation that I have described elsewhere[17] as being typical of the magical, institutionalistic paradigm.

The same approach can occur in an even more extreme form in groups that are oriented to social and political issues. Some such groups are critical of evangelism that aims for the conversion of individuals, and instead, they make the alteration of political structures the main content of their sermons. It should be clear by now that I do not take lightly the question of Christian responsibility for society, and that I do not dismiss structures as unimportant. But it is my impression that pulpit declarations are the worst possible way to make real progress in this field (especially if they are made at the expense of the conversion of the individual, or in front of empty pews).

Whenever I hear sermons by pastors who are influenced by this approach, I cannot help smiling. These pastors use strong words to condemn the world economic system, the dangers of genetic engineering, or socialism. Sometimes their sermons contain demands addressed to the political leaders. In one case I know of, a pastor even gave the American president an "ultimatum" in his sermon in Germany. (I can just imagine how impressed the president must have been all those miles away in Washington!) But when pastors preach this sort of sermon, I am aware that, in the pews, Grandpa Smith and Grandma Jones are sitting there, longing to give their lives to Christ if only someone would invite and help them to do so.

I find it amazing that the very people who are critical of the conversion of the individual are often the ones who, so to speak, give an altar call for *structures* to be converted. Who can be converted, if not the individual? Social structures cannot be converted. They are not mysterious personal forces; they are created by people, and they can only be changed by people. And a preacher must address the people in the audience, for example Grandpa Smith and Grandma Jones, and tell them how *they* can contribute to making the world a fairer place in the coming week, with the help of God and the support of the local church. But this would bring us back to the hard everyday work of church development—and that is precisely what these experts in verbal proclamation want to avoid. If in my sermon I *announce* more justice in the world—so they believe—I have made a major contribution. This approach can be summed up in one word: magic!

The third version of universalism outstrips the others by far in its—supposed—effectiveness. Where in version 1 we at least have to make the

---

17   Cf. p. 29.

effort to *drag* people into the kingdom of God by the sword, forced baptism, or other threats, and in version 2 it is at least necessary that a certain group of people *hear* us when we save the world through our proclamations, in this third version, the problem of church development is shifted entirely to the theologian's study. With the aid of (more or less) ingenious definitions and increasingly universalistic formulations, people are simply *declared* to be Christians. I must admit that I personally find this procedure, which aims to fulfill the great commission without having to bother with the everyday questions of church development, extremely enticing—evangelism can be achieved quite simply from a desk in the study!

All universalistic concepts that are developed on this basis have one thing in common: the dividing line between belief and unbelief is not crossed by *people* in real life—it is crossed with the aid of *theology*. In the minimal form, all (nominal) church members are declared to be Christians.[18] In the next stages, all doubters are declared Christians (because they have understood God more profoundly than those who are sure),[19] or, if the boundaries of culture are crossed, adherents of all religions are declared Christians (because we all believe in the same God).[20] In the final stage, all humans are declared Christians, irrespective of their attitude to Christ, Buddha, or Hare Krishna or whether they are religious or antireligious, church members or anti-church. The ingenuity of some of these theological acrobats is so great that nobody can escape the power of their definitions. What the *cogite intrare* in the Middle Ages could not achieve—to integrate all humans everywhere into the *corpus Christianum*—is now within the grasp of these universalists.

They quote the universal biblical statement, "God so loved the world" to support their position, but they overlook the fact that this verse continues with the specific statement, ". . . that whoever believes in him shall not perish."[21] God's free grace, his generous love really is available to the whole world—to all who believe. "Those who exclude themselves *are*

---

18 Michael Herbst describes this mechanism in the state church as follows: There are, indeed, members who are pleased that there is a church "in the same way as they are pleased that there is a doctor, a judge, and a health insurance scheme. Now there are theologians—not a few, and their numbers are increasing—who tell these church members that they are positively distanced Christians. Behind this monstrous phrase lies a cybernetic policy decision. It is regarded as the freedom of a Christian, achieved by the Reformation, that people can be Christians with no links to the church, no word of God, no sacrament, no prayer, and no witness. The state church lives on justification by grace, which means that those baptized are and remain Christians. The church is glad if they don't resign their church membership. Everything else is not so important. Even those who participate in absolutely nothing and express no faith whatever are Christians, even if only latent ones" (*Herbst: 1986*, p. 98).
19 For example in *Tillich: 1962 a*, p. 14.
20 For example H. R. Schlette (a follower of Karl Rahner), who writes that the religions are the "ordinary way of salvation" but the church is the "extraordinary way of salvation" (*Schlette: 1963*, p. 85).
21 John 3:16.

excluded; those who do not allow themselves to be included *are not* included."[22]

But theological universalists include all—not by evangelistic proclamation which calls people from unbelief to faith, but by changing the definition of what a Christian is. A typical example is the doctrine of universal reconciliation *(apokatastasis panton)*, which excludes the possibility that anyone could be lost. Thus, all decisions we make are illusory decisions, our responsibility is an illusory responsibility, and our freedom is an illusory freedom. In evangelism, people are thus not really saved, they are merely freed from an intellectual misconception. Separation from God is not really overcome, only the erroneous opinion that people are separated from God. Concepts like the "judgment" lose their significance, as judgment, to quote Helmut Thielicke, only "whispers the happy ending in our ear."[23]

The prototype of this sort of theological universalism was created by Paul Tillich, who invented the distinction between the *manifest* and the *latent* church. He wrote, "The existence of Christian humanism outside the Christian church seems to me to make this distinction urgently necessary. It cannot be that all who are alienated from the organized churches and the traditional symbols are regarded as unchurched. My life in such groups for half of my life span showed me how much of the latent church is in them: the boundary experiences of life, the question of transcendence and human limitations, the commitment to justice and love, a hope that is more than utopia, the acceptance of Christian values, a sensitivity for the ideological misuse of Christianity in church and state . . . The latent church is a term of the boundary on which to stand is the fate of countless Protestants in our days."[24]

Elsewhere, Tillich makes it clear that doubters in their doubts give a particular witness that they are standing for truth, and thus are at one with God—and are therefore "justified" in their thoughts. Tillich closes these deliberations with the remarkable sentence, "Thus I was gripped by the paradox that anyone who seriously denies God is, in fact, affirming him."[25] Atheism thus becomes impossible by definition. Tillich can

---

22   *Brunner: 1960 a,* p. 325.
23   *Thielicke: 1965,* p. 193. Heinz Zahrnt correctly points out that this tendency to a doctrine of universal reconciliation that runs through the theology of Karl Barth is merely a symptom of a deeper fault, "its lack of historicity" *(Zahrnt: 1966,* p. 141). "The revelation of God is for Barth no more a thrilling, changing drama between God and man with progress, setbacks, and alterations, with stages, phases, and eras, but merely an 'enlightenment' concerning a process that is long complete . . . There is hardly a theological system in which so much is said about events, happening, and history as in that of Barth, but there is also hardly any theological system in which so little happens, because everything has already happened in eternity" *(Zahrnt: 1966,* p. 143).
24   *Tillich: 1962 c,* p. 48f.
25   *Tillich: 1962 a,* p. 14.

hardly find enough paradoxes to illustrate his discovery: doubting the meaning of life is an expression of life's meaning, the experience of separation from God is an expression of his presence, even protest against God is a hidden demonstration for God.[26]

This procedure aims to show mercy to people who are alienated from God—and I willingly assume that this mercy arises from noble motives. But it has little in common with the mercy we learn from Jesus. When Jesus had pity on the masses, he did not declare them to be Christians—he sent out disciples to bear witness of the gospel and to show his mercy in practical service of love.

At this point I agree with Karl Barth, who accuses Tillich in his "all too generous generalization" of a "far too cheap universalism." When he reads Tillich's works, he sees a wide "faith and revelation steamroller" flattening everything, houses, humans, and animals.[27] In Barth's opinion, it is not permissible to treat revelation in this way. With enough aptitude and inclination for philosophical thought, he regards it as relatively simple to create this sort of synthesis, but he says that this procedure would "harmonize" what, in the real world, is "separate." Thus, Barth's reaction to Tillich's statements is, "What solutions! What perspectives! If only things were like that!"[28] The problem with all these attempts is that theology oversteps the mark. It tries to save people itself, without this salvation needed to *happen* in people's lives.

Danger to the Left: Quietism

The latter version of universalism is, interestingly enough, surprisingly close to the quietism of the spiritualistic paradigm. The interests of representatives of the institutionalistic and the spiritualistic paradigms are different at this point—universalists want to claim all people for the church, spiritualists want to escape any structural commitment to evangelism. But it is plain where these different motivations become allies. Both aim to make evangelism in practical terms superfluous. This is the point where the two hostile paradigms can agree.

It is thus not surprising that, on this issue, the same theologians can be claimed by representatives of both paradigms. One of these ambivalent figures is Paul Tillich. In terms of the formal structure of his thought he seems to me to be the systematic theologian of the 20th century who is closest to the bipolar paradigm presented in this book. However, because his approach is based on abstract ontological premises, he cannot share the personal categories that are fundamental in natural church development. So his theology remains a thought structure from which adherents

---

26 Cf. *Tillich: 1962 a*, p. 14ff; *Tillich: 1952*, p. 45.
27 *Barth: 1962*, p. 226ff.
28 *Barth: 1977*, p. 90.

of both the spiritualistic and the institutionalistic paradigms can quote passages to suit their own positions. It is no accident that Tillich speaks of God in purely abstract, neutral terms: "being itself," "the power of being," "the ground of being." In spite of all formal affinity to the bipolar approach described here, church development as a profoundly *personal* process is hardly imaginable on such a neutristic foundation.

For spiritualists, planned proclamation of the gospel which reaches people and addresses the needs of a particular target group is not a desirable thing. They regard it as far too "external." Within the spiritualistic paradigm, the concept of evangelism has no clear contours. It is not surprising that almost all mystic movements—in all religions—are noticeable for their lack of missionary zeal (with very few exceptions that only prove the rule).

But we can only really speak of quietism when an additional characteristic that is typical of spiritualism is also present—a characteristic that we have already come across in a different context.[29] Whereas the institutionalistic paradigm, as described for the second form of universalism, tends towards a "magic of words," spiritualistic thinking (again, in all religions) has a marked tendency to a "lack of words." "Undoubtedly, the great mystics were silent. They were far too aware of the limitations of language . . . The highest ecstasy is silent, it can find no symbol for its experience."[30]

It is not without reason that "silence" is one of the hallmarks of mysticism, and often this esteem for not talking is combined with the ideal of inactivity. In Christian circles, particularly in the issue of church development and evangelism, this means that we can hardly expect spiritualists to react enthusiastically to plans to reach a whole town or a whole nation with the gospel. For them, such plans have the aura of artificiality and manipulation. They will not necessarily resist such plans, and they may even join in if they value relationships with particular people involved in these projects. But they are not really part of the efforts, struggles, and conflicts that such an endeavor involves.

Spiritualists prefer to retreat to quietness and wait for revival—and this brings us to another key concept of quietist spiritualism: waiting. In some circles, this word seems to be a comprehensive symbol of the contribution that Christians can make to the challenges of our age. So they wait—and sometimes it is hard not to suspect that they may turn out to be *waiting for Godot*.

It seems to me that there is not much more we can say about the contribution of quietist spiritualism to church development.

---

29 P. 120.
30 *Praag: 1990*, p. 107.

The Bipolar Approach

But what is the approach of natural church development in view of these two misconceptions of evangelism?

First, the church growth movement has rightly affirmed the importance of "church-centered" evangelism.[31] This means a form of evangelism which is actively supported by the church,[32] and which has as its aim not an individualistic "decision," but integration into the Christian fellowship.

Second, I find the distinction proposed by Win and Charles Arn between "church growth by proclamation" and "church growth by attraction"[33] helpful. Whereas the majority of publications on the subject of evangelism concentrate on proclamation, in most cases—and most effectively— evangelism actually occurs by attraction. The life of the Christian fellowship and its practical expression of love is very important for evangelism.[34]

Third, our surveys in German-speaking Europe have confirmed the thesis that most people come to faith through personal relationships with friends, relatives, and work colleagues (the so-called *oikos* principle).[35] Interestingly, this happens both in churches that consciously work with the *oikos* principle and in churches that see the emphasis of their evangelism strategy in other areas (such as visitation or preaching). The more a church can utilize the dynamic potential of the *oikos* principle, the greater evangelistic potential it has.

Fourth, the bipolar approach implies a radical break with all coercive methods. This applies even where coercion is used in subtle ways, for example, by rhetoric or manipulative methods. However, those who are quick to call evangelistic methods manipulative should bear in mind that it is not only rhetorical force that manipulates. Boring meetings also

---

31   For more detail, cf. *Arn/Arn: 1982,* pp. 142-159. Cf. also *Wagner: 1986 a,* p. 37. Here, Wagner makes it clear that "church-centered" is the exact opposite of "closed and withdrawn."

32   Johannes Hansen makes a helpful distinction between "permanent" and "contingent" evangelism, and he describes the relationship between the two dimensions of evangelistic ministry as follows: "The emphasis will surely have to be on 'permanent evangelism,' without which 'contingent evangelism' would lose its power and even its meaning. Many prejudices against evangelism surely have their cause in the fact that 'evangelism' constantly occurs in special meetings, whereas the daily life of the church is largely introverted and is hardly able to accept new friends" (*Hansen/Möller: 1980,* p. 43).

33   Cf. *Arn/Nyquist/Arn: 1986,* p. 128ff.

34   This is not an invention of the church growth movement—it applied from the beginning of the history of the church, as is testified by the gentile statement that is reported by Tertullian: "See how these Christians love each other" (Apologeticum 39, 7). This in itself had a great evangelistic attraction.

35   According to our survey of 1,600 active Christians, 76 percent of those asked said that a friend, relative or colleague had had a decisive influence on their decision for Christ and the church.

have a highly manipulative effect—they manipulate people to leave the church!

Fifth, we should distinguish between "discipling" and "perfecting." It is not a symptom of a superficial view of the gospel[36] that evangelism is largely kept free from a discussion of the ethical consequences of the faith. Evangelism aims for a "relationship to a person, namely Jesus Christ, more than the acceptance of a detailed ethical code."[37] This does not mean that spiritual growth (perfecting) is unimportant and that Christians should abstain from ethical or political questions. But no ethical standards must be made into a precondition for conversion, neither explicitly nor implicitly.[38]

Sixth, this approach means that the subjects covered in evangelism must be determined by the interests of the hearers. Many of those who refuse to differentiate between discipling and perfecting unconsciously combine evangelism with the ethical questions that are important to *them*. Lesslie Newbigin rightly stresses that the "virus of legalism" can easily creep into evangelism if the evangelist feels called to "tell the potential Christians exactly what the ethical consequences of their conversion" will be.[39] If an evangelist speaks about ethical issues, they must be issues that are particularly important to the audience, not issues that are important to him or herself.

Seventh, the question of receptivity is of crucial importance for the process of evangelism. Not all people are equally receptive, and not all are receptive at the same time.[40] In church development, it is important to concentrate on those who display the greatest receptivity. To use a metaphor, instead of banging our heads against locked doors (which many Christians believe is implied by the commission to go to all people), we should walk through the doors that are already open.[41] When we have finished that, we can still try to break open the locked doors!

Eighth, we should not overrate the importance of the motivation that makes people come to Christ. The motives that lead people to seek the truth can be very complex and it is often difficult to distinguish between "spiritual" and "egotistic" ones. An interesting study by Jarrell

---

36 This fear is expressed by critics of the church growth movement such as David Bosch, Lesslie Newbigin, Orlando Costas, Robert Evans, and others (cf. *Wagner: 1981*, p. 133ff).

37 *Wagner: 1981*, p. 136.

38 Cf. *Wagner: 1981*, p. 140: "I know of many evangelists who do not insist, as a prerequisite to salvation, that unbelievers agree to tithe their income. But after they become Christians they learn that their new Lord expects them to tithe their income. This is not bothersome to the average Christian. Initial repentance and conversion means turning to Christ as the Lord of Life, and when, over a lifetime of discipleship, the Lord speaks and brings new requirements to their attention, they are cordially accepted."

39 *Newbigin: 1978*, p. 52.

40 Cf. *McGavran: 1980*, p. 259.

41 Cf. Acts 13:51.

Pickett[42] showed that the original motivation that made people come to Christ had next to no influence on their commitment level in their subsequent spiritual lives. How committed a person lives as a Christian largely depends on the care provided by the church *after* conversion, not on the original motivation.

Practical Illustration:
The Quality Characteristic
"Need-Oriented Evangelism"

In our surveys of growing and declining churches, we discovered that the difference in their practice of evangelism depends largely on the question of whether or not they are able to relate their evangelistic activities to the actual needs of those they aim to win. The quality characteristic we deduced from these observations we call "need-oriented evangelism."[43]

The *oikos* principle mentioned above is put into action by the church leadership helping all Christians to recognize their own personal networks of relationships with people who are not Christians (i.e., their "extended family").[44] Instead of making a great effort to contact people they do not know yet, the *oikos* principle suggests that Christians should use the contacts they already have. These are the "bridges" that God has provided.

The number of people that can be identified in this way is the "potential congregation," on which the evangelistic activities of the church concentrate. According to our surveys, the potential congregation is approximately six times as large as the actual number of active Christians. We can assume that many of these people are particularly receptive to the gospel. In the concept of "need-oriented evangelism," care is taken that the service of the church is oriented towards the felt needs of the potential congregation (e.g., help with homework, projects for the unemployed, groups for singles, sexual counseling, housing assistance, and so forth).

The evangelistic ministry of the church becomes particularly dynamic when it is combined with the quality characteristic "gift-oriented ministry" which was described earlier.[45] In this context, the gift of evangelism naturally has a special role to play. We can assume that approximately 10 percent of the active Christians in every church have this gift.

---

42 Cf. *McGavran: 1980*, p. 174. Pickett interviewed 3,947 people and asked about the motives that made them decide to follow Christ.
43 For a more extensive treatment cf. *Schwarz/Schalk: 1998*, pp. 105-115.
44 Cf. *Arn/Arn: 1982*.
45 Cf. p. 186f.

The problem is that most of them do not know it, and even if they know it, they do not have the time to practice it.[46] Normally, they are "tied down" with many other (not unimportant) tasks in the church, usually directed to serve other Christians.

The approach of gift-oriented ministry involves releasing these people to live for their real calling—and to relate the other gifts that the New Testament mentions more directly to evangelistic service. Wherever churches have set out to implement this pattern with a reasonable degree of consistency, the results have been extremely encouraging—and sometimes spectacular.[47]

---

46 I am relatively sure of the 10 percent hypothesis because it has been confirmed from three sources. First, this is the number that C. Peter Wagner gives for the churches in America (cf. *Wagner: 1979*, p. 176f). Second, this is exactly the value we calculated after evaluating more than 2,000 returned feedback sheets from our "Gift Test" (cf. *Schwarz: 1997*). Third, in all seminars I have conducted on the subject in different churches, there were significantly *more* than 10 percent of participants who had the gift of evangelism. The greater proportion in the third category can be explained by the fact that it is in the nature of such seminars that they largely attract Christians who are interested in and gifted for evangelism.

47 For a more extensive treatment of the whole subject, cf. *Schwarz: 1993 a*; *Schwarz/ Berief-Schwarz: 1995*.

Part 3

The Biotic Approach
to Church Growth

*Whereas part 1 of the book described the basic structures of the
institutionalistic, spiritualistic, and bipolar paradigms, and part 2
explained the relevance of the bipolar approach by reference to a
number of contentious doctrinal issues, part 3 now aims to concentrate on the effects that the bipolar paradigm has on practical
work for church development. The central element of what we have
considered up to now is the distinction between the dynamic and
the static poles of the church. We described the dynamic pole with
personal categories, and the static pole with functional ones.
This interdependence of personal and functional elements is the
secret of natural church development. The following pages do not
aim to enlarge on the practice of this strategy—this is done in
other publications—but rather on a number of basic theological
issues which result from what has been said so far, and which are
highly relevant for our practical work.*

1
The New Paradigm

What were described as the spiritualistic and institutionalistic paradigms in the first two parts of this book, I did not first deduce from a study of theological history. Rather, I have observed it in my practical work with churches, and particularly with pastors. I have noticed that there are certain thought patterns which often occur in people who have problems with natural church development. At first I could not make sense of these observations, but then I set out to find the theological roots of these patterns. The results of my search for an explanation of this phenomenon are the content of the first two parts of this book.[1]

Part 3 will now deal with the demonstrable effects of thinking in the wrong (that is, old) paradigms, and above all with the consequences that thinking in the new, bipolar, or biotic paradigm can have on our practical work for church development.

I find fairly often that pastors and churches make use of the practical tools provided by our institute, but attempt to integrate them into their old (i.e., institutionalistic or spiritualistic) paradigm. It is understandable that the results are less than satisfactory. Whereas representatives of the institutionalistic paradigm largely misunderstand these resources in a technocratic way and—in spite of a well-rehearsed litany of denying it—attempt to *make* the church grow, spiritualists tend to pick out those elements that emphasize spirituality and redefine them in a spiritualistic way (which is fairly easy), so that in the end they define "church growth" in the only way that is acceptable to them—as an internal, spiritual growth. This characterization is, of course, oversimplified—in reality, there are no such people as total technocrats or total spiritualists—but it does indicate real tendencies which can be observed in practical work for church development.

---

1   With these remarks, I do not wish to imply that everyone who has problems with natural church development is necessarily influenced by the spiritualistic or institutionalistic paradigm. There are also many other hindrances that have nothing to do with the paradigms described here. The converse, however, is true: everyone whose thinking is dominated by the spiritualistic or institutionalistic paradigm will have problems coming to terms with natural church development.

Even what I have called the new or bipolar paradigm can be studied better in practice than in theological books. I have experienced this paradigm in the form of Christian leaders who harmoniously combine both the personal, spiritual pole and the institutional, organizational pole within their person. It is my observation that leaders of healthy, growing churches are usually able to create a functional relationship between these two elements, which are fundamental for the paradigm of natural church development.

However, many people find it difficult to do so. For example, there are pastors who give personal spirituality and the church as an organism absolute priority. They feel that relationships are immensely important. They expect to experience God's supernatural intervention. They know how to react spontaneously and make the best of each moment. All these things are valuable—and they are important for church development. But if they are taken as absolutes and placed in opposition to the institutional, organizational pole, they are bound to lead into the spiritualistic paradigm.

There are other pastors who give the organizational pole absolute priority. They feel happiest when they can organize things. They have deep analytical insight into the empirical aspects of the church. They confidently draw up plans for church growth. All these things are valuable—and they are important for church development. But if they are taken as absolutes and placed in opposition to the personal, spiritual pole, they are bound to lead into the institutionalistic paradigm.[2]

One of hundreds of examples of pastors who manage to integrate both dimensions in their own personality is the leader of the Basileia Vineyard Fellowship[3] in Berne, Switzerland, Martin Bühlmann. When you are sitting with him, you get the impression that nothing in the world is more important for him than the individual. He says that the entire ministry, both personal and corporate, is built on relationships. He takes much time to form friendships with the members of his leadership team. He places great emphasis on counseling. When he is leading a church service, he is keen that the Holy Spirit should be actively

---

2   Within the bipolar paradigm, then, different personality structures are needed—people who are keen on "order" and people who are keen on "freedom." The transition between the legitimate striving to live in harmony with our (God-given) personality profile and the psychologically unhealthy extremes to the right and left can be defined fairly precisely. It is the point at which a love of order turns into a heteronomic security mentality (which is typical of the institutionalistic paradigm), or the point at which the love of freedom becomes an urge for total autonomy (spiritualistic paradigm). Both of these attempts are, theologically speaking, close to what the Bible calls "sin." The security mentality described is the exact opposite of the nature of faith, and the sinful nature of autonomism is revealed in its emancipation from God's orders.

3   The Basileia Vineyard Fellowship in Berne started as a "lay movement" within the Reformed (state) church, and is now part of the Vineyard churches.

present and able to work in ways that transcend all human planning. And everything must happen with much love.

But this is not all we can say about him. The very same person who is so keen on relationships with individuals can also get enthusiastic about plans and organizational structures. Bühlmann is a sober, calculating strategist. In each of his decisions he rationally considers what the outcome will be. When he thinks through alternative solutions to a problem, a whole sequence of scenarios with consequences for each possible decision goes through his mind.

The characteristic element of people like Martin Bühlmann is that these two poles are not seen as a contradiction. Bühlmann is not a schizophrenic who sometimes plays one role and sometimes the other, and who changes personality whenever he switches roles (although people who regard the two poles as contradictory may perceive it that way). I am not surprised that the church he leads has grown within a relatively short time from 30 to over 1,000 members—although these numbers are only a symbol of something far more important: a quality of spirituality and church life which has an effect far beyond Switzerland.

It is not my intention to concentrate on Martin Bühlmann as a person. I am sure that his personality and his ministry are also liable to include elements that are not so ideal, and not in accordance with the paradigm of natural church development. Nor do I wish to imply that everyone should be like him. I could equally well replace his name with others who illustrate the same principle. My concern is just to show by at least one authentic example that the thought paradigms described in this book are not abstract theological concepts—they have very practical effects.

There are people who place the quest for freedom and autonomy above all—and thus automatically tend towards the spiritualistic paradigm. There are others for whom the longing for security is the highest concern—and thus automatically feel most at home in the thought patterns of the institutionalistic paradigm. It is plain that, if the theological paradigm is reinforced by a corresponding psychological conditioning, it becomes very difficult for the person to change their position. Therefore it is fitting to speak not merely of theological paradigms, but of life paradigms.

The approach proposed here must be careful to avoid a fatal misunderstanding. The concern of the bipolar paradigm—as I indicated in part 1[4]—is the integration of the dynamic and the static poles, a functional relationship between the church as an organization and the church as an organism—and not a mixture of spiritualism and institutionalism!

Regarded from the point of view of church development, such a mixture would be a "fatal dose." There are representatives of the institution-

---

4   Cf. p. 47f.

alistic paradigm who have integrated elements of the spiritualistic paradigm into the practice of their faith, just as there are spiritualists who
display decidedly technocratic tendencies in some areas. The logical inconsistencies that arise from such a mixture then become a starting point
for using paradox thought patterns that have the function of bringing the
theological inconsistencies back into a (assumed) logical coherence.
Since paradox thinking is often regarded as proof of the theological
"depth" of a statement, proponents of a mixture of institutionalism and
spiritualism can state their position self-confidently, just as if everything
were in perfect logical order. Wherever the synthesis of institutionalism
and spiritualism is justified with this form of paradox dialecticism,
church development has a hard time.

I can vividly remember numerous encounters with Christians who
mix spiritualistic and institutionalistic elements in an unholy disorder
(seen from the point of view of my paradigm) in their thinking. One example is a Lutheran pastor who is deeply influenced by sacramentalism
(institutionalistic paradigm), but who seeks his spiritual food in monas-
tic retreats that encourage a strongly dualistic form of devotion (spiritualistic paradigm). He has a tendency to an almost fundamentalist approach to the Bible (institutionalistic paradigm), but sometimes the same
person treats the Bible in a totally eclectic way (spiritualistic paradigm).
In private conversation he makes revolutionary, rebellious comments on
the spiritual state of his church (spiritualistic paradigm), but at the same
time he shows an almost servile mentality of subjection to the leadership
of his denomination (institutionalistic paradigm). His personal lifestyle
is rather ascetic, and he regards this as desirable for all Christians (spiritualistic paradigm), but in the administration of the sacraments he pays
no regard to the faith or moral standards of the recipient, and even justifies this attitude with great passion (institutionalistic paradigm). He re-
charges his spiritual batteries in large charismatic meetings where nobody knows him, and he is happiest when the Holy Spirit acts in ways
that go against all planning and organization (spiritualistic paradigm),
but he is emotionally completely fixed on the liturgically ordered form of
service in which he regards most elements as absolutely mandatory (institutionalistic paradigm).

He has wide theological interests, is well-read, and—not surprisingly—has developed a special love for paradoxes. He never tires of using new Latin and Greek words to describe the mysteries of God and of
his own existence. And it breaks his heart that nobody in his church understands his concerns!

I must add that he is a man of deep faith and an extremely pleasant
person who expects revival from the depths of his heart and is committed to pray for it. However, it cannot surprise us that, in spite of the devoutness of its pastor, his church is making very little progress towards
church growth.

Let me put it plainly. I believe that it is easier to win an ultra-liberal pastor who believes neither in a personal God nor in the claims of Jesus nor in the presence of the Holy Spirit, for Jesus, and then for church development, than to win the above brother in Christ who has known Jesus, the Father and the Holy Spirit for many years, and has long integrated all three into his sacramentalist, spiritualistic, paradoxical life paradigm.

I am convinced of the importance of theological *thinking* in what this book calls a paradigm shift. But it would be naïve to reduce the relevance of this concept to the rational level. There are people whose thinking is admirably functional, but emotionally they are still trapped in the old (spiritualistic or institutionalistic) paradigm. We should not speak of a paradigm shift until the new paradigm is the decisive factor in our whole personality, our feelings, our dreams, our subconscious. The more we live in a new paradigm, the more we notice that we are seeing the world with new eyes. We discover things we have never seen before. We have a completely new attitude to developments we were already aware of. We sense how inadequate our terminology has been. We read the Bible with different eyes. I would even go so far as to say that we experience the same God we already served in a new way.

Such, at least, was the experience of Martin Luther when he had the experience that we today call the Reformation breakthrough, which was a classical example of a paradigm shift.[5] We can learn from Luther that this is not so much a one time experience—his so-called "tower experience" should not be interpreted this way—but that it is rather a long, drawn-out process in which we must not only learn, but also *unlearn* a lot of things. That is what makes paradigm shifts so slow and difficult.

Learning from Creation

The term "paradigm shift" is not a specifically Christian term; it also plays an increasing role in scientific discussion. In the last decades we have seen in all branches of science—especially in physics and biology—that the mechanistic paradigm that has been dominant since the 17th century (which understood our world as a totally determined environment for humans who work like machines) has been called into question. The mechanistic view regarded material as the basis for all existence, and the material world was thought to consist out of a multitude of separate objects which combine to make one complicated whole. Therefore people thought that the best way to understand a complex phenomenon was to separate it into its smallest units and to study each separate unit in isolation. This approach, known as reductionism, is so deep-seated in our western culture that it is often regarded as being *the* methodology of science.

---

5   Cf. p. 55.

The new paradigm which now rebels against the inherited thought pattern in the sciences starts from a different point. It regards the universe as an indivisible, dynamic whole in which the individual parts are related to each other in a multitude of ways. If we want to understand the whole, we must above all study this network of interrelationships. Whereas in earlier times the human organism was explained by analogy with a machine—for example, Descartes compared the nerves with water pipes, the spaces in the brain with storage containers, the muscles with mechanical springs, and so forth[6]—now, the opposite procedure is adopted. Biology is taken as a pattern to learn principles that can be transferred to other areas.

This rediscovery of biology is simply a rediscovery of the phenomenon of "life." Whereas the mechanistic scientist, the technocrat, finds it difficult even to define life, the concept of life has become the key to the new paradigm. Now we discover that the basic principles that are characteristic of the phenomenon of life "appear again and again, from the smallest microscopic dimensions right up to the cosmos itself."[7]

This does not, however, mean that the rediscovered *organic* thought pattern and the *technical* way of thinking are in opposition to each other. The revolutionary element of the emerging scientific paradigm is the fact that the two aspects are interrelated. A model of this bipolar approach can be seen in the way the human brain works. In many experiments it has been demonstrated that the two halves of the brain can be assigned to different functional areas.[8]

The left half of the cerebrum—which controls the *right* half of the body—is normally the thinking, logical, rational, and verbal half. The right half of the cerebrum—which controls the *left* half of the body—is the artistic half; it sees and stores images, remembers melodies, creates poetry. It is the intuitive, creative side. It is interesting to note that in western culture the values and activities associated with the left half of the brain and the *right hand* are assigned a positive value. In most Indo-European languages, the right side is associated with good, just, and virtuous and the left with evil, danger, and suspicion. The word "right" itself means "correct," "fitting," and "just," whereas the Latin word for "left," *sinister*, means something that is evil and threatening. Even the words for the law and for the right hand side are sometimes identical

---

6   It must be said, however, that the mechanical perspective does have a limited justification, as living organisms really do, to some extent, work like machines. But this does not mean that they *are* machines. The mechanical approach only becomes dangerous when it is regarded as a complete explanation of the phenomenon of life.

7   *Vester: 1988*, p. 28.

8   Recent research seems to indicate that the different specializations of the two halves of the brain are preferences rather than absolute distinctions, although the overall concept of the complementarity of the halves of the brain was confirmed. Cf. *Kinsbourne: 1978*.

(e.g., *Recht* in German, *droit* in French, *right* in English). But this preference for the right has caused an imbalance in the psychological make-up
of our society.

The hallmark of the new scientific paradigm that is influenced by
biology is the interrelationship of polarities that are placed opposite each
other. Bipolarity is frequently found in nature, for example in electricity,
in magnetism, and in the sexes. The law of polarity assumes that for every force there must be a counter-force. This is one of the major principles
of the phenomenon of "life."

In figure 16 I have assigned a small selection of polarities that I have
discovered in different areas of science to the concepts "left" and "right."
The parallels to the concepts assigned to the headings *organism* (left) and
organization (right) in our theological paradigm[9] are plain to see.

left	right
organic	organizational
soft	hard
animate	inanimate
biology	technology
intuition	rationality
heart	head
female	male
holistic	analytic
inductive	deductive

Fig. 16: Polarity as a law of life.

One indication of how fruitful this integrational approach is can be seen
in the new scientific discipline of *bionics*[10] (a combination of a biological
and a technical view). This discipline sets out to examine to what extent
biological patterns—that is, the basic principles of life—can be used as
models for technical or social issues.

From a theological point of view, this new respect for nature and its
principles is nothing else than a rediscovery of God's creation. The principles discovered in biology by modern scientists bear—whether the scientists realize it or not—the Creator's signature. This explains why the
two "new" paradigms, in science and in theology, are so similar to each
other.

---

9   Cf. p. 16f.
10   Cf. *Vester: 1988*, pp. 217-233.

Technical and Organic Thinking in Church Development

In the work of our institute, I have noticed that a purely quantitative approach is not adequate to describe the growth dynamics of a church. It is, of course, possible to use graph paper and growth curves to represent the level of church attendance and other quantitative elements, but this gives us no information about the church's quality (unless we assume that a high attendance at church services automatically implies high quality). As remains to be shown,[11] in natural church development we assume that *qualitative* growth in the areas we have called the "eight quality characteristics" will have a positive effect on quantitative growth.

To represent this sort of growth process, I had to look for a form which would integrate both aspects, quality and quantity. In this quest, I found an illustration in Frederic Vester's book *New Horizons of Thinking*[12] helpful as a way of pointing out the integration of organic and technical thinking. Whereas the arrow can be used as a symbol for the linear, deductive methodology of technical thinking, Vester uses the circle to represent the holistic, inductive method of thought that arises from a study of organic life (see below, fig. 17).

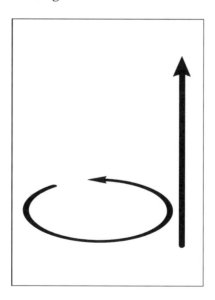

Fig. 17: Circular (organic) thinking and linear (technical) thinking—without any communication between the two.

---

11   Cf. pp. 240f and 248f.
12   *Vester: 1988*, p. 52.

The concern of natural church development is to relate these two aspects to each other. We saw in the first chapter[13] that where the New Testament speaks of the church, it uses both perspectives: technical, architectural imagery (the building up of the church) as well as biological, organic imagery (the growth of the church). As a symbol for a combination of the two approaches, we can use the helix (or spiral) (see below, fig. 18).

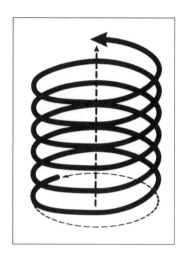

Fig. 18: The helix as a symbol of biotic thinking (a synthesis of the circular and linear perspectives).

These illustrations make it clear how easily such terms as *building up* the church and church *growth* can be misunderstood, in that they can be taken as mutually exclusive alternatives. I therefore agree with Klaus Eickhoff, who suggested the term *church development*,[14] which includes both the organic and the technical aspects.

In order to harness this combination of growth and building, organic and technical thinking in our practical work, we have developed the so-called *church helix* in our institute (fig. 19). The spiral line with the arrow indicates quantitative growth; the shaded area shows how strongly each quality characteristic is developed in the church (qualitative growth).

We can *build up* the quality of the church (eight quality characteristics), but the quantity (church attendance) can only *grow*. It is not in our power to "make" the attendance at church services increase, but it is pos-

---

13   P. 14ff.
14   Cf. *Eickhoff: 1992*, p. 24: "The term *church development* aims to do justice to both concepts, the architectural, constructional image on the one hand and the organic on the other. The church is better compared with a garden than a building site."

sible to take practical action to improve the quality of the church in the eight areas (e.g., by seminars, organizational measures, working materials, prayer times, and so forth).

Fig. 19: The integration of qualitative and quantitative elements in the church helix.

Technocratic or Biotic Functionality?

Both "new" paradigms—in theology and in science—have a common enemy: technocracy. The fact that adherents of both new paradigms concentrate their arguments on what we have called the "danger to the right" does not imply that the "danger to the left" is less problematic. The reason is rather that our western society, ecclesiastical and secular, has a strong tendency to the "right." Thus it is sensible to criticize particularly what we have called the institutionalistic paradigm, and what in science is called technocracy.

But what takes the place of technocracy? Within the new scientific paradigm, the concept of *cybernetics*—which originally came from theology—has acquired a central importance. It represents the conscious attempt (at least in bio-cybernetics) to be "oriented towards the systemic coherence, the functioning, and the survival guidelines of nature."[15] In this way, scientists make use of principles that are agreed to be many times more effective than anything created by humanity. The scientist can only observe with surprise the fact that these principles are immensely effective. The Christian, however, knows the reason why they

15   *Vester: 1988,* p. 1.

are so effective: they can be traced back to the handiwork of God, the creator.

In order to describe the cybernetic approach, different terminology is used by different scientists: systemic, holistic, ecological, autopoietic, and so forth. Whenever I use the term *biotic* in natural church development, I mean it as a shorthand for this integrated way of thinking.

This approach gives a deeper meaning to what we have called functionality. In principle, we could interpret this word in a purely technocratic way—by doing what we ourselves regard as useful. However, a technocratic interpretation of functionality is the exact opposite of what I mean by the term. Functionality in the sense proposed in this book means following the principles that God gave to his creation. This is based on the insight that we humans are not able to gain a complete picture of the complex effects that a specific decision has on a whole range of areas. What may seem to us to be functional can, in the long term, turn out to be decidedly counterproductive, and thus not functional at all. But when we follow God's principles, we know from the outset that the long term effects are in keeping with his will. Therefore I like to speak of biotic or cybernetic functionality—functionality in accordance with the *kybernetes*, God himself.

Perhaps a practical illustration will help to explain the difference between technocratic and biotic functionality. I will deliberately use an example from an area remote from church life—zoology—and only afterwards will I apply the principle to the life of Christian churches and their development.

Frederic Vester reports about attempts to save a herd of elephants threatened with extinction.[16] A nature protection area is created to preserve the population level of the elephants. The desired result is actually achieved. The elephant population, normally kept at a constant level by predators and disease, actually increases unhindered within the protection area. The available vegetation is, for a time, sufficient for all the elephants. But the more the herd increases, the more the vegetation is reduced by grazing. As soon as a critical level of the elephant population is exceeded, the point is quickly reached at which the last acacia tree has been grazed. Now, conditions change abruptly. It is not just the population increase that stops: the whole herd suddenly dies! The very measure that was designed to protect the elephants—and in the short term was successful—led in the medium term to the extinction of the herd.

Similar phenomena can be observed in a wide range of areas. Many artificial measures adopted in biological or social systems lead, in the medium or long term, to the exact opposite of what was originally intended—for example the acquired resistance of insects and bacteria to pesticides and antibiotics or, on the macroscopic level, the energy crisis. We look for solutions that are insufficient—for example, state subsidies that

16   *Vester: 1988,* p. 70.

merely shore up obsolete economic enterprises, thus eventually causing whole regions or branches of business to collapse all the more violently.

The same mistake we saw in the example of the "protected" herd of elephants—the "rescue action" that is not in keeping with natural laws—happens in thousands of cases in our churches. In the short term, our efforts may lead to the desired results, but the long term results for the growth of the church are found to be detrimental.

In part 2 of this book we encountered many illustrations of the technocratic, and therefore counterproductive, mechanism that lies behind the institutionalistic misconception. The structure was always the same. An action that was intended to safeguard the church as an organism led—at least in extreme cases—to its destruction. The similarity with the example of the "protected" herd of elephants is not an accident—it is just another expression of the same thought pattern. Because the technocratic measures in both cases do not adhere to the biotic principles of the system, there is, in the short term, an *apparent* success, but in the end, the result is the very opposite of what was intended. The common element in such measures is that they concentrate on one problem in isolation—which is typical of technocratic thinking—rather than taking into account its biotic network of interrelationships with other areas.

"The Simpler, the More Accurate"

Within the mechanistic paradigm, the rule of reductionism is applied: the more exact the information about the details is, the better the overall system can be understood. The object of investigation is thus increasingly split up, and people believe that this enables them to understand the system better. There are church researchers who can fall into an almost ecstatic desire to isolate hundreds of subtly differentiated factors, and they never tire of pointing out that each one has a whole range of exceptions.

For the biotic approach, the exact opposite applies. The important thing is not the precise information about every detail, but rather a grasp—however vague—of the whole picture and its underlying principles. Frederic Vester writes that the heart of the biotic—he calls it: cybernetic—approach lies "in the application and observation of simple qualitative rules and basic principles and in the evaluation of the dynamics of the system on the basis of these principles. From a certain degree of interrelationships onwards, the amount of detail in a model has no importance. Therefore, the simpler such a model is, the more rudimentary it is, the truer it will be."[17]

For responsible church growth planning it is not necessary to know all the details. Too much information could even be counterproductive, as it could easily distract us from what is really important: that we allow

17 *Vester: 1988*, p. 78.

ourselves to be guided by a few quite simple and very practical basic biotic principles.

When our institute carries out an analysis of a church, we ask a lot of specific questions about innumerable details in the church. This is not in order to give detailed, pre-programmed instructions for each area of the church, but rather to find out which two or three areas represent the church's main problems. Our aim, therefore, is not to record as many details as possible as accurately as possible, but rather to gain a deliberately rough—and *therefore* accurate—picture of the whole. Planning always proceeds from the overall picture to the specifics. An analysis of the structural principles that govern the way the details are interrelated and interdependent is more important than the details themselves.

Biotic Principles and Biblical Wisdom

Although the word *interdependence*—which is a key term in the new scientific paradigm as well as in natural church development[18]—is not a biblical term, the underlying content is closely related to what the Bible calls "wisdom." Examining a phenomenon not in isolation, but rather in its complex interrelationships, and not forgetting the order that God, the creator, has revealed to us—that is the essence of the biblical concept of wisdom.

It is characteristic of the Old Testament wisdom writings[19] that they do not deal with an explicitly "religious" sphere. "There is everyday life, involving paid employment, decisions to be made without God's commandments dictating every step, human relationships with wives, children and friends, behavior towards superiors and subordinates."[20] The "wise" person in the Old Testament sense is not a "philosopher or speculative theoretician" reflecting about God and humanity. "In all the refinement of creative formulations in the wise sayings and songs, wisdom remains eminently practical and concerned with the art of living."[21] Walter Zimmerli correctly observed that the Old Testament is "an unashamedly human book" in that it assigns such writings, which deal largely with the "everyday aspects of human life," an "inalienable right to belong to the canon."[22]

---

18   Cf. pp. 233-251.
19   They include Proverbs, Ecclesiastes, and in a wider sense the Book of Job and a
      number of psalms (e.g., Psalms 37 and 73).
20   *Zimmerli: 1982*, p. 136.
21   Ibid. p. 92. Cf. also Gerhard von Rad: "Like all nations, Israel thought of 'wisdom' as
      an eminently practical knowledge of the laws of life and the world that is based on
      experience. The Hebrew word translated as 'wise' and 'wisdom' refers to the experi-
      ence and specialist knowledge of, for example, a boatman, a metal ore worker, a
      political adviser, and so forth" *(Rad: 1982, p. 430f).*
22   *Zimmerli: 1982*, p. 136f.

The world the wise person considers is a world of hidden order. "For all God's authority over the world, as a world of justice it obeys Yahweh's God-ordained order (which does not function automatically, but is kept to by Yahweh himself)."[23] But the Old Testament also says that wisdom can become a temptation. There is a danger that the wise person who deals with wisdom (Gerhard von Rad impressively describes the *eros* of this relationship)[24] "believes to possess the order of the world."[25] It is no accident that Jeremiah 9:23 exhorts: "Let not the wise man boast of his wisdom or the strong man boast of his strength." Just as political and military strength can lead to the temptation to seek an ungodly security,[26] the wise person is easily tempted to think that "by means of his or her knowledge of life and the world, he or she is assured of life and the world."[27]

It is characteristic of the Old Testament concept of wisdom that it moves "within the horizon of creation."[28] The teaching on wisdom emphasizes that God made creation "by wisdom."[29] This is the same concept as in the statement in Genesis 1 that God's work was good. "The heavens declare the glory of God," we read in Psalm 19:1. Such statements, which use the order of the world to point to the supernatural author of this order, should not be interpreted in the sense of a "proof of God's existence,"[30] but they are certainly reminders that God's creation shows the handwriting of the Creator—even though it can be interpreted in different ways, and even misconstrued.

This leads us to a phenomenon which has special significance in our context. The dynamics that God implanted in his creation can be studied both by believers and by unbelievers. When an unbeliever discovers these dynamics, this does not make his or her observations wrong—they remain dynamics created by God. I point out this rather obvious fact because it has a highly theological relevance to the efforts of the church growth movement (which are sometimes heavily criticized) to learn from other disciplines, such as biology, sociology, economics, and so forth.

It is a striking fact about the wisdom literature in the Old Testament that it is international in a way that no other Old Testament writings are, and that a wealth of related concepts have been discovered in the writings

---

23 *Zimmerli: 1982*, p. 140.
24 *Rad: 1970.*
25 *Zimmerli: 1982*, p. 141.
26 Cf. Isaiah 28:15.
27 *Zimmerli: 1982*, p. 141; the Book of Ecclesiastes has a similar skeptical, thoughtful attitude to any "wisdom euphoria."
28 Ibid. p. 31.
29 Cf. Proverbs 3:19: "By wisdom the Lord laid the earth's foundations, by understanding he set the heavens in place."
30 Cf. the Thomasian proof *ex gubernatione rerum*, which is generally known as the *teleological* proof of God, but which could equally be called a *cybernetic* proof.

of countries around Israel.[31] Even in Israel's estimation of its own role in the world, wisdom was "something international and interreligious."[32] First Kings 4:30 quite openly states that there was wisdom outside Israel, for example in Egypt and among the "men of the East." The close links between Israel and the wisdom of Egypt is seen not only in Solomon's intermarriage with the Egyptian royal family; it can also be clearly demonstrated by a study of Proverbs 22:17–23:12.[33] Here, an excerpt from the Egyptian teaching of Amenemope[34] is given with slight (but important) revisions. The additions made by the editor of Proverbs give us insight into the way Old Testament wisdom sees itself.

It is clear from the outset that the faith of the Old Testament sees a different supernatural power behind the underlying order of the world than the faith of Egypt.[35] The Old Testament faith knows, "in the soberly perceived order of daily life, only One who could be addressed by its petitions and its praise, Yahweh ... When it entered the land, Israel stepped into a world in which high gods were praised as creators of the world and the glory of their creation was extolled. It ... entered this world with the provocative creed on its lips, 'Yahweh is his name.' Within this creed, it largely expressed its praise of creation with words taken over from the outside world. But these words were understood in relation to the One, Yahweh, who alone is to be praised, and besides whom there is none other. This was not just a formal, philosophical occurrence. It was the basis on which Israel understood the whole of creation, a realm which it entered with its faith in Yahweh and in which it assigned everything it discovered to him. This, then, was the context in which wisdom was developed, and Israel itself ... was surely conscious of its international character."[36]

On this basis, Egyptian wisdom literature could be assimilated. The natural observation of the diligence of the ant[37] and the miracle of bird flight[38] could be quoted in both contexts. But even observations of human life, for example, that laziness brings poverty,[39] that a hot temper

---

31 Cf. *Zimmerli: 1982*, p. 136.
32 *Rad: 1982*, p. 442.
33 On the subject of this section, cf. *Zimmerli: 1982*, p. 136f.
34 Cf. *Römheld: 1989*.
35 In more recent studies of Egyptian "wisdom," the concept of *Maat* has been shown to be especially significant. *Maat*—comparable in its function with the Persian/Indian sun God *Mithra*—is a sort of religious symbol of the "world order." It includes the order of the cosmos as well as the order of human life. But *Maat* is not only regarded as a concept, but also as a divine being. When a person subjects his or her life to *Maat in* the right way, he/she places his/her life within the right order, and thus becomes successful. Therefore, what seems to be a secular order of life in Egyptian teaching actually has a deeply religious background. Cf. *Zimmerli: 1982*, p. 137.
36 *Zimmerli: 1982*, p. 138f.
37 Proverbs 30:25.
38 Proverbs 30:19.
39 Proverbs 10:4.

causes arguments,[40] and that a foolish son brings grief to his parents[41] could be assimilated unaltered into the sayings of the Old Testament.

In the same way, the excerpt from the Egyptian teachings of Amenemope mentioned above was included in the collection of Old Testament proverbs which was published in the name of Solomon. Here, too, we cannot overlook the fact that the creed "Yahweh is his name" has become an integral part of the teaching. Even in the introduction, the Old Testament editor added a comment about the aim of the wisdom teachings that is not to be found in the Egyptian original: "So that your trust may be in the Lord, I teach you today."[42] Where the Amenemope text forbids the changing of boundaries by an appeal to the moon god, Proverbs 23:11 justifies the same commandment with the words, "for their Defender is strong; he will take up their case against you." Thus, the creed "Yahweh is his name" is repeatedly combined with the (international) wisdom sayings without the need to change any of the individual sayings, which are included in the Old Testament as they are in the Egyptian version.

The process adopted here, which we can get a complete picture of by comparison with a fully preserved non-biblical source text, seems to me to be characteristic of the Old Testament concept of wisdom. The insights of international wisdom are not rejected just because somebody else discovered them first; rather, they are traced back to their true "author," to Yahweh himself, and thus they can be instrumentalized for his purposes.

This concept arises as early as the first page of the Bible, the creation text in Genesis 1. The passionate "concern to demythologize the cosmic elements"[43] is mainly apparent in the way the heavenly bodies that were so revered in the Babylonian empire are, so to speak, strung up like lanterns in the hand of the divine Creator and given a functional meaning— simply to give light.[44] The words "sun" and "moon," which were evidently mythically loaded, are not even mentioned in the text; "in a striking instrumentalization of these heavenly powers," the text merely speaks of the greater and the lesser light.[45]

The way in which the Bible traces supposed (or real) supernatural powers back to God, and at the same time instrumentalizes them in the hand of the Creator and robs them of their pagan religious qualities, seems to me to be a prime example of how we, as Christians, should treat the insights we find outside the realm of Christianity. It is a fact that the biotic principles have not only been recognized by Christians, and

---

40 Proverbs 15:18.
41 Proverbs 10:1.
42 Proverbs 22:19.
43 *Zimmerli: 1982*, p. 26.
44 Cf. *Zimmerli: 1982*, p. 27: "Thus, an assertion of the governing function of the stars is not avoided. But this government has no authority over conscience, it merely 'governs the day and the night,' and its governing function is to 'separate the light from the darkness.'"
45 *Zimmerli: 1982*, p. 26.

that it is not only serious scientists that talk increasingly about these dynamics—but that many religious or semi-religious movements, such as New Age, also work with similar insights, and sometimes quite successfully.

Many Christians who notice this react as follows: because the New Age movement uses these concepts (and therefore, presumably, invented them), they are pagan and therefore evil. Thus we must set ourselves apart from them, and consequently we must also set ourselves apart from Christians who work with similar concepts. Proponents of this approach do not seem to realize that, in the last analysis, they are actually setting themselves apart from something that God himself has given us in his wisdom.

I give so much space to these arguments because I have frequently heard them from fellow Christians. I suspect that some of the principles proposed in this book seem questionable to them because some New Age books may contain similar thoughts. Knowing that this is a sensitive area in Christian circles, I would like to make five comments:

First, I did not learn the principles of natural church development from the New Age movement (nor from secular scientists), but rather from my observations and surveys in churches. It was only afterwards that I discovered parallels in other areas, and thus "borrowed" the terminology of secular cybernetics and introduced it into the discussion of church growth (e.g., the principles of symbiosis, energy transformation, and so forth). However, the fact that my insights came in this order is a pure accident. It could have been the other way around—I could have discovered these concepts by secular study or in a New Age book— which would not have affected their theological justification.

Second, as we have seen, in the Bible wisdom teaching is international and interreligious. Christians and non-Christians find the same handwriting of God when they study his ordinances. This phenomenon is an integral part of God's creation. Thus there is no reason why we should not learn from non-Christians. They may have discovered something that we Christians would have discovered long ago if we had not been hampered by our ghetto mentality. The New Testament principle, "Test everything, hold on to the good"[46] shows us the way we should deal with such knowledge.

Third, the attempt to instrumentalize the insights of non-Christians for the cause of Jesus is not without its dangers. (On the other hand, constantly chasing our own tails is also extremely dangerous, and these dangers are often underestimated.) Christians with insufficient discernment who study non-Christian philosophies that have a pagan-religious background can easily be drawn into the sphere of influence of these religious teachings.

---

46   1 Thessalonians 5:21.

Fourth, we must therefore consider how best to face these dangers. I do not consider it a satisfactory answer if we react to these real dangers by rejecting all wisdom spoken by unbelievers or adherents of other religions, simply because they are not Christians. Those who take this approach can no longer pray for the sick (so that they will not be confused with pagan "spirit healers"), and strictly speaking, they should not even engage in missions (because "missions" is becoming increasingly a key-term of non-Christian movements).[47] But that is not the path the Bible shows us. The best protection against the corruption of the church seems to me to learn to distinguish between the insights themselves and their religious background.

Fifth, it is clear that this solution requires a certain amount of discernment. It is a major problem that this sort of discernment is not cultivated in the context of the spiritualistic and institutionalistic paradigms with their "either-or" structure. Especially the institutionalistic thought pattern, with its inability to distinguish between the bipolar paradigm and the spiritualistic heresy, has a fateful effect at this point. How can people learn to discern between different concepts if they are deliberately kept in ignorance, blinded by a simplistic scheme of black and white? I am convinced that our ability to discern will grow in direct proportion to the extent to which we cultivate the discerning, critical approach inherent in the bipolar paradigm.

There is a very clear difference between the way the New Age movement deals with biotic principles and the way the Christian faith deals with them. For New Age, these principles are divine beings (the *tao*, *wakan-tanka*, the *original principle*, the *cosmic spirit*,[48] and so forth), whereas for the Christian they are instruments that God has given us. They are not divine beings, they are created by God. The error of New Age is to worship "created things rather than the Creator";[49] biblical faith on the other hand aims to "declare the glory of God"[50] in his creation (and even in the biotic principles contained in it).

The difference between New Age and the Christian faith can be aptly illustrated by a comparison between lyrics from two songs. One is a verse from Mozart's music for the drama "Thamos, King of Egypt"; the other is from the (deservedly more famous) "sun song" by Francis of Assisi.

---

47 Cf. for example Gerd Gerken, who is regarded as a "trend guru" for management theory as influenced by New Age: "The meta-trend of management is developing in the following direction: 'Companies are becoming faith fellowships.' The trend is away from the command principle to missions and passion" *(Gerken: 1990,* p. 79.).

48 For example, Fritjof Capra, who is an international leader of the New Age movement, thinks it is "not too far-fetched" to assume that all structures, "from sub-atomic particles to the galaxies, from bacteria to humanity" are "manifestations of the self-organizing dynamism of the universe which we . . . have identified with the cosmic Spirit" *(Capra: 1988,* p. 331).

49 Romans 1:25.

50 Psalm 19:1.

Mozart's song addresses the sun directly, and even worships it:

> *Oh sun, the night, enemy of light, flee from you!*
> *Egypt now brings you new sacrifices . . .*
> *Highest Godhood, mild sun,*
> *Here Egypt's devout pleading!*
> *Protect the King's new crown,*
> *May it always be upright!* [51]

Francis also speaks of the sun, and he gets enthusiastic about it. But his worship is not addressed to the sun, but to the Lord:

> *Be praised, my Lord,*
> *With all your creatures,*
> *Especially with Brother Sun*
> *Who brings the day and lights our way;*
> *He is fair and shining in his glory:*
> *Oh highest one, the sun is a parable of you.*[52]

The text used by Mozart is basically along the same lines as what we now call New Age—the sun is God—whereas the words of Francis show how we should treat this so-called god. We should not turn our eyes away in indignation, or even call it "satanic." Instead, we should lift up our eyes, and praise the glory of the Lord for the splendor of the sun.

After we Christians have already let them steal our rainbow—we should not allow them to steal the sun as well.

---

51   Thamos, King in Egypt, KV 345.
52   Quoted in *Fietz/Schwarz: 1984*, p. 3.

2
Natural Church Development

Natural (or biotic) church development is an attempt to study nature, and thus God's creation, to discover principles that are applicable far beyond the realm of biology. This appeal to the biological world, the "largest and most successful organizational system we know,"[1] involves the use of *analogy*[2] as a method of perception. This analogy is not concentrated on the external appearances; rather it attempts to "press on to the underlying basic principles."[3] Frederic Vester, who has tried to harness the bio-cybernetic approach to enable us to understand the functional mechanisms of society as a whole, writes: "Even more productive than the study of biological structures and functions is what we can learn from the organization of biological processes, from the specific dynamics of their development and decomposition, their growth, their communication, and their self-regulation."[4]

---

1   *Vester: 1988*, p. 132f. Frederic Vester characterizes the nature of the bio-cybernetic approach, which is also our frame of reference, as follows: "By cybernetics (from the Greek *kybernetes*, helmsman) we mean the recognition, control, and self-regulation of interlinking, networked processes with a minimum expenditure of energy. Although this term has proved fruitful for new thought patterns, it has been devalued in many ways and often confused with control engineering and computer systems (although nothing is less cybernetic than the data processing mechanisms of a computer). Where do the cybernetic principles have their true origin? There is no doubt that it is in the area of living organisms where we can study them *in natura*; and not, as is so often assumed, in the world of computers" (*Vester: 1988*, p. 53). However, in order to avoid misunderstandings, in natural church development we use the term "biotic" instead of "cybernetic." Cf. p. 224.
2   This sort of analogy is especially to be found in the Old Testament wisdom literature. The wisdom teachers "discover analogies between processes in nature and processes in human life. These sayings contain comparisons of completely different areas, in which analogous phenomena occur, which can therefore be combined. The organizing mind attempts to group comparable phenomena together" (*Rad: 1982*, p. 437).
3   *Vester: 1988*, p. 48.
4   Ibid. p. 227. It is no exaggeration when Vester writes: "We can therefore confidently predict that cybernetic thinking, thinking in regulatory cycles and networked feedback systems, introduced into science by Norbert Wiener, will open up a similar sort of new era as was introduced in the 16th century by Copernicus with the fundamental change in mankind's understanding of its own position in the universe" (*Vester: 1988*,

However, it would be an oversimplification to regard the reference to biology (i.e., the principles of living organisms) in natural church development merely as a "transfer" of the secular concept of cybernetics to the sphere of the church. The biological approach is inherent in the Bible. It is noticeable how frequently analogies from nature are used to describe the principles of the kingdom of God. In commentaries on the New Testament parables it is sometimes suggested that Jesus used these analogies because his hearers lived in an agricultural society and were thus particularly "receptive" to such analogies. But I feel that this is only a partial explanation. If Jesus were among us today, he would hardly replace these parables from nature with those from the world of computers (e.g., "The kingdom of God is like a computer program: the output depends on your input"). Such (technocratic) analogies would be misleading, even if it were true that people are more "receptive" to this sort of imagery today. When the New Testament refers to organic dynamics, this is far more than metaphors that could be substituted by other imagery—rather, it speaks about *real principles* that operate in the world of nature as well as in the kingdom of God.[5]

A fine example of this approach taken by Jesus is found in Matthew 6:28: "See how the lilies of the field grow." The word "see," however, does not fully cover the implications of the Greek word *katamathete*; it omits an aspect that is important in our context. The word implies more than just seeing or looking; it is "the intensive form of *manthano* in the meaning of precise examination, observation, comprehension, consideration."[6] Even the word *manthano* has the basic meaning of "setting your mind to something," "appropriating something mentally so that it has a certain effect,"[7] a meaning that is heightened by the prefix *kata*. The sense here, then, is not mere looking, but "conscious examination and study."[8]

Taking this understanding into account, the verse quoted does not speak about "meditative observation."[9] Jesus is referring "to the order in nature that bears witness to the abundance of options and resources available to the Creator."[10] We are not asked to concentrate on the lilies themselves, but rather on their *growth mechanisms* ("how the lilies . . . grow").

---

p. 92). It seems to me that what Vester here puts into words for science applies by analogy to ecclesiology—understood as the study of the principles that determine the life and growth of *ekklesia*.

5   Here, following on from what was said on pages 226-230 about Old Testament wisdom, we must remind ourselves that wisdom is also a positive concept in the New Testament (cf. Matt. 11:19; Luke 11:49; 21:15; Acts 6:3; Rom. 11:33; 1 Cor. 1:24, 30; Col. 3:16). Above all we must point out the function of Jesus as a "wisdom teacher" (cf. *Bultmann: 1979*, p. 73ff).

6   *Rengstorf: 1942*, p. 416.

7   Ibid. p. 393.

8   Ibid. p. 416.

9   Ibid. p. 417.

10   Ibid.

We are to study and examine them, to meditate on them, and take our direction from them. All these aspects are included in the imperative verb form *katamathete*, and we are told that we need to do so in order to understand the principles of the kingdom of God. This approach describes exactly the procedure of natural church development.

God Is the Helmsman

Our concern in natural church development is not to try to be the *kybernetes*, the helmsman, and to develop the church with our own wisdom and in our own strength. Our theological starting point is to allow God to be the *kybernetes*, and to let him show us the "rules of the game." Nature teaches us what disastrous consequences it has if a technocrat plays *kybernetes*,[11] and the same applies to the church. Nothing can do more to liberate us from such a "can-do" mentality than the recommendation (or command) of Jesus to learn from biological processes.[12] In the "parable of the seed that grows by itself," we read: "The kingdom of God is like a man who casts seed upon the ground; and goes to bed at night and gets up by day, and the seed sprouts up and grows—how, he himself does not know. The earth produces crops *by itself*; first the blade, then the head, and then the mature grain in the head. But when the crop permits, he immediately puts in the sickle, because the harvest has come."[13]

According to Rainer Stuhlmann, the word *automate* which is translated "by itself" is "the key . . . to understanding the parable."[14] It would not be consistent with Hebrew thought to interpret *automate* as referring to the intristic self-regulation of nature. In the context of the parable, the word means "with no apparent cause," and the underlying thought is "performed by God," for the Jews saw "growth as a miracle from God."[15] In his commentary on this passage, Walter Grundmann writes: "We cannot force it [the kingdom of God] to come about, neither by an action of repentance and law fulfillment, as the Pharisees thought, nor by bold violence, as the Zealots dreamed,"[16] nor, we could add, by sacramentalist formulas or technocratic methodology.

---

11 Frederic Vester describes the illusion behind technocratic thinking as follows: "It would be easy to think that nothing is easier than to enter all the factors in our biosphere, including human behavior and our economic and industrial resources, into a supercomputer so that we find out what buttons to turn to play God a bit, to play at being the helmsman, the *kybernetes*, who will release us from the treadmill of the progressive destruction of our environment and our own race. But we do not even know a fraction of the contributing factors, let alone the way these factors are actually interrelated" *(Vester: 1988,* p. 72).
12 For more detail, see pp. 254-257.
13 Mark 4:26-29; my italics.
14 *Stuhlmann: 1972/1973,* p. 153.
15 *Grundmann: 1977,* p. 131.
16 Ibid.

By contrast with the Hebrew contemporaries of Jesus, modern science regards this *automate* as a growth mechanism that can be explained immanently, that is, on the basis of the inherent laws of nature.[17] The discovery of such automatisms in all areas of life—ecology, economy, medicine, education, and so forth—is a key to understanding secular cybernetics. Adherents of cybernetics believe that if they discover such growth automatisms (also known as self-organization or self-regulation) and then organize their work to be in harmony with them, they will be able to achieve maximum results with a minimum of effort.[18] Instead of adding new energy from outside, the existing energy is utilized. One illustration is so-called "gentle" or "cybernetic" medicine. Instead of using technical or chemical resources to replace the self-healing functions of the body, this approach primarily uses resources to support the body's self-healing powers.[19] Similar illustrations could be given for all areas of life, including management.[20]

At this point, however, we must ask the theological question of what relationship there is between the *automatisms* in modern secular cybernetics and the *automate* in the parable of the seed (and everything else we learn in the Bible about God's order of creation). My answer is as follows: Whereas the secular scientist understands these mechanism in a purely immanent way (and this is certainly one possible interpretation), the

17 This (immanent) approach is, however, not shared by scientists who give the laws of life a (pseudo-)religious significance (e.g., New Age) by identifying them with whatever they, within their own thought system, regard as "God."

18 In various seminars on natural church development, I have heard it said that this approach is akin to the "free market economy" glorified by capitalism, the proponents of which also assume that everything works best when the "self-regulating forces" of the market are interfered with as little as possible. The following comment must, however, be made: it is certainly right that capitalism has discovered many self-regulating forces and displayed an ability to use them. That is the reason why it is far superior to any form of central command economy. However, what we today see happening in capitalism can be explained far better with *technocratic* categories than with *biotic* ones. This has to do with the fact that the aim of many capitalists—the maximization of profits at any cost, even against the laws of nature—is absolutely unbiotic. Whereas the short-term consequences of wrong behavior (i.e., behavior not in harmony with nature) can provide a feedback and therefore regulate themselves (e.g., a society that produces too much waste is in danger of suffocating in its own refuse, so it automatically looks for solutions), this does not apply to the long-term consequences (e.g. the environmental damage that will only be felt in coming generations). As the biotic feedback to the people causing the problem does not occur, the state must intervene at this point. The "free market" on its own does not regulate such damage. But this state intervention should happen in such a way that, as far as possible, it supports society's self-healing powers rather than being a substitute for them, and thus weakening or even destroying them.

19 Cf. the comments made by Frederic Vester on "self-regulating medicine" or "cybernetic medicine" (*Vester: 1988*, p. 197f).

20 Cf. Gerd Gerken: "Business enterprises are fit for turbulence when they are organized in a largely self-organizing way. The central question of the future is: How do we organize self-organization?" (*Gerken: 1990*, p. 105).

Christian knows that behind this order is none other than God the creator himself.

Scientific knowledge has progressed far since the days of Jesus' contemporaries, but the theological *interpretation* of what the scientists discover can still be the same as in the days of the New Testament. Behind the cybernetic mechanisms—and behind the whole of the created order —we detect the Creator's handwriting. The fact that we can *explain* these mechanisms very well today only detracts from their divine nature in the eyes of those who see God's actions exclusively in those phenomena that contradict natural laws (which are, in fact, his created order!). This approach would lead us to regard God as the "God of the gaps": what we cannot (yet) explain scientifically is assigned to God, whereas the things we can explain are removed from his sphere of influence. Where Friedrich Nietzsche proclaimed the death of *this* (concept of) God, we must agree with him. [21] Whether a particular phenomenon can be explained scientifically tells us a lot about the quality of science, but nothing at all about whether God's action lies behind this phenomenon or not. We will return to this point in the section on "church development and science."[22]

The starting point of natural church development—similar to that of secular cybernetics—is the quest to discover and apply growth automatisms in the work of the church. Instead of trying to "make" the church grow in our own strength (that is, with great effort), we prefer to utilize the growth automatisms which God's word shows us and which we find confirmed by our experience. The further church growth research progresses, the more we will be able to explain these mechanisms. However, this will not stop us from seeing God's hand in them and praising him for them!

Some theologians stop thinking (or drift into completely foggy thoughts) as soon as they have spoken of what God alone can do for church growth. For me, this is the point where things start to get exciting. Releasing God's growth automatisms in the church does not mean that we sit back and do nothing. As will be explained more fully in the next chapter, our approach involves a very specific distribution of roles with regard to what we humans can (and should) do and what God alone can do. Because natural church development is designed as a guide for humans (and not for God!), I have, of course, concentrated on the things that God wants *us* to do.

---

21 Cf. *Nietzsche: 1964*, p. 98: "Into every gap they had placed their madness, their stop-gap that they called God." But the fact that, in place of God, Nietzsche placed the *superman* ("All Gods are dead, now we want the superman to live") is an entirely different matter (Ibid. p. 84).

22 Cf. p. 257ff.

What Is a Strategy?

To be able to see clearly what natural church development is, it is important to understand the distinctions among five categories: testimonies, models, principles, programs, and strategies. These concepts are often confused and sometimes used synonymously, so I will explain briefly how they are used in the context of this book.

- *Testimonies* are here taken to be relatively unstructured accounts of personal experiences a person has had with God. It is typical of such testimonies that they emphasize elements that do not fit into the principle-oriented approach. They are thought to be more "edifying" if they show how God has again set aside all principles.[23] This category also includes the "edifying" testimonies of growing churches, of which there are a considerable number today. The more those giving the testimony wish to glorify God, the less they describe the principles that have led to growth. As a result, these testimonies normally cannot be transferred to any other situation. They have only one aim in mind: to show that God is working in our lives and our church.

- The term *model*, on the other hand, does imply the concept of transfer to other situations. People describe their experiences in a way that makes it easy for others to discover a certain underlying pattern. When a model is being presented, the intention—by contrast with a mere testimony—is to encourage others to imitate the experience. But this imitation is directed not so much to the underlying principles, but very clearly to the church which serves as a model. This is based on the recognition that the best way to understand the principles behind a growing church is often to start by imitating the model, and to grasp the principles in this very process. After a certain period of imitation—we hope!—there comes a time of detachment in which imitators are mature enough to apply the principles learned to a variety of new situations.

- This leads on to what is meant by the term *principles*. They are a sort of distilled result gained by abstraction from hundreds of models. The

---

23 Almost every event can be represented from two different points of view: either in such a way that it appears as something quite out of the ordinary or in such a way that it appears completely "normal." For example, if I drive from Los Angeles to San Francisco, I could—justifiably—describe it as an event accompanied by a thousand miracles ("Whenever I drove through the lights at green, the traffic on the other road waited. I just managed to reach the gas station before I ran out of gas!"). I could, however, claim with equal justification that it is quite normal that I arrive safely in San Francisco ("Of course the traffic has to wait when the lights are red. When I saw that gas was getting low, I went to the next gas station!"). If the two accounts are laid side by side, it might appear that they were describing different journeys. But they are simply the same trip seen from different perspectives.

process of abstraction explains why, for many Christians, principles are regarded as less colorful and attractive than practical models or pulsating real-life testimonies. But this abstraction is the great advantage of principles. We do not have to filter them out of complex situations ourselves, by going through the long process of separating the uniquely individual features of a testimony from the elements that can be transferred to other situations. Principles are by definition based on this kind of background work. By contrast with models and testimonies, they are universally applicable. However, we need to apply them to our own situation and put them into practice, which is sometimes quite complicated.

- This is where the category begins that I would call a *program*. By program I mean the application of principles to a specific situation. Each church must develop a practical, specific program from the principles of church development that it either learns from church growth research or deducts from models, a program suited to the church's local situation. Helping to apply principles to specific situations is the typical job of a church consultant. He or she does not need to discover the principles, nor be an expert on the local church situation. The consultant is a mediator between the principles and the situation and thus helps the church to develop a program that fits. As many situations are similar (at least in some respects), it is possible to apply programs, once developed, in different churches; how well the programs can be transferred depends on how similar the starting situations really are. A program provides specific steps in a specific time frame for the specific situation.

- The last of the five concepts, *strategy*, is in a way located between principles and programs. Whereas principles merely describe universally valid individual insights but do not integrate them into any methodology, strategy goes a step further. The individual principles are forged together into a systematic overall concept, with methodological considerations playing a major role. However, a strategy is not a program and does not provide a step-by-step sequence. It merely offers a rough framework within which churches can develop their own programs.

All five categories have a certain justification (because they all fulfill different purposes), but the main emphasis of the work of our institute is in the area of principles and strategy. What we call "natural church development," for example, is a typical example of a strategy. The eight quality characteristics of growing churches, which have frequently been referred to, are typical illustrations of what we call principles. They have been abstracted from the study of hundreds of churches, and we have observed that they apply on a universal level. The raw material for these studies included testimonies and models, although we had to take great care to separate elements specific to the situation and elements that can be reproduced elsewhere—a distinction that is often (understandably) more difficult for the people involved than for outside observers.

Some of the services we provide, however, come under the category of programs. As we have found that certain methodical instructions are felt to be helpful in different situations, we have summarized them in written form. One example is the *Learning Love Process*—in the accompanying leaders' manual we give specific instructions on how the material can be covered in one, three, six, or twelve sessions.[24] Where we provide such programs, our aim is to encourage the users not to take them legalistically, but to feel free to adapt them to suit their individual situations best.

It seems to me a significant problem that these five categories are not distinguished clearly enough in discussion on church growth. Some testimonies are put forward as principles, and principles are relativized and regarded as mere testimonies of experience. Programs are confused with principles, models with programs, strategies with models, and so forth. Thus it is understandable that the aversion that many people (rightly) have to a legalistic application of programs is also directed against principles, that the general framework of a strategy is criticized for not providing a definite program, and so on. In popular discussion and in the literature on growing churches there is great confusion over these terms—which is why I am so concerned to state how I use them. If my definitions encourage a few people to use these terms in the same way, I will be pleased.

The strategy of natural church development is made up of three building blocks: first, the eight quality characteristics; second, the six biotic principles; and third, the minimum strategy.

First Building Block:
The Eight Quality Characteristics

The content of the eight quality characteristics has already been described in some detail, so here I can restrict myself to a number of more formal aspects. The emphasis placed on the eight quality characteristics makes it plain that natural church development has a qualitative approach.[25] The primary question is not, "What can we do to get more people attending

---

24 *Schwarz/Berief-Schwarz: 1995.*
25 The biotic concept of the qualitative approach should not, however, be confused with similar sounding lines of argument in which the emphasis on quality only serves to justify the lack of quantity. Authors such as Donald McGavran, C. Peter Wagner and others have rightly protested vehemently against such self-justifying strategies and deliberately emphasized the significance of quantity: "The numerical approach is essential to understanding church growth. The Church is made up of countable people and there is nothing particularly spiritual in not counting them" (*McGavran: 1980*, p. 93). The point of natural church development is not to play quality off against quantity but to show that real quality (as against supposed quality) generally does have an effect on quantity.

services?" but rather, "What can we do to grow in quality in each of these eight areas?" Behind this approach is the assumption that qualitative growth has quantitative effects. So far, our surveys have strongly supported this assumption. We have not (yet) discovered a single church which had a quality index of 65 or more (50 being the average in a given country) in all eight areas which was not also growing in quantity.[26] This seems to confirm the biblical principle that a good tree *will* produce good fruit.[27] Natural church development therefore does not approach the question of church growth from the perspective of its quantitative *effects*, but (deliberately) from the perspective of the underlying spiritual and strategic *causes*.

However, I must add that this distinction of cause and effect is somehow artificial. This way of speaking is, perhaps, justified to make ourselves understood in a world accustomed to the absolute validity of the law of causality, but it does not really do justice to our subject. The more we understand the biotic (and thus interrelated) principles of church development, the more we will notice that the concept of cause and effect is problematical. I am not saying that it is not legitimate to search for the causes of specific (positive or negative) developments in the church. This very quest is a major part of the work of our institute. But I would take issue with the idea that occurrences in the church can be adequately explained by using the linear, causal logic that is typical of the world of computers. In some areas—for example, for machines and robots—this sort of input/output thought structure is appropriate. But it is not adequate for organic systems—and the church belongs to this category.

In biotic thinking it is in many cases not possible to say what is the cause and what the effect. For example, we have seen that pastors of growing churches tend to plan to stay in their churches much longer than pastors of stagnant or shrinking churches.[28] There is some evidence that this decision of the pastor to stay for a long time is in itself a positive growth factor (in other words, one of the causes of the growth).[29] However, it is possible to argue that the growth of the church is the cause of the pastor's wish to stay at this place. Which of the two is right?

My guess is that both assumptions are right and that—here and in other areas—it is futile to attempt a technocratic distinction between cause and effect. The resulting principle is that growing churches have a

---

26 It seems to me that our procedure of examining the quality of churches on the basis of the eight quality characteristics fulfills one of the wishes expressed by C. Peter Wagner in the 1986 book *Church Growth—State of the Art*: "We need to develop ways to measure church quality as well as measuring membership growth" (*Wagner: 1986 b*, p. 34).

27 Cf. Matthew 7:17.

28 In the declining churches we analyzed, 31 percent of the pastors stated that they wish to remain in the church as long as possible; in growing churches, 71 percent expressed this wish (cf. *Schwarz: 1987*, p. 66ff).

29 Proposed, for example, in *Wagner: 1985 b*, p. 67f.

pastor who stays at the church for a long time—period. This consciously leaves the question of cause and effect unanswered. It is typical of biotic, circular processes that cause and effect merge into complex growth dynamics.

The mere fact that we carry out an analysis of a church has effects on the life of the church and therefore influences the results of the analysis— just as the temperature of a thermometer has an effect (albeit minimal) on the temperature of its surroundings, or a measuring device connected to an electric circuit alters the resistance of that circuit, or a person who looks in a mirror to study his or her facial expression changes that expression. A survey that sets out to study *effects* can itself become a *cause* for certain effects.

We can see how closely cause and effect are interlinked when we try to make sharp distinctions between the eight quality characteristics. On paper and in diagrams it is fairly easy, but in practice we find it impossible. To some extent, each quality characteristic contains the heart of all other elements; conversely, none of the elements can be put into practice effectively if we do not also work on the other areas. For example, how can we work on the quality characteristic "gift-oriented ministry" without at the same time re-arranging church leadership (quality characteristic 1), and without it having effects on the structures of the church (quality characteristic 4). If we look closely, we will find that each one of the other seven quality characteristics is affected by our actions in the area of "gift-oriented ministry"—including the areas of "evangelism" (quality characteristic 7) and "relationships" (quality characteristic 8).

Our institute has the possibility of monitoring churches over a longer period and observing the changes against time. We soon found it to be a rule that when a church changes just one of the quality characteristics (positively or negatively), this has—empirically demonstrable— consequences for all other areas. That does not surprise us, because one of the important concepts we have learned from God's creation is *interdependence*. If we think in terms of interdependence, we can no longer be taken in by the sort of simplistic cause-and-effect causality that is typical of technocratic thinking.

The term "quality characteristics" describes those principles that are valid for all kinds of churches in any situation. A leadership that concentrates on *empowering* others, a ministry that is *gift-oriented*, a spirituality that is *passionate*, church structures that are *functional*, a worship service that is felt to be *inspiring*, small groups that are *holistic*, evangelism that is *need-oriented*, and relationships that are *loving*—all these aspects are fundamental for any church worldwide that wishes to experience qualitative and quantitative growth.

My concern in this list is, of course, not so much the terminology as the *content* that these words—however imperfectly—aim to convey. I am also not concerned about the number *eight*. One book on church growth contains 16 different lists with essential characteristics of growing churches, each list stemming from a different author.[30] The shortest of these lists names three characteristics, the longest 15. A lot of these differences arise from the fact that the different authors made the same observations, but then fitted them into different theoretical frameworks. Thus it is possible for two characteristics to be combined into one concept, or for one characteristic to be split up into two, six, or even twenty sub-characteristics, each of which is then called a quality characteristic. The way these characteristics are divided and labelled is therefore, in the last resort, largely a methodical question. When I look at all the characteristics in the 16 lists mentioned above, I have the distinct impression that almost all points are directly or indirectly included in our eight quality characteristics.[31]

The shortest list of quality characteristics I know of was given to me by the Korean pastor, David Yonggi Cho, in a telephone conversation: "Pray and obey." That is certainly one way to summarize the issue. What Cho means with "pray" largely corresponds with our quality characteristic of "passionate spirituality," and the term "obey" undoubtedly covers the work on all the other seven elements on our list!

However, the advantage of our eight quality characteristics over the other lists I know of seems to me to lie in the clear expression of the typically biotic aspect of each element (i.e., the aspect that aims to activate the self-organizational dynamics). The nouns included (leadership, ministry, spirituality, and so forth) can be found in just about every church, but the concepts underlying the adjectives (empowering, gift-oriented, passionate, and so forth) are the decisive secret of growing churches. In other words, the key is that we work biotically in every single area.

Second Building Block:
The Six Biotic Principles

It is at this point that the second building block of natural church development comes into play. Whereas the eight quality characteristics are concerned with the content, that is, with the question "What?", the biotic principles are concerned with the question "How?" To put it in a nutshell: the more we apply the biotic principles in each of the eight areas mentioned, the greater the growth potential of a church will be.

The six biotic principles are meant to be rules that can help us in every issue to make decisions. This principle-oriented approach sets natural church development apart from a legalistic *casuistry* ("Follow exactly this method and your church will grow!") on the one hand and mere

---

30 *Reeves/Jenson: 1984*, pp. 155-160.
31 Cf. especially the similarity to the lists of C. Peter Wagner *(Wagner: 1985 a)* and Robert E. Logan *(Logan: 1989)*.

pragmatism ("The end justifies the means!") on the other. Rather, each decision should be made in such a way that it is in harmony with God's principles of growth. Underlying this approach is the recognition that church growth does not proceed according to a script that is fixed in all its details, but rather as a constant interplay of individual goals and continually changing situations. In this process, in which we can easily lose our bearings, the biotic principles are meant to be a help in making the right decisions.

With regard to the authority they claim, the biotic principles are (not accidentally) close to the Old Testament wisdom teaching. In his *Theology of the Old Testament*, Gerhard von Rad vividly describes the task of the wisdom teacher. He wants to give people practical help in their many everyday decisions, but "not with divine commandments, for which he was not authorized because his directions were largely drawn from experience. What he could offer to help those younger than himself was largely advice (*'ezah*). Such advice demands no obedience, it must be tested; it appeals to the judgment of the hearer and aims to convince him; it aims to make the decision easier."[32] To underline this character, I have deliberately not given the six biotic principles names that sound biblical; rather, I have chosen terms that are used in biology and ecology.[33]

It is my experience that whenever I have the chance to ask pastors of growing churches about each of these biotic principles—even if they have never before heard anything about them—they are spontaneously able to give me countless illustrations of how they apply these principles in their churches. This brings me back to one of the starting points of natural church development: I have not thought up these principles, I have *observed* them in healthy churches. My contribution was merely to give them a name and to integrate them in a methodically structured overall strategy.

- *Biotic principle 1: Interdependence.* This principle, which we have come across frequently in this book, simply means that we should understand the church as a complex organism in which all parts are linked with all others. The way the different parts are integrated into the whole is more important than the parts themselves.[34] It is therefore important to gain an ever deepening understanding of the nature of this network, rather than just considering isolated activities or an individual segment of church development.

- *Biotic principle 2: Multiplication.* Behind this principle lies a recognition that unlimited increase in size (permanent addition) is not biotic.

---

32   *Rad: 1982*, p. 447.
33   Cf. *Vester: 1988*, pp. 81-86.
34   Interestingly, this fact was discovered by Friedrich Engels, who designed his *Dialectics of Nature* as a "science of the overall context": "In nature, nothing happens in isolation. Each aspect has an effect on others, and vice versa, and it is usually the fact that this all-round movement and interplay is forgotten that prevents our nature researchers from seeing the most simple things clearly" (*Engels: 1973*, p. 453).

At some point, all growth has its natural limits. But in a network system, permanent multiplication is possible and desirable. A plant does not permanently increase in size; instead, it produces new plants, which themselves produce new plants. It is our task to create a structure that enables the work not only to be extended, but to be multiplied. Examples of the way this principle can be applied in church life are expressed in words like "delegation," "department head," "co-leader," "cell division," "church planting," and so forth.

- *Biotic principle 3: Energy transformation.* This principle is concerned with harnessing and controlling the contrary forces existent in the environment. Instead of destroying the forces of nature by using counter-force ("boxer mentality"), the principle of energy transformation utilizes them by using leverage. Apart from the small force needed for redirection, hardly any energy need be expended to achieve the goal.[35]

- *Biotic principle 4: Multi-usage.* In nature, whenever an organism has fulfilled its function, it is automatically integrated into a new cycle and thus fulfills a new function. The same applies in the church. We should take care that any measures we adopt can simultaneously benefit different areas. In the church, as in nature, there should be no "waste." What the technocrat regards as "waste" can, within the larger whole, have an important role to play. Frederic Vester writes: "It is obvious that in such processes we can make no progress with the one-dimensional thinking we were brought up with. This thinking only knows beginning and end, clearly defined cause and effect. In cyclical processes, however, the distinction between raw material and waste evaporates automatically, just as cause and effect merge in a cybernetic cycle."[36]

- *Biotic principle 5: Symbiosis.* Symbiosis is a close association between different organisms for mutual benefit (synergism). Any monoculture is a typical example of technocratic thinking, blind to the symbiotic effect of diversity. Technocrats love to demonstrate by mathematical calculations that a monoculture uses less energy and costs less. But they overlook, for example, the stabilizing effect that hedges, ponds, and bogs have on the whole ecological system.[37] As a result, the genetic variety in the fields is lost, which involves the risk that whole crops can be destroyed by a single pest. In the end, *more* energy must be expended per unit of harvest than for biologically oriented methods of cultivation which harness the energies of the existing

---

35 Cf. *Vester: 1988*, p. 83, who calls this the *jiujitsu* principle: "The jiujitsu principle is the main means used by nature to keep the energy flow at a minimum and at the same time achieve the most harmonious state of order for the system."
36 Ibid.
37 Cf. *Vester: 1988*, p. 249.

variety. Transferred to the church, this means that a variety of forms is far more effective than the monoculture of a single, dominant form. The decisive factor is to bring these different forms into a symbiotic relationship to each other.

- *Biotic principle 6: Functionality.* A healthy organism automatically rejects forms that are not conducive to its health. Nothing in nature is an end in itself, always a means to a higher end.[38] All life in God's creation is characterized by its ability to bear fruit. In natural church development functionality means first of all to check on the quality of the church by examining its fruit. We can best tell whether an activity was really functional or we just imagined it to be so if we examine the results. A good tree *does* produce good fruit, and fruit is not invisible (neither in the Bible nor in science).

The biblical, theological legitimacy of the six principles is, I hope, clear to the reader from the overall context of this book. Of course it would be relatively easy to find numerous biblical illustrations for each of them. But a list of "proof texts," so popular in certain Christian circles, would not be consistent with the approach to the Bible that I advocate.[39] However, when we begin to consider the general message that runs throughout the Bible, its thought structures and principles that are expressed in ever-changing illustrations, we will learn much of what we here call "biotic principles."

I would like to illustrate this by reference to *one* principle, the concept of energy transformation. I chose this one because I am frequently told in my seminars that this principle surely cannot be "biblical." But it seems to me to be more the (esoteric-sounding) *name* rather than the specific *content* that prevents some Christians from accepting this principle as "biblical." The Bible is full of illustrations of how energy transformation works.

A typical example of the harnessing of contrary forces for the cause of God is the sermon of Paul on the Areopagus, reported in Acts 17. Here, Paul uses an idol statue as the starting point for his evangelistic message. The Book of Acts bears witness to the effect of the principle of energy transformation on almost every page. What men and women do with evil intent is transformed into something good. The persecution scatters the church—and this scattering becomes the "seed of Christianity," as Tertullian later concluded from this and other contexts. Here we see clearly the difference between the secular understanding of these dy-

---

38 Cf. *Vester: 1988*, p. 32: "The perspective of our aim 'capacity to survive' forces us ... to the conclusion that nothing is really an end in itself, only a means to an end. That means preserving or allowing to come about those constellations which will increase the guarantee that the goal, which is basically a goal *without* end, can be reached. Every goal that is an end in itself, such as permanent economic growth, is therefore directed against the system and, in the last resort, against ourselves."

39 Cf. p. 121ff.

namics (as purely immanent phenomena) and their theological interpretation: Christians know, even in this sort of situation, that God is at work behind the scenes.

This is especially shown in the greatest of all models of this principle: the crucifixion of Jesus. What seemed to be the ultimate triumph of Satan—God's Son hanging on a cross—God turned into the greatest victory over Satan in human history. This principle illustrates the logic expressed in the words coined by Augustine, *victor quia victima* (victim, but victor). Again, we see how inadequate it would be to understand these dynamics in purely immanent terms. The person who turns defeat into victory is God himself.

The cross, the crown of thorns, and the persecution of Christians are illustrations that indicate the final, deepest, and most dramatic dimension of this principle. In the everyday life of the local church, however, its application is normally far less spectacular. When Paul says of himself that he became a Jew for the Jews, that he became subject to the law for those who were subject to the law, and that for those who were without the law he became as one without the law,[40] he is giving us a less dramatic (but strategically no less important) illustration of the same principle. It is striking what (functional) reason Paul gives for his behavior: ". . . so that by all possible means I might save some."

What I have merely hinted at for the principle of energy transformation applies equally well to the other five biotic principles. Even if the terminology is not used by the biblical authors, the underlying content is expressed almost continually in the Bible. This is not surprising, for we are not dealing here with rules made up by men and women, but with principles based on the observation of God's creation.

When I am invited to hold a seminar about natural church development, my concern is not to persuade the participants to adopt a specific *program.* I do not wish to lend credence to the technocratic illusion that a static set of step-by-step instructions is the solution to all our problems. My concern is rather to train the participants in a biotic way of *thinking.* On the basis of a series of case studies, we discuss how the six biotic principles can influence the way we make decisions. In such discussions I have discovered that our intuition tends to lead us (perhaps especially those of us who have studied theology)[41] to decide in non-biotic ways, rather than thinking biotically. It is only when we have worked with this approach for some time that we notice how our intuition gradually changes. We then no longer need the biotic principles to help us; we can make the right decisions intuitively. It all depends on what we allow to determine our intuition!

---

40   Cf. 1 Corinthians 9:20.
41   We can certainly say of the normal training schemes for pastors (and the whole tradition of western academic training) that they are usually relatively unbiotic. One cause for this is the reductionist view of science which was described in the last chapter (pp. 218 and 225).

If we think more deeply about these six principles, we will notice that in the final analysis they are just variations on a single theme: "How can we create conditions in which the growth automatisms God uses to grow his church can be better released?" When it comes down to it, all the church growth principles in the world (C. Peter Wagner told me that 146 principles have been counted so far) can be reduced to this one rule. We could call it the basic principle behind natural church development.

Third Building Block:
The Minimum Strategy

Whereas the quality characteristics describe the *content* we need to work on (What should we do?) and the biotic principles tell us about the *method* (How should we do it?), the third building block, the minimum strategy, examines the right *timing* (When should we do it?). Here, we are dealing with a strategy, as the answer to this question is not defined in a fixed time plan that applies to all churches. Instead, each church can get help to find out itself when the right time will be for which activity. As no church can work on all eight quality characteristics in the same intensity at any one time, it is important to find out the time when the energy invested is most likely to bear "fruit." That is precisely where the minimum strategy aims to help.[42]

Fig. 20: The strategic significance of the minimum factor within the church helix: in this case, the minimum factor is structures.

Figure 20 again shows the church helix mentioned in the last chapter. The shaded areas indicate how well the individual quality characteristics are

---

42   For a more extensive treatment, cf. *Schwarz: 1996*, pp. 49-60.

developed, and the spiral arrow represents the numerical development of the church attendance figures. In simplified form, natural church development is based on the following assumptions: The church will grow quantitatively until the arrow meets the least developed quality characteristic (minimum factor). If the church wants to continue to grow, it should deal with this quality characteristic. If it is successful in developing the quality in this area, quantitative growth will resume and continue until the arrow meets the next minimum factor. Then the church should concentrate on a qualitative improvement in this area. Thus, the development of the church is a constant interplay between qualitative and quantitative factors.

The minimum strategy is taken from biology. It goes back to the discoveries made by Justus von Liebig in agriculture about 150 years ago. These discoveries have been applied to the dynamics of social systems by Wolfgang Mewes and others.

The "minimum-oriented" fertilization discovered by Liebig led to a breakthrough in agriculture and enabled biological production to be dramatically increased. Liebig discovered that four minerals are necessary for the growth of plants: nitrogen, lime, potash, and phosphoric acid. As long as these minerals are present in the environment in sufficient quantity, the plant grows automatically. However, its development ceases when the supply of one of the minerals is exhausted (fig. 21). If this shortage is overcome, for example, by fertilization with the mineral, the plant again grows until growth is stopped by a new shortage (fig. 22).

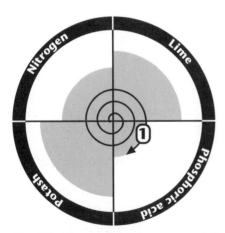

Fig. 21: Three of the four essential minerals for growth are in adequate supply (nitrogen, lime, potash), but the growth of the plant is hindered by a lack of phosphoric acid.

Fig. 22: Once phosphoric acid is added, the plant continues to grow until its growth is hindered by a lack of nitrogen.

If, however, the farmer continues to fertilize the soil with phosphoric acid because this was successful in the past, the result is an excess of phosphoric acid (fig. 23). Because of this excess, the soil is poisoned with overacidity. The more effort the farmer invests, the more the harvest is reduced, and the greater is the damage to the environment. But if the fertilization is concentrated on the new shortage (fig. 24), growth can resume.

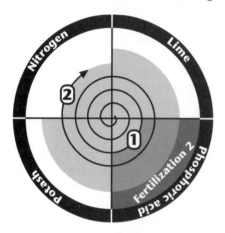
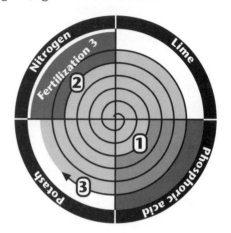

Fig. 23: If the farmer now goes by experience and continues to fertilize the soil with phosphoric acid (a method that evidently worked in the past), the fertilizer will—at best—be wasted; it may even be harmful, as the overacidity may poison the soil. In reality, the growth of the plant is hindered by a lack of nitrogen.

Fig. 24: However, if fertilization is now concentrated on the new minimum factor, there are two consequences. First, growth can resume; second, the excess acid is automatically taken out of the soil, so that it is no longer poisoned.

In our ministry we have experienced how helpful the minimum strategy can be for the right timing in church development. Some church growth experts, however, have criticized this concept and remarked that churches should concentrate on their strengths, rather than investing their energy in their weaknesses.

I feel that both approaches are right, but that it is important to note that they apply to different areas. Where we are talking about programs, which can be chosen at will, it is true that we should fortify our strong points and not pay much attention to our weak areas. For example, if one of the strong points of a church is its aesthetically sophisticated liturgical worship with organ music, this strength should be built on, for example by making a greater effort to reach people with cultural interests, rather than trying to introduce tamborines and clapping alongside the organ. The same applies to all areas of church life that are not absolutely essential to the growth of the church (neither tamborines nor organ music are essential to a healthy church).

But when we are dealing with absolutely *essential* characteristics of a church—and our eight quality characteristics belong to this category—the principle of concentrating on our strengths no longer applies. If just one of the quality characteristics is missing or poorly developed—for example "functional structures"—it will not help us if we increase our strengths in other areas, such as "passionate spirituality," as the growth is not hindered by a defect in the area of spirituality, but by nonfunctional structures. We must first take action to restore the health of the organism before we can continue to grow in the areas where we are strongest.

In practical work, we have achieved the best results by combining the two approaches: we use the existing strengths of the church to tackle its weakest point (minimum factor). Personally, I try to make this practical in church seminars by usually starting with the spiritual gifts that God has given to the church members. As every Christian has at least one gift, these gifts are the strengths that already exist in every church. Then we consider, as a second step, how to use the gifts we have identified in the area that we have diagnosed as the minimum factor.

This procedure is a typical illustration of what natural church development is all about. We do not try to force a church into the mold of a previously thought-out program. Instead, we start with what God has already given the church, and we ask: "How can we use it better than we have done so far, to the glory of God and for the growth of his church?" The more fully we keep to God's own principles, the firmer the ground under our feet as we set about this quest.

3

Can We "Make"
the Church Grow?

There is perhaps no question in the field of church development debated with greater emotion than this: Can we "make" the church grow?[1] My concern here is not to give an account of the present status of this debate, because there isn't any "present status." Anyone who studies the literature dealing with this subject will find that the same clichés are articulated again and again, but that we hardly find any progress in the discussion—not to mention any agreed-upon solution. But what else should be the sense of a theological discussion, if not to answer the question at issue clearly, and then to build constructively on it?

In this chapter I wish to demonstrate that this question *must* be unanswerable as long as we base our thinking on the spiritualistic or institutionalistic paradigm. Within the bipolar paradigm, we can regard it as already answered. But, for understandable reasons, the answer cannot be accepted by proponents of the institutionalistic and spiritualistic thought patterns (unless they change their paradigms). We can safely assume, then, that there will be many more books written about the subject in the coming years, and that these contributions will still not make any major progress in the discussion.

The Perspective of the Biotic Paradigm

Let us look back at our bipolar paradigm. After all that has been said so far it is logical to say that the institutional pole of the church can be "manufactured," whereas the church as an organism cannot. It has also become clear that working on the institutional/organizational pole may

---

1   We should not, however, confuse this topic with the question of the contribution we make to our own salvation, so hotly debated since the dispute between Pelagius and Augustine. In this book, I am not talking about cooperation in our own salvation, but exclusively about our cooperation in church development. It would be disastrous if the same formulations that have been developed in the one discussion were transferred to a wholly different issue.

stimulate the emergence and growth of the church as an organism. The task, then, is to structure the organizational pole in such a way that it can most effectively serve the development of the church as an organism.

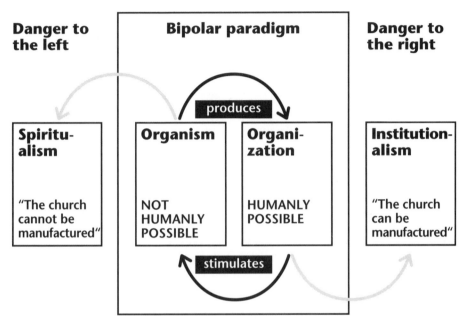

Fig. 25: Whereas organizations can be manufactured, this is not true of the church as an organism.

If things are that easy, why does this discussion make no headway? The problem is that it is largely carried out by proponents of the spiritualistic and institutionalistic paradigms. Spiritualists, as we have repeatedly seen, tend to separate the organic pole from the organizational one. So it is consistent with their thought pattern when they say: "We cannot 'manufacture' the church," for the church as an organism really cannot be manufactured by human means. Extreme spiritualists can be satisfied with this answer and lean back in their quietist armchairs. But those who sense that this cannot be all there is to say (and they are the majority) may remain fairly stubborn in their dogmatic answer: "We cannot 'manufacture' the church," but then they set about manufacturing something anyway, however halfheartedly. What they are actually manufacturing, and why they are manufacturing it if the church cannot be manufactured by our actions, is never really clear. But as spiritualists do not normally take theological reflection very seriously, they are satisfied with a general appeal to the "mysterious ways of God."

Representatives of the institutionalistic paradigm have a different starting point. As they identify the organization with the organism (thus making the organic pole superfluous), they really should say: "We can 'manufacture' the church." Their whole thinking, which I described in a wide variety of areas in part 2 of this book, really is geared to this concept. We have seen that this attitude does not necessarily lead to activism, but can manifest itself in a whole variety of ways, ranging from the establishment of universalistic definitions through the creation of a rigid order of church discipline to the recitation of mysterious formulas. However, adherents of this paradigm will vehemently deny that they regard the church as something that can be "manufactured" by human actions, in spite of their contradicting practice. How can we explain this phenomenon?

The solution seems to me to lie in the fact that representatives of the institutionalistic paradigm cannot—theologically—admit to themselves that they have at all times tended to "manufacture" the church, and still do so. They simply assert in spite of the facts that the opposite is true. We can only explain the passion with which some of them oppose the (alleged or real) "can-do" mentality of the church growth movement by assuming that the repressed parts of their own psychological make-up are breaking out. How else can we understand sacramentalism, clericalism, monopolism, or traditionalism, if not as an expression of an extreme "can-do" mentality?

Whereas spiritualists can paper over the inconsistencies in their lives with mystical, mysterious reasoning, adherents of the institutionalistic paradigm tend to use paradox theological formulas, as we have seen, which serve the same purpose. Finally, both of them, in spite of their different starting points, say very similar things: "We *can* do nothing at all to further the growth of the church. But nevertheless, we *should* do something!"

I have heard statements like this in innumerable lectures, and I have never witnessed any hearers who left the room because of the illogical premise (I myself did once). Usually the reaction is different. People have become so accustomed to regarding these statements as "spiritual" and "edifying" that, depending on their devotional style, they nod their heads, smack their lips, or gaze at the ceiling. But however listeners socialized in Christian circles react, their reactions show that they regard these statements as expressions of deeply felt devotion. What I write here is not a malicious caricature; it is based on countless observations in Christian meetings.

Agriculture as a Model

The Bible points us again and again to biological (or more precisely, agricultural) analogies when it tells us of the principles of the kingdom of God. We can show wonderfully in agriculture the logical (rather than paradoxical!) connection between the technical and the biological, between organizational and organic elements.[2]

Natural church development tries to harness the logic behind the agricultural analogy for practical work in the church. We know that, on an organizational, technical level we can—and should—do much! What we do in this area has an effect on the organic level, and thus on the harvest. But we know, too, that the dynamics here are different from the technical dynamics involved in machinery. Organic life—whether it be a plant, a human being, or the organic pole of the church—is something completely different from human-made things (machines, computers, robots, and so forth). The principles with which we can explain the functioning of a robot are fundamentally different from those that apply to growth in the area of organic life.

An oak tree grows out of a minute seed in the acorn. An elephant develops from a small fertilized ovum which looks very much like the ova of other mammals. Robots are not incubated from robot eggs; they must be made up of prefabricated parts in a factory. They do not reproduce by means of cuttings or sexual reproduction, and they cannot regenerate themselves after they have been damaged. They work by push buttons and do exactly what we have programmed them to do—a response that is not true of the organism of a human being, nor of the organism of the church.

Hans Jürgen Dusza summarizes the dynamics that is in the background of the bipolar paradigm very aptly: "Our efforts in planning only remove the obstacles that hinder this non-manufacturable growth of the church . . . Church growth cannot be compared with the construction of a machine, but rather with the organic growth of a plant. The church lives like a body; it does not rattle like a machine."[3]

But beware! There are many people who use similar words to those used by Dusza or myself, but they mean something completely different. The consequence they draw from the fact that we cannot manufacture growth is, in the last resort, to say that there are no strategically relevant principles at all concerning church growth. They speak of the "seed that grows by itself," but then we find that they have no more to say about methods for church development. Yet in the Bible we find much more in the way of instructions for church growth than just this one parable. Or they emphasize—rightly—the biblical principle: "Do not worry!" but neglect just about every other biotic principle the Bible teaches us. Thus, they don't worry about the future of the church—but in view of the fact that they permanently neglect about twenty other biblical principles, they have every reason to worry! This tendency to perceive selectively, which is linked with a tendency to obey selectively, can best be overcome

---

2   Cf. p. 16ff.
3   *Dusza: 1989*, p. 436.

in relation to our subject matter by letting the agricultural analogy have a deep effect on us.

The *locus classicus* of this subject is found in the words of Paul in the First Letter to the Corinthians: "I planted the seed, Apollos watered it, but God made it grow. So neither he who plants nor he who waters is anything, but only God, who makes things grow. The man who plants and the man who waters have one purpose, and each will be rewarded according to his own labor. For you are God's fellow-workers; you are God's field, God's building." [4] When we reflect on such agricultural analogies, many things become crystal clear:

First, it becomes evident what any farmer knows even without these words—what they can do, and what they can't do. Farmers can plant, water, and harvest. Not only that—they *should* do these things, otherwise there will be no harvest. But farmers know that they cannot make the crops grow. We can "make" a robot, but we can't "make" the church.

Second, a farmer who works hard can expect to have a greater harvest than someone who doesn't spend much energy in sowing and reaping. But the greater harvest is in no way guaranteed. In spite of all the hard work, a single storm or frost can destroy all the crops. If we work hard for church development we do, of course, increase the probability of reaping a greater spiritual harvest—but we will often find that in spite of all our work and commitment, we see hardly any fruit.

Third, every farmer knows that hard work is in vain if it is not in harmony with the laws of nature. If we sow seed at the wrong time, add too little water or too much fertilizer, then we will have a poor harvest no matter how hard we work. We need the experience that comes from training, careful observation, and ceaseless experimenting. Even in church development, hard work, commitment, and motivation are not all that is needed; the right *know how* is just as important. What are the principles governing the growth of the church? If we permanently neglect these principles, we should not be surprised if the church does not grow.

Fourth, no farmer expects that what he or she has just sown can be harvested the same day. A considerable time must pass between sowing and reaping, sometimes several years. It may be possible to build a robot overnight; organic processes generally take longer. In the church we should also be skeptical of instant programs that follow the logic of robots rather than the logic of life. What seems, in the short term, to bring scanty results—sowing minute seeds in the ground and letting them "die"—bears most fruit in the long term.

The whole issue of whether we can "make" the church grow is only a problem for people who have let themselves be infected by the logic of robots. For farmers, it is the plainest thing on earth that they cannot "make" the crops grow, but that there is a lot of work that they can do to

---

4   1 Corinthians 3:6-9.

remove hindrances to growth. That is not a "paradox," a "dialectic" statement nor an "unresolvable tension"; it is purely logical—not the logic of a robot, but the logic of nature.

Church Development and Science

Those who have difficulty with the question of whether we can "make" the church grow will also find it difficult to accept using scientific methodology in the area of church development. The same vehemence that is directed against the alleged "can-do" mentality of the church growth movement is understandably directed against attempts to study the church with empirical methods.

At this point, the negative view of anthropology in some parts of Protestant theology, which has not come to terms with Old Testament wisdom teaching, has a devastating effect.[5] In the chapter about the new paradigm we have already seen how closely natural church development is related to the biblical—and especially Old Testament—concept of wisdom.[6] "That is wisdom: the effort of will to achieve a rational clarification and order in the world a person finds himself/herself in, the will to perceive and define the order in the processes of human life and natural phenomena."[7] It is therefore no accident that Proverbs 1:5 speaks of wisdom as helmsmanship, an expression translated in the Septuagint as *kybernesis*.

It is also characteristic that the early wisdom of Israel, which Gerhard von Rad calls the "wisdom of experience,"[8] is far removed from claiming to be the product of a special divine revelation. "It was rather a matter of logic and common sense, and thus it was wholly non-inspirational."[9] Common sense, not faith, was needed to check the statements and to agree that pride comes before a fall, that vegetables eaten with love are better than an ox eaten with hate, that stolen bread becomes like gravel in the mouth, and so on. Wisdom was "a wholly worldly business,"[10] although we must add that, for Israel, Yahweh was directly behind the order detected by observation.[11]

The way the wisdom teaching came to be is not merely similar to the way church growth principles are discovered and formulated today—it

---

5 This is especially true with regard to the so-called "dialectial theology." It is all the more remarkable that the young Dietrich Bonhoeffer was one of the first theologians influenced by this approach who pointed out, in his dissertation "Sanctorum communio" (*Bonhoeffer: 1960*) completed in 1927, the connection between theology and sociology in ecclesiology.
6 Cf. pp. 226-230.
7 *Rad: 1982*, p. 438.
8 Ibid. p. 430.
9 Ibid. p. 456.
10 Ibid. p. 450.
11 Ibid.

is identical. As Gerhard von Rad writes about Old Testament wisdom, "A great number of identical or similar processes had to be observed before a certain set of principles gradually emerged."[12] The starting point is the presupposition "that there must be an order behind everything," and this presupposition shows the underlying faith "which knows of the deep, hidden secret of God's preservation and guidance."[13] The empirical approach of natural church development is founded on the same presuppositions. In our quest to discover by empirical means the principles behind the growth (or shrinking) of churches, we are in good (biblical) company. Michael Herbst is right to emphasize that it is no contradiction to the nature of the church "that the measurable things in it are measured and the visible things are recorded and evaluated."[14]

What we have *formulated* as principles should not to be identified with the principles of God himself. Our perception is imprecise, our empirical methodology may be flawed, our conceptual framework imperfect. However, the principles themselves that underlie the imperfect formulations really are God's principles, in the same way that the laws of nature are God's laws. They were created by none other than God—and those who study and describe them will find that, in the process, they learn more about the way it pleases God to act.

For me, there is hardly anything that is more "edifying" than research into church growth. It is fascinating to examine the conditions in which churches are developing, and gradually to discover a hidden pattern behind phenomena that, at first, seem to be completely unstructured. I am, however, aware of the fact that many Christians, probably most, find the very things I regard as edifying to be completely "unedifying." We have repeatedly come across the fact, especially in our description of the spiritualistic paradigm, that a lot of Christians can only see God at work when a specific phenomenon cannot be explained by any principles.

Here, it seems to me that the idea many of us have of "edification" is influenced more strongly by journalism than by the biblical edification concept. "News is what's different" is the first commandment for newspapers. It would be a deadly sin for a journalist to emphasize what *normally* happens. The exceptions to the rule must be emphasized—they are what people read about. This addiction to the sensational (along the lines of: "Pope begins lesbian link with the late Mao Tse-tung") has had a massive influence on Christians. When I describe dramatic exceptions to the principles of natural church development in my seminars, I can see the eyes of many Christians shining. But when I explain the principles themselves—which are far more important from a spiritual and strategic point of view—many find it "not edifying" at all.

---

12   *Rad: 1982*, p. 432.
13   Ibid. p. 440.
14   *Herbst: 1987*, p. 105.

On a human level I can understand this because the journalistic principle "News is what's different" simply gives credit to a psychological fact. What I find hard to accept is that this understandable hunger for sensation is given a wrong dignity by assuming that these exceptions are more spiritual than what God normally does. It is not "edifying" in the biblical sense if we get a cold shiver in our spine (or a warm feeling in the stomach, depending on the content) when we read a headline. It is edifying when the church of Jesus Christ is demonstrably built up.

Church Development or Revival?

In the description of the spiritualistic paradigm in part 1 of this book, I briefly mentioned Christian groups that put forward an expectation of revival—as a sort of *alternative* to natural church development. Church development has, at best, a limited justification for these groups; the real thing for them is the (actual or supposed) coming revival.[15] As I fairly often come across this line of argument, I would like to make a few comments on it against the background of what has already been said.

First, in my discussions with Christians influenced by this approach I have never managed to find out exactly what the goal of the anticipated revival is. Is revival a synonym for effective church development? If that is the case, I wonder why revival is so often put forward as an alternative to principle-oriented work on church development. If it is not the case, I wonder if, when revival comes, the eight quality characteristics (or other principles of natural church development) are not needed any longer. Does revival mean that the leadership does not need to be empowering, that the ministry of Christians should not be gift-oriented, that spirituality should not be passionate, and so forth? Does revival mean that in all these areas we need not work biotically, but can work technocratically or chaotically instead, and that this is what God intends? This surely cannot be the case. Doesn't revival mean that we will be more effective in all eight areas than we are today? If that is so, revival really is a synonym for effective church development. Yet in the judgment of these Christians, it is not. It must, then, be something different. The question is, what?

Second, in many cases it is found that the thought patterns of the spiritualistic paradigm have had a major influence on the expectation of revival. It is true that spiritualism is completely different from natural church development. Thus, the arguments put forward by proponents of this direction are more or less dominated by spiritualistic dualism and a mystic concept of the Spirit. Sometimes it is suggested that the difference between the revival approach and church development is that revival is implemented by God, whereas church development is human-made. This point would

---

15   Cf. p. 37f.

be true if the concepts under discussion were influenced by technocracy, but it is certainly not true of natural church development. The central concern of natural church development is to do as much as possible to enable God's Spirit to work unhindered in our churches, so that he can grow the church. (This *includes* putting our finger on spiritualistic hindrances, revealing them for what they are and rejecting them!)

Third, proponents of this direction often make the same mistake we described in part 1 of this book: they give absolute priority to *one* quality characteristic ("passionate spirituality") at the expense of the other seven. Sometimes this really is the main hindrance to church growth, and the church would be well advised to concentrate particularly—even one-sidedly—on this area for a time. But in many cases, "passionate spirituality" is not the minimum factor of the church, and growth is blocked by other factors (such as disfunctional structures, a ministry that is not gift-oriented, a questionable evangelistic concept). Concentrating the church's resources on spirituality in these cases can even be counterproductive. The Christians are exhorted to pray more, spend more time with the Bible, deepen their commitment to Jesus, believe his promises more (because it is thought that these things will automatically lead to revival). But since the church is disobedient to God in other areas, and the hindrances to revival are to be found *there*, the Christians do not, of course, experience an answer to their prayers for revival. This can be terribly frustrating, because the reason for the lack of revival is not sought in the neglect of so many principles of church development. The cause for the unanswered prayers is either projected onto God himself ("Why don't you send us revival, even though we are so committed?"), or it is projected onto the Christians and the fact that their spiritual life is evidently not committed enough to bring about revival. This is the point where a quest for passionate spirituality changes into spiritualism.

Fourth, I find again and again that people connect revival with such phenomena as healing, prophecy, dancing, and so on. I really am in favor of these things taking place in our churches. But we should not assign them an exaggerated spiritual or strategic importance—we should see them for what they are. If people dance for joy, they are dancing for joy. If a prophecy is shared, a prophecy has been shared. Of course these things have an effect—but the effect is not that church growth results automatically from these occurrences. The mistake of this sort of expectation of revival lies in the way that segments of church development—sometimes even non-essential segments—are regarded as the whole picture.

Fifth, the way proponents of this direction deal with historical (or contemporary) models of revival seems to me to be rather adventurous. In terms of the important distinction between testimonies, models, principles, programs, and strategies which I explained in a different context,[16]

---

16   Cf. p. 238ff.

there is often total chaos. Usually, what we have called testimony is presented as a principle or as a program. The result is that people try to transfer those aspects of a model that are not transferable. On the other hand, the principles which research shows to be behind the revival are not really noticed, and they are not transferred into the local situation. Our research of churches that experience a revival clearly indicates—besides much that cannot be transferred—high values for all of the eight quality characteristics. I know of no "revival" church that can do without any one of these eight principles. One problem, however, is that many leaders of successful churches consciously report on their work in categories of a testimony rather than talking about the underlying principles. In many cases they use spiritualistically influenced patterns which contain partial truths (and usually make a favorable impression on the listeners), but are not helpful as transferable concepts.

Sixth, church growth involves spiritual, institutional, and contextual factors. In many cases, revivals are influenced by contextual factors (e.g., a periodically occurring openness for new ideas, such as the gospel, in certain groups of the population, often stimulated by a political or economic crisis).[17] Whereas spiritual and institutional factors can largely be reproduced, this is not true of contextual factors. Taking our lead from *that* sort of model is questionable from the outset, and making changes in contextual conditions an aim for the church is, to say the least, confusing.

Seventh, it often seems that one motive of the advocates of the revival approach is the idea that, when the revival comes, church growth will occur without any work—or at least with far less work. Personally, I find this concept understandable because work is strain. But this concept is certainly not a very spiritual one. It seems to me that here the "old Adam," which prefers to shy away from hard work and conflict, is simply getting the better of us. The Bible nowhere hints at this idea. Or do the things Jesus, Paul, and others teach us about *our* share in church development no longer apply when revival comes? Do all analogies with agriculture (with the implications of hard work) cease to be valid when there is a revival? Can we expect to have less work at harvest time of all times? (For revival is surely a time of harvesting.) I don't know who first thought of this idea—it certainly wasn't Jesus. If what many people think of as revival actually happens, one of the first consequences will surely be that we have more work, more conflicts, and more problems.

Eighth, I find it remarkable that proponents of this expectation, despite their opposition to strategic work and planning, seem to believe in the importance of our actions in at least *one* area—the area of psychology. I have been in a number of churches and interdenominational meetings in

---

17   Of course, favorable contextual factors will only contribute to church growth if the spiritual and institutional factors are also favorable.

which the leaders pull out all the stops to increase the expectations of Christians in the audience (i.e., to stimulate their expectation of revival). In principle that is not a bad thing, for it is good and biblical to expect great things from God. But on such occasions I find myself wondering to what extent the proclamation of totally groundless (and spiritualistically molded) future forecasts is equated with "boldness of faith." In actual fact, many of these practices have nothing to do with boldness of faith, but represent just a fairly transparent amateur psychology that may motivate people in the short term, but which is likely to be demotivating in the long term. The psychology of the expectation of revival is the area in which spiritualists—while waiting for a revival that does not come—are most in danger of resorting to technocratic methods which promise magic results.[18]

I do not, of course, dispute that God can and sometimes does act in ways that cannot be described in terms of principles. But I object when that sort of divine action is regarded as more valuable than the things he does that are in harmony with the principles we have studied. The essence of the difference between the revival approach described above and natural church development is the notion that when revival comes, all principles (which spiritualists would call "human" and I would call "divine") will no longer apply, but that everything will happen in a totally different way.

Let us assume for a moment that this day will really come. Then we are faced with the question of how we can prepare for it. By cultivating the field in accordance with the principles God shows us in his Word—or by letting it run wild? By trying to put church growth principles into practice as well as we can—or by picking our favorite principle and ignoring the others? By working with passion for church development—or by doing it halfheartedly because we are really waiting for something else?

To avoid misunderstandings, let me add that in many growing churches I have ministered in, an expectation of revival is linked with consistent work for church development. In churches that approach revival in *this* way we can study and learn all the quality characteristics we have identified (at least I have studied them there). The same applies to churches who do not only expect, but actually *experience* revival. Their leaders may not reflect on their work in the same way as this book does, they may use different terminology and a different theological framework, they may not be conscious of some of the principles they use—but in these churches the work is going forward in the sense of what we call

---

18   Cf. *Praag: 1990*, p. 153: "We must realize . . . that mystics have special experiences that are distributed throughout their whole lives, often with long gaps. Is it not then self-evident that human impatience will try to stimulate these experiences? Where this happens, magic is only a short step away. Mystics are sometimes subject to the same temptations as people who are gifted as mediums: They find it difficult to accept a long gap between occurrences of their 'special state.'"

natural church development. The expectation of revival is the "tonic" that motivates Christians to do all they can in all eight areas. And they do it with all their hearts!

If revival is understood in this way, I am a passionate advocate of this approach. But if our expectation of revival leads us to work only halfheartedly for church development, then I would question it. Like so many other half-truths propounded by spiritualistically influenced people, it seems to me that it gets in the way of God's intentions. It absorbs the energy of willing Christians whose commitment is so urgently needed for church development.

4
Thriving in the Third Millennium

A t the beginning of the 20th century in Europe, the "century of the church"[1] was optimistically proclaimed to be under way. But the general mood in the western world has now swung completely the other way. If we regularly read and evaluate Christian news magazines, we will find the following trend expressed: we are living in a world that is less and less spiritual; Christian traditions are crumbling everywhere; Christian values are decreasing on every side—in other words, things are getting more and more difficult.

From the point of view of the institutionalistic paradigm, this analysis of the situation is understandable. But what can we say on the basis of the bipolar paradigm? To put it briefly, the change of paradigm we can currently observe in society may be threatening for those who identify "faith" with their old paradigm. But from the point of view of church development, we can be thankful for the period we are moving in.

Secularization:
A Threat to the Institutionalistic Paradigm

What is today called "secularization"—the fact that people in the western world are leaving the "age of the cathedral"[2]—is simply a mass exodus from the institutionalistic paradigm. For the first time in church history, a church that justified itself in an institutionalistic way, is in danger of becoming irrelevant because the world (how impudent of it!) has left the sphere of influence of these thought structures. It is tragic that most Christians do not understand this process and still dream of the sort of "unified world" that was typical of the "age of the cathedral."

Historical thinking, which is one of the foundations of the new paradigm (as we have seen, neither representatives of the spiritualistic nor

---

1   Cf. *Dibelius: 1928.*
2   *Seitz: 1979*, p. 172.

the institutionalistic paradigms really think historically), is a direct consequence of the secularization process of recent times. In *this* area, advocates of secular historical thinking and advocates of the new theological paradigm are in agreement. In *this* area, they are allies against the heteronomic tyranny of the institutionalistic age which now, by the grace of God, is gradually drawing to a close.

Atheism was provoked by a wrong transcendent theism. If in a lot of western countries people leave the church in large numbers, they are in most cases not leaving a personal faith and a healthy Christian fellowship. Very often they have never experienced anything like this. They are merely taking their leave of the institutionalistic misconception of the faith and the church. People who have only come to know the institutionalistic variety of Christianity (or, more rarely, only the spiritualistic one), are almost inevitably *driven* to atheism. If I personally were given a choice merely between Christian spiritualism, Christian institutionalism, and atheism, I know what *my* answer would be. I would be on the side of those atheists who invest their lives to fight against the condescension and superstition of false religion.

What we have described as the institutionalistic paradigm in our typology is basically the image that most non-Christians—rightly or wrongly—have of "the church." Sometimes this impression is not fair because most churches do not only show institutionalistic tendencies— we also find personal faith, meaningful fellowship, and need-oriented service in them. But the institutionalistic tendencies are predominant, and it is they that are addressed in atheism's criticism of religion. As far as I know, no serious discussion of personal faith in the context of the bipolar paradigm has yet been undertaken from an atheistic point of view. The whole rhetoric of atheism is directed against the old, heteronomic paradigm with the corresponding concept of God. When atheists declare that *this* God is dead, I totally agree with them.

The deep-seated influence of the institutionalistic paradigm on Christianity, especially in those countries which still have a state church system, can be studied in the language used to describe the changes in the world today. People speak of the *post-Christian* age (implying that the "age of the cathedral" was a "Christian" age); they speak of the *new* heathens (implying that people who where living in the compulsory churches of the past centuries were not heathens); they speak of the *re*-evangelization of Europe (implying that the earlier methods used to establish the church in Europe were evangelism); they speak of Germany *becoming* a mission field (as if it were not a mission field in past centuries); they speak of the western world as being *no longer* Christian (implying that it was Christian in the past).

The (often unconscious) use of such vocabulary shows more clearly than any official statements what thought structures are dominant. We can only understand these expressions by assuming that many people, even if they reject the idea in other contexts, still instinctively use as their criterion the concept of a past "Christian age." This becomes even clearer when they speak of their hopes for the future. Their statements are full of words like "again" and "back" and "restore," but these words do not imply a return to the apostolic age—they refer to a *restoration* of our Christian culture (ideal are the Middle Ages), which has unfortunately disintegrated. Whenever people use language like that (and a lot of Christians still do!), we are reminded how persistently the standards of the institutionalistic age still live in our minds. So far we are certainly not living in a *post*-institutionalistic age.

New Religiosity: The Trend Towards Spiritualism

The decline of the institutionalistic paradigm which we can observe to-day must not, however, be taken to mean that it is being replaced by the bipolar paradigm. What we see is a different trend. Some of those who are turning from the institutionalistic paradigm are seeking refuge in atheism (the by-far smaller number), but others are turning to a revival of spiritualism (of a Christian or pagan variety).

The famous suggestion by Dietrich Bonhoeffer that we were entering a "religionless age"[3] was a gigantic misinterpretation. Religion is in a boom period. Bonhoeffer shrewdly recognized that what we have called the institutionalistic paradigm was coming to an end in our age, but he underestimated the resilience of spiritualism. The renewed interest in religion which we can observe at every hand today is nothing else than a revival of the spiritualistic paradigm. While some incorrigible theologians (who are wrongly called "modern") still try to persuade us that modern men and women are "without religion," a large proportion of modern people are, in fact, more than willing to absorb anything that smells vaguely religious.

The tragic thing for Christianity is that just at the time when the revival of interest in (non-heteronomic) religion was taking place, that is, at the end of the sixties and the beginning of the seventies, many theologians were devoting their energy to drawing the practical consequences from the erroneous forecasts made by Bonhoeffer and others. Instead of offering a form of faith that satisfied people's longing for spiritual experience, they concentrated on removing, in the name of "modern man," all allegedly mythical elements from the Bible and from preaching, claiming that these elements were not in keeping with our times. When they had finished this process of "demythologization" and replaced the vivid language of the Bible with an abstract, philosophical terminology, they were surprised that "modern man," in whose name they had done it, hardly understood a word. They had not noticed that the terminology most

---

3   Cf. *Bonhoeffer: 1952*, p. 178f.

people speak is far more "mythical" than many theologians care to admit. The result is that we are now largely unprepared for a situation in which most people have an immense religious longing.

Against this background, it is understandable that a movement such as New Age could grow so rapidly. It catered to the interests of people who had had enough of the objectivistic, institutionalistic misconception of Christianity. While many Christians were still proclaiming a "religionless age," the New Age movement declared the "Age of Aquarius." In my view, we can only understand the success of the New Age if we recognize that this movement succeeded in harnessing the dynamics of the global paradigm shift for its own ends. It is no accident that the literature of the New Age is full of terms like "paradigm shift," "gentle medicine," "soft management," "spirituality," and so forth. New Age has recognized the signs of the times—which, apart from a few and remarkable exceptions, we cannot say of the Christian church.

Spiritual and Secular Mega-Trends

What are the signs of the times? The days when there was a single dominant trend are well and truly past. We would do well to accept that in future there will be a variety of different, even contradictory trends. In our context, I feel that the following developments are of special significance:

- *Mega-trend 1: The trend towards multiple option Christianity.* Whereas in the past a single form of church life was thought to be appropriate, this has now changed dramatically, and it will continue to change in the coming years. In a similar way to the growing secular trend to a multiple option society, the need for a multiple option Christianity will also grow. This plurality is certainly better than the medieval ideal of unity, but we must also recognize that it has a certain ambivalence. Along with the growing variety of Christian groups, there will also be a growth of groups that we can justifiably call "sects."[4] It is of crucial importance how and by whom the increasing demand for variety within Christianity is met. In the years before us, the surviving relics of the medieval concept of unity (parochial structures, denominational boundaries, and so forth) will become less and less important for an increasing number of people. The question they will ask (whether we like it or not) will be: Where are my needs best met?

- *Mega-trend 2: Revival of Christian spiritualism.* I have already mentioned that, in this century which has been wrongly labelled as "religionless," pagan spiritualism is on the upsurge. This also applies to Christian forms of spiritualism, however questionable we may think

---

4   On this concept, cf. p. 167ff.

them. I anticipate that Christian churches that are dominated by the spiritualistic paradigm will see considerable growth in the years ahead. Their approach is in keeping with the trend. I do not, of course, see it as my calling to support this trend—wherever I have contact with such groups, I hope to provide a corrective input. The more a spiritualistically influenced church studies the bipolar approach, the greater is the chance that it will eventually overcome its spiritualistic implications.

- *Mega-trend 3: Restoration of the institutionalistic paradigm.* Research into the death experience has shown us that people faced with death can display an enormous energy, which may appear almost super-human. We can expect to see this phenomenon in proponents of the institutionalistic paradigm. Precisely because most trends (both secular and spiritual) point in the opposite direction, some adherents of this paradigm will make an even greater effort to establish their case. We must therefore expect—in spite of tendencies to "reconciliation" between Christian groups that were formerly enemies—that there will also be a revival of divisiveness, slander, and accusations of heresy.

- *Mega-trend 4: Flight into pragmatism.* On the other hand, some Christians who are tired of these arguments will take refuge in a pragmatism that is hostile towards all sorts of theology. Seeing what intractable divisiveness can be caused by theology, they will try to avoid theological controversies. These Christians are in danger of being used by advocates of all sorts of ideologies—because they do not understand their backgrounds, or, for opportunistic reasons, do not *want* to understand them.

- *Mega-trend 5: Discovery of a national perspective.* One of the most hopeful trends that is evident today and will hopefully grow in the coming years is the way Christians of different backgrounds come together to develop a national vision. This process has already taken place in many countries, and initiatives in this direction are meeting a growing interest. I consider this to be a "trend" initiated by God himself. Whereas natural church development tries to apply biotic principles in the local church setting, the national movements aim to apply the same principles for a whole country.

- *Mega-trend 6: From addition to multiplication.* It will be one of the hallmarks of the coming years that innumerable new churches will be planted—both within the existing denominations and outside them. Currently, about 1,600 new churches are planted worldwide each week,[5] and we can expect this trend to accelerate. Particularly in Europe, with its centuries-old heritage of monopolistic state churches, where this trend is by definition a break with tradition, the idea of the multiplication of new churches will gain in popularity in an increasingly

---

5   Cf. *Wagner: 1981*, p. 58.

pluralistic society. We must expect this trend to produce not only positive results—there will be many questionable developments as well. Some of the new churches will arise as a conscious protest movement against the existing ones, and they will be characterized by an "anti-everything" attitude. These churches will fight against the established churches—without realizing that, in fact, they have the same ideological starting point as those they criticize. There is perhaps no other area where a paradigm shift would do so much good as it would here.

The Chances for Church Growth

We can undoubtedly say that the chances for church growth today are better than they were, say, a hundred years ago. We must remember that there was a time—the much extolled "Christian" age—when expressing the sort of ideas we find, for instance, in a book like this, would have been a sure way to be burned at the stake.

"Never before in the history of humanity has there been a non-political, non-military movement that has grown as fast as Christianity in our times,"[6] C. Peter Wagner writes. Ecclesiastical traditions that are wrongly thought to be the essence of Christianity are waning, but a personal faith in Jesus has better chances today than some years ago. It is an empirically demonstrable fact that in areas where the influence of the established churches has greatly decreased—for example, the big European cities—the conditions for church development are better than in areas that are regarded as "ecclesiastically intact."[7]

If we, as Christians, want to use the trends we see today in the cause of church growth, we should take the following factors into account:

First, we should stop longing for a return to the medieval "golden age." The spiritual bondage that many Christians display at this point, which cannot be explained rationally, is sometimes so strong that only a liberation of exorcistic dimensions can bring deliverance. Many things that Christians tenaciously cling to are irretrievably past. We do not want to go *back* to things of the past—we want to go *forward* to new experiences that we ourselves do not yet know!

Second, it is crucially important to what extent we understand the implications of what we have called the principle of energy transformation.[8] I personally tend to regard the trends and developments we see in

---

6 *Wagner: 1986 a*, p. 11.
7 This does not mean that the inhabitants of these cities are more pious than people, for example, in rural areas. More likely, the opposite is true. The fact that the chances for church growth are greater in areas that are less influenced by church traditions is mainly due to contextual factors. People who are less rooted in tradition tend to be more flexible and mobile, subject to less social control, and more open for new ideas—including the Christian faith.
8 Cf. p. 245ff.

the church and the world as being largely positive. But even those who interpret these trends exclusively in negative terms will have to consider how they can use them for the purposes of the kingdom of God. I believe that this question can be an issue of life or death for the church, especially in our approach to New Age or similar movements.

Third, as Christians we should not be afraid of being confused with other movements. When we begin to speak the language of our audience (or even our adversaries), some people may misinterpret us. The more we go out of our way to find new, creative ways to win as many non-Christians as possible, the more we will have the painful experience that the real resistance comes from other Christians. We must learn not to be blown off course by this resistance. To illustrate, the bait on the hook does not need to be to the taste of the angler (nor the angler's friend); the only thing that matters is whether the fish likes it. As long as we permit the sort of church we are developing for tomorrow to be more influenced by the taste and expectations of clericalistic, traditionalistic, or fundamentalist Christians than by the questions and needs of those we want to reach, all our efforts for church development will be nothing but spiritual cosmetics.

Fourth, it is important in the coming years that we actually *do* the things we have seen to be right. This may seem to be a platitude, but here is usually the cause of our problems. It is just not true that a correct understanding of *what* we should do automatically shows us *how* we should do it. Declaring a principle is not the same as acting on it. If we really want to act on our insights, we must devote our energy to finding out what methods will be helpful. Everything else, including a book like this, is just *propaedeutics*.

This is the point where the usefulness of a book is exhausted. As we have seen, the different paradigms described are not just thought paradigms; they are life paradigms. This means that we cannot expect a paradigm shift to take place in our thinking alone. It is not difficult to understand the new paradigm. But it is far more difficult to accept the effect it has on our lives.

The management expert Tom Peters writes: "Before the new technology is introduced, the thought patterns of the past decades must be changed."[9] This statement is in harmony with the approach advocated in this book, but I am convinced that the thought patterns of the past decades—or, in our case, centuries—can only be changed to the extent to which what Peters calls the "new technology" is put into practice at the same time. In other words, new thinking and new practice do not develop one after the other (which would be technocratic); they develop simultaneously.

It is always difficult to give up something we have grown accustomed to, especially when the new things that are to replace them are not

---

9   *Peters: 1988, p. 124.*

clearly visible yet. Hardly anyone is willing to embark on such a process of their own free will. Only an existential crisis can put enough pressure on us to cause us to adopt a new paradigm. I am therefore convinced that God will send his people many crises in the coming years to prepare them for the tasks he wants them to fulfill.

The time before us is sure to be more and more turbulent. Conflict will increase rather than decrease. That is normal for a time with conflicting paradigms—until the new paradigm overcomes the resistance of the old. Never yet has it been possible for new developments to be established without facing major resistance from advocates of the old ways, who cling more and more tenaciously to the old structures as the new ways become more and more established.

There are Christians who think it is an illusion to suppose that the concern behind natural church development can be fulfilled by means of reforms. They believe that we should not try to improve existing conditions, but rather set up a better version. They compare all efforts to reform the existing system with the rearrangement of the furniture on the doomed Titanic. What is really necessary, they argue, is not a reformation, but a revolution.

Maybe they are right.

Bibliography

This list contains only those titles that are quoted in this book. The footnotes give the name of the author and the year of publication (according to the edition quoted). With these pieces of information the full title of the books can easily be identified.

Aland, K.: Kirchengeschichtliche Entwürfe, Gütersloh 1960.

Albertz, H.: Endlich begreifen. Heinrich Albertz im Gespräch mit Christian A. Schwarz, in: Abakus-Magazin 3/1980.

Arn, W. / Arn, Ch.: The Master's Plan for Making Disciples. How Every Christian Can Be an Effective Witness Through an Enabling Church, Pasadena 1982.

Arn, W. / Nyquist, C. / Arn, Ch.: Who Cares About Love? How to Bring Together the Great Commission and the Great Commandment, Pasadena 1986.

Baden, E. / Knospe, G. / Schmidt, H. / Schnell, H. / Wilken, W. (Ed.): Missionarischer Gemeindeaufbau, Berlin 1961.

Bainton, R.: The Left Wing of the Reformation, in: Journal of Religion 21/1941.

Bainton, R.: Martin Luther, 2nd edition, München 1983.

Barth, K.: Dogmatik im Grundriß, 2nd edition, Zollikon-Zürich 1947.

Barth, K.: Die Kirchliche Dogmatik I,2, 4th edition, Zollikon/Zürich 1948.

Barth, K.: Rudolf Bultmann. Ein Versuch, ihn zu verstehen (Theologische Studien, Heft 34), Zollikon-Zürich 1952.

Barth, K.: Die Kirchliche Dogmatik I,1, 7th edition, Zollikon/Zürich 1955.

Barth, K.: Theologische Fragen und Antworten. Gesammelte Vorträge III, Zollikon 1957.

Barth, K.: Antworten und Fragen an Paul Tillich, in: P. Tillich, Gesammelte Werke VII, Stuttgart 1962.

Barth, K.: Einführung in die evangelische Theologie, 2nd edition, Gütersloh 1977.

Beutel, M.: Leidenschaft einüben. Ein geistliches Energieprogramm, Emmelsbüll 1995.

Beyer, H. W.: diakonia, in: Theologisches Wörterbuch zum Neuen Testament II (edited by G. Kittel), Stuttgart 1954.

Biedermann, A. E.: Christliche Dogmatik, Berlin 1884.

Bohren, R.: Unsere Kasualpraxis – eine missionarische Gelegenheit (Theologische Existenz heute Nr. 83), München 1960.

Bohren, R.: Dem Worte folgen. Predigt und Gemeinde, München/Hamburg 1969.

Bohren, R.: Daß Gott schön werde. Praktische Theologie als theologische Ästhetik, München 1975.

Bohren, R.: Die Laienfrage als Frage nach der Predigt, in: R. Bohren, Geist und Gericht. Arbeiten zur Praktischen Theologie, Neukirchen-Vluyn 1979.

Bonhoeffer, D.: Widerstand und Ergebung. Briefe und Aufzeichnungen aus der Haft, München 1952.

Bonhoeffer, D.: Sanctorum Communio, 3rd edition, München 1960.

Bonhoeffer, D.: Gesammelte Schriften V, München 1972.

Bonhoeffer, D.: Nachfolge, 12th edition, München 1981.

Brunner, E.: Das Mißverständnis der Kirche, Stuttgart 1951.

Brunner, E.: Dogmatik I, 3rd edition, Zürich 1960 a.

Brunner, E.: Dogmatik II, 2nd edition, Zürich 1960 b.

Brunner, E.: Dogmatik III, Zürich 1960 c.

Brunner, E.: Wahrheit als Begegnung, 3rd edition, Zürich 1984.

Bultmann, R.: ginosko, in: Theologisches Wörterbuch zum Neuen Testament I (edited by G. Kittel), Stuttgart 1953.

Bultmann, R.: Jesus Christus und die Mythologie, Hamburg 1964.

Bultmann, R.: Die Geschichte der synoptischen Tradition, 9th edition, Göttingen 1979.

Busch, E.: Karl Barth und die Pietisten. Die Pietismuskritik des jungen Karl Barth und ihre Erwiderung, München 1978.

Capellmann, C. / Bergmann, W.: Pastoralmedizin, 19th edition, Paderborn 1923.

Capra, F.: Wendezeit. Bausteine für ein neues Weltbild, München 1988.

Chadwick, H.: Die Kirche in der antiken Welt, Berlin 1972.

Cho, P. Y.: Gebet: Schlüssel zur Erweckung, 2nd edition, Hochheim 1988.

Conzelmann, G.: charisma, in: Theologisches Wörterbuch zum Neuen Testament IX (edited by G. Friedrich), Stuttgart 1973.

Deschner, K.: Abermals krähte der Hahn, Hamburg 1972.

Dibelius, O.: Das Jahrhundert der Kirche, 5th edition, Berlin 1928.

Douglass, K.: Gottes Liebe feiern. Aufbruch zum neuen Gottesdienst, Emmelsbüll 1998.

Durant, W.: Die großen Denker, 7th edition, Zürich 1945.

Dusza, H. J.: Gemeindeaufbau und Gemeindeleitung, in: Deutsches Pfarrerblatt 89, 1989.

Echternach, H.: Es stehet geschrieben. Eine Untersuchung über die Grenzen der Theologie und die Autorität des Wortes, Berlin 1937.

Ecke, K.: Fortsetzung der Reformation. Kaspar von Schwenckfelds Schau einer apostolischen Reformation, Gladbeck 1978.

Egelkraut, H.: Pietismus und Reformation, in: K. Heimbucher (Ed.), Luther und der Pietismus, Gießen 1983.

Eggers, U.: Gemeinschaft lebenslänglich. Deutsche Hutterer in den USA, Witten 1985.

Eickhoff, K.: Gemeinde entwickeln für die Volkskirche der Zukunft, Göttingen 1992.

Engels, F.: Dialektik der Natur, Berlin 1973.

Engen, Ch. v.: The Growth of the True Church. An Analysis of the Ecclesiology of Church Growth Theory, Amsterdam 1981.

Eppler, E.: Ende oder Wende. Von der Machbarkeit des Notwendigen, 3rd edition, München 1979.

Feuerbach, L.: Das Wesen der Religion, Berlin 1981.

Fietz, S. / Schwarz, Chr. A.: Ist Frieden möglich?, Greifenstein 1984.

Fritzsche, H. G.: Lehrbuch der Dogmatik I. Prinzipienlehre, 2nd edition, Berlin 1982.

George, C. / Logan, R. E.: Leading and Managing Your Church, Old Tappan 1987.

Gerhard, J.: Loci theologici I, Berlin 1863.

Gerken, G.: Management by Love. Mehr Erfolg durch Menschlichkeit, Düsseldorf 1990.

Gibbs, E.: I Believe in Church Growth, London 1981.

Gollwitzer, H.: Vortrupp des Lebens, München 1975.

Gollwitzer, H.: Befreiung zur Solidarität. Einführung in die Evangelische Theologie, München 1978.

Grundmann, W.: Das Evangelium nach Markus, 7th edition, Berlin 1977.

Haarbeck, A.: Theologie des Gemeindeaufbaus. Eine kritische Auseinandersetzung mit Fritz und Christian A. Schwarz, in: R. Weth (Ed.), Diskussion zur Theologie des Gemeindeaufbaus, Neukirchen-Vluyn 1986.

Hampe, J. Ch.: Die Autorität der Freiheit I. Gegenwart des Konzils und Zukunft der Kirche im ökumenischen Disput, München 1967.

Hansen, J. / Möller, Chr.: Evangelisation und Theologie. Texte einer Begegnung, Neukirchen-Vluyn 1980.

Hauck, F.: koinoneo, in: Theologisches Wörterbuch zum Neuen Testament III (edited by G. Kittel), Stuttgart 1950.

Hauschildt, K.: Wer gegen den Strom schwimmt, in: idea spektrum 31/1989.

Heintz, P.: Anarchismus, in: Die Religion in Geschichte und Gegenwart I (edited by K. Galling), 3rd edition, Tübingen 1957.

Herbst, M.: Grundentscheidungen im Gemeindeaufbau. Die Berufung zum normalen Leben des Christen in der Gemeinde, in: R. Weth (Ed.), Diskussion zur Theologie des Gemeindeaufbaus, Neukirchen-Vluyn 1986.

Herbst, M.: Missionarischer Gemeindeaufbau in der Volkskirche, Stuttgart 1987.

Heussi, K.: Kompendium der Kirchengeschichte, 15th edition, Tübingen 1979.

Hiebert, P. G.: Set and Structures. A Study of Church Patterns, in: D. Hesselgrave (Ed.), New Horizons in World Mission, Grand Rapids 1979.

Hiebert, P. G.: Conversion in Cross-Cultural Perspective, in: H. J. Schmidt (Ed.), Conversion: Doorway to Discipleship, Kansas 1980.

Hild, H. (Ed.): Wie stabil ist die Kirche?, Gelnhausen/Berlin 1974.

Hoekendijk, J. Chr.: The Call to Evangelism, in: The International Review of Missions 39/1950.

Huber, W.: Der Streit um die Wahrheit und die Fähigkeit zum Frieden. Vier Kapitel ökumenischer Theologie, München 1980.

Hunter, K.: Foundations for Church Growth, New Haven 1983.

Jäger, A.: Mut zur Theologie. Eine Einführung, Gütersloh 1983.

Joest, W.: Erwägungen zur kanonischen Bedeutung des NT, KuD 12/1966.

Josuttis, M.: Der Pfarrer ist anders. Aspekte einer zeitgenössischen Pastoraltheologie, München 1982.

Jüngel, E.: Gott als Geheimnis der Welt, Tübingen 1977.

Käsemann, E.: Exegetische Versuche und Besinnungen I, Göttingen 1960.

Kantzenbach, F. W.: Orthodoxie und Pietismus, Gütersloh 1966.

Kierkegaard, S.: Der Liebe Tun I, Köln/Düsseldorf 1966.

Kinsbourne, M. (Ed.): Asymmetrical Function of the Brain, New York 1978.

Köhler, W.: Das Marburger Religionsgespräch, Leipzig 1929.

Kopfermann, W.: Abschied von einer Illusion. Volkskirche ohne Zukunft, 3rd edition, Wiesbaden 1991.

Kraus, H.-J.: Reich Gottes: Reich der Freiheit, Neukirchen-Vluyn 1975.

Kraus, H.-J.: Systematische Theologie im Kontext biblischer Geschichte und Eschatologie, Neukirchen-Vluyn 1983.

Krause, B.: Verheißungsorientierter Gemeindeaufbau in der Volkskirche, in: B. Schlottoff (Ed.), Gemeindeaufbau provokativ, Neukirchen-Vluyn 1989.

Kreck, W.: Grundfragen der Ekklesiologie, München 1981.

Krusche, W.: Die Herausforderung durch die konkrete Situation, in: Lutherische Rundschau, 20. Jahrgang 1970.

Lindberg, C.: The Third Reformation? Charismatic Movements and the Lutheran Tradition, Macon 1983.

Lochmann, H.: Dogmatisches Gespräch über die Kirche, in: Theologische Zeitschrift, Jahrgang 28, Heft 1, 1972.

Lochmann, J. M.: Platz für Prometheus, in: Evangelische Kommentare 5/1972.

Logan, R. E.: Beyond Church Growth, Old Tappan 1989.

Lohfink, G.: Wem gilt die Bergpredigt?, Freiburg/Basel/Wien 1988.

Lohse, B.: Epochen der Dogmengeschichte, 5th edition, Stuttgart 1983.

Lucius, E.: Die Anfänge des Heiligenkultes in der christlichen Kirche, Tübingen 1904.

Luther, M.: Vorrede auf die Episteln Sankt Jakobi und Judas, in: Der Glaube der Reformatoren (edited by F. Lau), Bremen 1964.

Luther, M.: Ausgewählte Schriften I (edited by K. Bornkamm and G. Ebeling), 2nd edition, Frankfurt 1983.

Luther, R.: Neutestamentliches Wörterbuch. Eine Einführung in Sprache und Sinn der urchristlichen Schriften, 18th edition, Bielefeld 1976.

Margull, H. J. (Ed.): Mission als Strukturprinzip. Ein Arbeitsbuch zur Frage missionarischer Gemeinden, Genf 1965.

McGavran, D.: Understanding Church Growth, Grand Rapids 1980.

Michel, O.: oikodomeo, in: Theologisches Wörterbuch zum Neuen Testament V (edited by G. Friedrich), Stuttgart 1954.

Möller, Chr.: Lehre vom Gemeindeaufbau I, 2nd edition, Göttingen 1987.

Möller, Chr.: Lehre vom Gemeindeaufbau II, Göttingen 1990.

Moltmann, J.: Kirche in der Kraft des Geistes. Ein Beitrag zur messianischen Ekklesiologie, München 1975.

Montgomery, J.: Eine ganze Nation gewinnen. Die DAWN-Strategie: Entstehung – Praxis – Perspektiven, Lörrach 1990.

Newbigin, L.: The Open Secret, Grand Rapids 1978.

Niesel, W. (Ed.): Bekenntnisschriften und Kirchenordnungen der nach Gottes Wort reformierten Kirche, München 1938.

Nietzsche, F.: Also sprach Zarathustra, Stuttgart 1964.

Nigg, W.: Heimliche Weisheit, Zürich 1959.

Oppen, D. v.: Das personale Zeitalter, Stuttgart 1960.

Ortlund, R. C.: Let the Church Be the Church, Waco 1983.

Ozment, S.: Mysticism and Dissent. Religious Ideology and Social Protest in the Sixteenth Century, London 1973.

Peters, T. / Waterman, R.: Auf der Suche nach Spitzenleistungen. Was man von den bestgeführten US-Unternehmen lernen kann, 9th edition, Landsberg 1984.

Peters, T.: Kreatives Chaos. Die neue Management-Praxis, Hamburg 1988.

Pfister, F.: Der Reliquienkult im Altertum, Gießen 1912.

Pöhlmann, H. G.: Abriß der Dogmatik, 3rd edition, Gütersloh 1980.

Pokorny, P.: Der Kern der Bergpredigt. Eine Auslegung, Hamburg 1969.

Praag, H. v.: Die acht Tore der Mystik, München 1990.

Prenter, R.: Die Realpräsenz als Mitte des christlichen Gottesdienstes, in: Festschrift W. Elert, Berlin 1950.

Rad, G. v.: Weisheit in Israel, Neukirchen-Vluyn 1970.

Rad, G. v.: Theologie des Alten Testaments I, 8th edition, München 1982.

Reeves, D. / Jenson, R.: Always Advancing: Modern Strategies for Church Growth, San Bernardino 1984.

Rengstorf, K. H.: manthano, in: Theologisches Wörterbuch zum Neuen Testament IV (edited by G. Kittel), Stuttgart 1942.

Richter, L.: Mystik. Begriff und Wesen, in: Die Religion in Geschichte und Gegenwart IV (edited by K. Galling), 3rd edition, Tübingen 1960.

Römheld, D.: Wege der Weisheit. Die Lehren Amenemopes und Proverbien 22,17-24,12, BZAW, Berlin/New York 1989.

Schlatter, A.: Die Preisgabe des Dienstes, in: O. Schmitz (Ed.), Pietismus und Theologie. Beiträge zu ihrer Verständigung, Neukirchen 1956.

Schlette, H. R.: Die Religionen als Thema der Theologie. Überlegungen zu einer "Theologie der Religionen", Freiburg 1963.

Schmidt, K. D.: Grundriß der Kirchengeschichte, 7th edition, Göttingen 1960.

Schwarz, Chr. A. / Schwarz, F.: Programm des neuen Lebensstils, Gladbeck 1981.

Schwarz, Chr. A. / Schwarz, F.: Die Friedenslüge. Plädoyer für Wahrhaftigkeit, 3rd edition, Neukirchen-Vluyn 1983.

Schwarz, Chr. A.: Praxis des Gemeindeaufbaus, Neukirchen-Vluyn 1987.

Schwarz, Chr. A. / Schwarz, F.: Theologie des Gemeindeaufbaus. Ein Versuch, Neukirchen-Vluyn, 3rd edition 1987.

Schwarz, Chr. A.: Gemeindegründung – die Strategie der neunziger Jahre, in: B. Schlottoff (Ed.), Gemeindeaufbau provokativ, Neukirchen-Vluyn 1989.

Schwarz, Chr. A.: Grundkurs Evangelisation. Leise werben für die Gute Nachricht, Emmelsbüll 1993 a.

Schwarz, Chr. A.: Der Gemeindetest. Kybernetisch Gemeinde bauen, 2nd edition, Emmelsbüll 1993 b.

Schwarz, Chr. A. / Berief-Schwarz, B.: Leiterhandbuch zum Grundkurs Evangelisation, 2nd edition, Emmelsbüll 1994.

Schwarz, Chr. A.: Anleitung für christliche Lebenskünstler, 2nd edition, Emmelsbüll 1995.

Schwarz, Chr. A. / Berief-Schwarz, B.: Leiterhandbuch zum Liebe-Lern-Prozess, 2nd edition, Emmelsbüll 1995.

Schwarz, Chr. A.: Natural Church Development. A Guide to Eight Essential Qualities of Healthy Churches, Carol Stream 1996.

Schwarz, Chr. A.: Der Gabentest. So entdecken Sie Ihre Gaben, 8th edition, Emmelsbüll 1997.

Schwarz, Chr. A.: Der Liebe-Lern-Prozess. Die Revolution der Herzen, 4th edition, Emmelsbüll 1998.

Schwarz, Chr. A. / Berief-Schwarz, B.: Leiterhandbuch zum Gabentest, 2nd edition, Emmelsbüll 1998.

Schwarz, Chr. A. / Schalk, Chr.: Implementation Guide to Natural Church Development, Carol Stream 1998.

Schweizer, E.: Gemeinde nach dem Neuen Testament, Zürich 1949.

Schweizer, E.: Gemeinde und Gemeindeordnung nach dem Neuen Testament, Zürich 1959.

Schweizer, E.: sarx, in: Theologisches Wörterbuch zum Neuen Testament VII (edited by G. Friedrich), Stuttgart 1964.

Schweizer, E.: Heiliger Geist, Stuttgart 1978.

Seeberg, E.: Luthers Theologie in ihren Grundzügen, 2nd edition, Stuttgart 1950.

Seeck, O.: Entwicklungsgeschichte des Christentums, Stuttgart 1921.

Seitz, M.: Praxis des Glaubens, 2nd edition, Göttingen 1979.

Sider, R.: Andreas Bodenstein von Karlstadt. The Development of his Thought 1517-1525, Leiden 1974.

Simson, W.: Gottes Megatrends. Sechs Wege aus dem christlichen Ghetto, Emmelsbüll 1995.

Singer. P.: Praktische Ethik, Stuttgart 1984.

Stauffer, E.: hina, in: Theologisches Wörterbuch zum Neuen Testament III (edited by G. Kittel), Stuttgart 1950.

Störing, H. J.: Kleine Weltgeschichte der Philosophie, 7th edition, Stuttgart 1950.

Strunk, R.: Zielsetzung im Gemeindeaufbau, in: R. Weth (Ed.), Diskussion zur Theologie des Gemeindeaufbaus, Neukirchen-Vluyn 1986.

Stuhlmann, R.: Beobachtungen und Überlegungen zu Markus IV 26-29, NTS 19, 1972/1973.

Thielicke, H.: Theologische Ethik I, 3rd edition, Tübingen 1965.

Thielicke, H.: Der evangelische Glaube. Grundzüge der Dogmatik I, Tübingen 1968.

Thielicke, H.: Der evangelische Glaube. Grundzüge der Dogmatik III, Tübingen 1978.

Tillich, P.: In der Tiefe ist Wahrheit, 4th edition, Stuttgart 1952.

Tillich, P.: Gesammelte Werke IV, Stuttgart 1961.

Tillich, P.: Gesammelte Werke VII, Stuttgart 1962 a.

Tillich, P.: Religionsphilosophie, Stuttgart 1962 b.

Tillich, P.: Auf der Grenze, Stuttgart 1962 c.

Tillich, P.: Systematische Theologie I, 3rd edition, Stuttgart 1964.

Tillich, P.: Systematische Theologie II, 8th edition, Darmstadt 1984.

Vester, F.: Neuland des Denkens. Vom technokratischen zum kybernetischen Zeitalter, 5th edition, München 1988.

Wagner, C. P.: Frontiers in Mission Strategy, Chicago 1971.

Wagner, C. P.: Your Spiritual Gifts Can Help Your Church Grow, Glendale 1979.

Wagner, C. P.: Church Growth and the Whole Gospel. A Biblical Mandate, San Francisco 1981.

Wagner, C. P.: Your Church Can Grow. Seven Vital Signs of a Healthy Church, 2nd edition, Ventura 1985 a.

Wagner, C. P.: Your Church Can Be Healthy, 5th edition, Nashville 1985 b.

Wagner, C. P.: Lektionen aus der weltweiten Erweckung, Mainz 1986 a.

Wagner, C. P.: The Church Growth Movement after Thirty Years, in: W. Arn / E. Towns / C. P. Wagner (Ed.), Church Growth – State of the Art, Wheaton 1986 b.

Wagner, C. P.: Die Gaben des Geistes für den Gemeindeaufbau, Neukirchen-Vluyn 1987.

Wagner, C. P.: Gemeindegründung. Die Zukunft der Kirche, Mainz 1990.

Wallmann, J.: Kirchengeschichte Deutschlands II. Von der Reformation bis zur Gegenwart, Frankfurt/M. 1973.

Wallmann, J.: Philipp Jakob Spener und die Anfänge des Pietismus, Tübingen 1986.

Walser, M: Halbzeit, München/Zürich 1964.

Weber, O.: Grundlagen der Dogmatik I, Neukirchen-Vluyn, 3rd edition 1964.

Weiss, K.: symphero, in: Theologisches Wörterbuch zum Neuen Testament IX (edited by G. Friedrich), Stuttgart 1973.

Weth, R. (Ed.): Diskussion zur Theologie des Gemeindeaufbaus, Neukirchen-Vluyn 1986.

Younghusband, J.: Orchester: Vom Barock bis zur Gegenwart, Köln 1991.

Zahrnt, H.: Die Sache mit Gott. Die protestantische Theologie im 20. Jahrhundert, München 1966.

Zimmerli, W.: Grundriß der alttestamentlichen Theologie, 4th edition, Stuttgart 1982.

Index